Edwin L. Kennedy

Edwin L. Kennedy
Reinvesting in Education

By David Neal Keller

Ohio University Press
Athens

© copyright 1993 by Ohio University Press
Printed in the United States of America
All rights reserved

Ohio University Press books are printed on acid-free paper ∞

Library of Congress Cataloging-in-Publication Data

Keller, David Neal.
　Edwin L. Kennedy : reinvesting in education / David Neal Keller.
　　p.　cm.
　Includes bibliographical references and index.
　ISBN 0–8214–1053–9
　1. Kennedy, Edwin Lust, 1904–　.　2. Businessmen—United States—Biography.　3. Benefactors—United States—Biography.
4. Philanthropists—United States—Biography.　5. Universities and colleges—United States—Finance.　I. Title.
HC102.5.K46K45　1993
361.7′4′092—dc20
　[B]　　　　　　　　　　　　　　　　　　　　　　　　92–42155
　　　　　　　　　　　　　　　　　　　　　　　　　　　　　CIP

Contents

	Acknowledgments	vii
	Preface	ix
	Prologue	xi
One	Volunteer of the Year	1
Two	An Early Resolve	8
Three	Gaining Confidence	22
Four	Family Ties	33
Five	Tumbling Wall	41
Six	The Right Niche	51
Seven	Fate's Interventions	68
Eight	A New Dimension	77
Nine	The Lehman Mystique	90
Ten	A Hard-Core Philosophy	105
Eleven	Contrasting Personalities	117

Twelve	Preserving a Culture	140
Thirteen	Conflicts of Interests	147
Fourteen	Continuing Commitments	164
Fifteen	Riding the Cycles	176
Sixteen	Renewed Motivations	193
Seventeen	Reminiscence	209
	Epilogue	217
	Documentation	221
	Index	227

Acknowledgments

The enjoyable task of writing a biography of Edwin Kennedy was possible only through the excellent cooperation of the many persons who were interviewed, and those who assisted through correspondence and by gathering resource material, often at great sacrifice of time. Through the entire project, my wife, Marian, helped in many ways, not the least of which included her support, suggestions, and constructive editorial criticism. The hospitality of Ed and of Christa and Jeff Cook made visits to their home more pleasure than work. Both Ed and Christa also searched files and stacks of accumulated papers on many occasions to locate requested documents. Susanne Cook not only gave information from the viewpoint of a granddaughter, but also wrote the book's preface. Gladys Linville was gracious in an initial interview and in answering innumerable telephone questions about her brother afterwards. Ed's brothers, Robert and Richard, and their wives also provided follow-up research on my behalf, as did Ruth's niece, Nancy Bletzer. Mildred Bond, a family friend who lives in Canton, compiled data from county courthouse records and other sources. Special thanks go also to Ohio University administrators George Bain, head of Archives and Special Collections; Sheppard Black, Special Collections librarian; Peggy Black, former director of

University News Services; Marie White, assistant to the president; and Jack Ellis, vice president for development; and to Sylvia Yankey, director of development at Hiram College, and Ronald G. Webber, development officer at Ohio Northern University. Claudia Grant of the Christian Church (Disciples of Christ) central office in Columbus arranged for research by the organization's historical society to obtain information on the Teachout Foundation and its founder. Elizabeth Zoernig gathered important material on Kerr-McGee, and arranged for interviews at the company's Oklahoma City headquarters. Kelly Thompson, former president emeritus of Western Kentucky University and chairman of its College Heights Foundation, provided written material and personal recollections of the late Roy Martin, one of Ed Kennedy's closest friends for many years. To those persons and the others who helped during compilation of resource material, I extend my sincere gratitude.

David Neal Keller

Preface

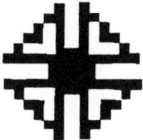

And there he was, perched on the edge of our dock on Calabogie Lake, Ontario. There I was behind the wheel of the boat; the boat that would gradually drag my grandfather through the water until it gained enough speed to yank him up onto his skis and send this eighty-four-year-old man sailing across the water's surface. It was a sight that sent onlookers scurrying to grab their cameras to snap a shot of Calabogie's local celebrity still waterskiing after all those years. As I turned to catch a glimpse of him jumping the wake of the boat and then zooming past docks and beaches filled with amazed viewers, I smiled with knowing pride. For me, it was just another day in the life of my dynamo, my grandfather.

So there he was, and there he has always been, smiling in the audience at piano recitals or quizzing me before a spelling bee. He has shown me the world from the Darien Jungle in Panama to the Isle of Skye in Scotland. But it is as my teachers in life where he and my late grandmother bestowed their greatest gifts. As John C. Baker noted in 1976, "I have never known any couple less selfish and more convinced that they were not born for themselves alone." It is their lesson in giving and their joy in sharing that have become synonymous with Ed and Ruth Kennedy. It is their humanity that will never be forgotten.

In the words of Ohio University President Charles Ping, "Ed Kennedy has lived an ideal: Life held not simply as a possession to own and enjoy, but as a trust to be used. The unspoken assumption of his life is the conviction that from him to whom much is given, much is expected. And so it has been."

Giving has been a way of life for my grandfather, although the act was not always easy, and the road to success was far from simple.

Susanne C. Cook
June 1992

Prologue

In the spring of 1992, America's anguish over perceived internal problems muffled a short-lived optimism stemming from the end of a Cold War that had persisted for more than forty years. One of several reasons attributed by a team of Associated Press pollsters was media exposure of errant leaders. Magnified by the bitter in-fighting of political candidates, such revelations indeed contributed to the feeling of distress. But the veil covering chicanery in business and government—in some instances collaborative—had been unraveling steadily during the preceding decade. Names such as Boesky, Milken, and Keating inflamed memories of bilking unsuspecting citizens from their life savings, crippling financial institutions, buying favorable legislation, and corrupting the nation's basic investment processes.

Numerous articles, television specials, and books rightly spotlighted the guile of such arrogant personalities. Left backstage, however, were many others who represented the antithesis of this deceit. Having built careers on reputations of integrity, they, even more than the rest of us, resented those who cast shadows of shame on their professions. Prominent among these figures whose word was still their bond was Edwin L. Kennedy.

Throughout a business career that began on the eve of the Great Depression in 1929 and had not fully ended sixty-three years later, Kennedy masterminded a wide variety of dealings, often converting adversities into opportunities, without a single sacrifice of honor. Business leaders, past and present, interviewed across the nation for this book, invariably offered that characterization, without prompting by the author. Most also attested to the perpetual optimistic perspective he still retained on his eighty-eighth birthday. It is hoped, therefore, that this biography, while not intended to be a statement on veracity, will in some small measure help offset the hopelessness induced by a lingering public negativism.

Wall Street was the hub of pursuits that sent Edwin L. Kennedy around the world, sometimes at a dizzying pace. In the scurry of business and philanthropic ventures, he enjoyed many friendships, some brief, others spanning several years, a few continuing for a lifetime. Those in the latter group became so important to Kennedy that his biography would be incomplete without what might appear to be brief diversions into other careers.

Uncomfortable with blatant confrontation, Kennedy quietly rejected business friendships solicited by persons he appraised as self-serving or dishonorable. Perhaps his most thinly disguised displeasure was evidenced when a young Manuel Noriega sought his friendship in 1970. Recognizing a sinister personality behind the broad smile of Panama's future dictator, Kennedy limited their relationship to what he considered the minimum acceptable for owning an enterprise in that country.

Kennedy admitted to making occasional, though rare misjudgments of people, but insisted that his wife "was never wrong in that respect." Many persons spoke of the strong influence both Edwin and Ruth Kennedy had on the lives of others, through companionship, anonymous acts, and support of education. The couple's own mutual respect and devotion was such that twelve years after Ruth died, Edwin still weighed what he felt certain her opinion would be whenever he made a decision.

David Neal Keller

Chapter 1   Volunteer of the Year

Few individuals in the history of higher education have given so much of themselves. Few have had so significant an impact on such a variety of educational institutions.

—President Ronald Reagan
October 15, 1985

"I have learned that the only things we really own in this life are those that we intelligently give away. Underscore *intelligently*." The speaker was Edwin L. Kennedy, reiterating a belief he had expressed many times during the previous three decades. In the audience were close friends, educators, political figures, family, and other guests gathered in Washington, D.C. to honor the still-dapper octogenarian as the Council for Advancement and Support of Education's 1985 Volunteer of the Year. The nonprofit organization had established its annual award two years earlier to recognize the vital role volunteers play in education. Kennedy was selected for the third citation from a field of forty-five men and women nominated by American and Canadian colleges, universities, and primary and secondary independent schools.

Standing characteristically erect behind the Sheraton-Washington ballroom podium on this October 22, 1985 evening, Ed Kennedy spoke in the quiet, albeit confident tones that had become a respected hallmark of his enterprising career.

At eighty-one, the retired partner of Lehman Brothers investment banking house had been water skiing two months earlier. Although no longer an active participant in Lehman affairs, he commuted regularly from his New Jersey home to a lower Manhattan office, where he worked independently on some holdover corporate board matters, personal financing, and ideas for new business ventures.

His response at the moment, however, pertained entirely to volunteerism, which he described as lying "at the very heart of our way of life." This assiduous focus on the subject at hand was another stamp of the Kennedy personality. Pointless straying from the topic of discourse, whether in a speech or a discussion, was a trait he rarely could abide. Persons who had served with him on various business and educational boards, many of whom were in the audience, would attest to that fact. Kennedy greatly respected disparate opinions, but irrelevant patter was one of two vexations likely to provoke a polite, yet humbling reply, made all the more poignant by its deliberate, low-key delivery.

The other sure-fire irritant was any hint of deceitfulness.

"Ed Kennedy always maintained unshakable high standards of ethics in a financial world where integrity too often is compromised," observed Dr. John C. Baker, a retired president of Ohio University—Kennedy's alma mater—who attended the recognition banquet. Eight years older than Kennedy, Baker had been involved in the first stage of his educational volunteerism, and had since become one of his four closest long-time friends.

Two others in that elite group, Boston financier Ora C. Roehl and Texas entrepreneur Walter R. Davis, echoed Baker's words. The latter, who didn't complete high school but built a fortune in oil and real estate, also had become an important patron of higher education, crediting Kennedy with influencing his decision to join in that effort.

"I remember walking with Ed on the way to Bankers Trust soon after we met, and he used that banking tie-in to explain his philosophy about never really owning anything until you give it away," Davis had recalled. "He said you can *use* your assets for your own benefit, but the manner in which you eventually dispose of them establishes their real value. He considered helping young people become educated a worthy consignment with mushrooming benefits, and I became convinced he was right."

Ed Kennedy had shared that philosophy also with the most important person in his life, who had died five years before the 1985 tribute in the nation's capital. Long after she succumbed to cancer, memories of Ruth Zimmerman Kennedy indeed continued to influence her husband's decisions, just as her thoughts and suggestions had done throughout the forty-eight years of their marriage.

Through personal as well as financial inflations and depressions, Ed and Ruth Kennedy viewed themselves as a team, working to carve a career, rear a family, and contribute to society. He was quiet to the point of sometimes being mistaken for a loner, she expansive, frequently out-spoken. Each admired these qualities in the other. During both the struggles of the thirties and later affluence, they remained so attuned to each other's thinking that either could, and often did make an immediate decision knowing the backing of the other would be forthcoming.

Ruth's sense of humor could buffer any threat of stodginess in investment banking. Whenever Edwin felt himself becoming overly immersed in finance at the sacrifice of family, he was rescued by thoughts of an incident that occurred midway through his career at Lehman Brothers:

> One evening Ruth and I watched a television program in which a traveling husband and his wife exchanged telephone kisses to close their conversations when he was away from home. Ruth asked, "Why don't we ever do that?" Well, I passed it off with some lame answer. But a few days later, my secretary interrupted an important Lehman meeting to tell me my wife was on the phone. This greatly concerned me, because Ruth never broke our rule that partners' meetings were not to be interrupted by phone calls, except in the instance of an emergency, or something equally important. So I rushed out of the meeting, picked up the phone, and immediately heard a loud, sensuous kiss. Then she hung up the phone.

In many ways, Ed and Ruth Kennedy came to measure success in the expanding friendships that blossomed from their multifarious interests around the world. They described events and enterprises in terms of people. Even brief encounters were seldom forgotten. Ruth maintained the better mental inventory of names—reinforcing a common husband-wife pattern still unaccounted for by psychologists—but both cherished vivid memories of those relationships, many of which helped shape significant decisions in their lives.

Roy C. Martin, the fourth member of Kennedy's quartet of closest friends and the man he credited with igniting his career-long fascination with the oil business, was considered an adjunct member of the family until his death in 1988 at the age of ninety-two.

Christa Teichmann, a teenage German girl who worked for the Kennedys during a visit to America, returned later and became as much a member of the family as their son Eddie. She was, in fact, referred to and treated as their daughter, and when she married Jeffrey Cook and they had a daughter, Susanne, Edwin and Ruth Kennedy gained a son-in-law and granddaughter, adding to the family group that also included Eddie's children, Dan and Patty.

Long-remembered advice from early teachers was repaid to society in the form of educational endowments. A critical $50 loan in the twenties appreciated to the value of an important college building and more in the eighties. A chance meeting at an Indian trading post sparked an interest that grew into one of the world's finest collections of Navajo weavings and Native American jewelry, placed in a university museum in the nineties.

In financing these and many other endeavors, Edwin and Ruth Kennedy expressed another deeply felt philosophy that "the most noble charity of all is to prevent a man or woman from having to accept charity." Having come from poor families, they were intent on establishing gifts in a manner that would encourage young persons to help themselves, and to lay cornerstones of projects on which other donors could build. They did not believe in fluttering money into the winds of fate.

As a consequence, Edwin and Ruth decided early that there would be few charitable donations in their wills. They had worked hard for their wealth and wanted a full return on every dollar they gave away. That meant determining its use during their lifetimes. Establishing a foundation, the Kennedys reasoned, simply turned over control to future directors who might be more interested in perpetuating the organization than getting the best use from its funding. They had observed this situation within well-meaning boards who lost sight of their original objectives.

So the Kennedys apportioned their gifts strategically, meaning where they believed recipients could realize maximum benefits and in ways that would have catalytic and compounding effects. "We prefer to distribute our money, particularly that given to colleges and universities, when and where needs arise that we consider vital," Ed Kennedy often explained. "And we prefer to use it as incentives for others to participate. Making it too easy is a mistake."

With that as their philosophy, Edwin and Ruth Kennedy proceeded to give away the major part of what they owned, despite their insistence that "tax laws have made charitable giving increasingly difficult." Although meticulous in keeping records to conform with those laws, they never totalled the amount given over a period of years. When they discovered that two young friends of Eddie and Christa could not afford to attend college because their father pumped gasoline for a living, they sponsored one at Hiram College and the other at Virginia Military Institute, without mentioning it to anyone outside their immediate family. Many similar individual gifts, provided quietly and anonymously without taking tax deductions, never will be identified.

Never seeking the limelight of gratitude, they reacted negatively to blatant displays of material wealth so often flaunted in New York City. They had not set out to acquire money as a source of power or influence. Once asked to name the goals he sought in life, Kennedy answered, "a family, a home for gracious living, and the respect of my fellow man." Ruth, who rarely veiled her true feelings, purposely avoided a neighborhood couple whom she believed to be "always trying to impress people with their money," explaining to daughter Christa, "They are phonies."

John Baker, active in Harvard and New York business circles both before and after his tenure as a university president, explained this distinguishing quality of the Kennedy personalities another way:

> Ed and Ruth never "went Manhattan." Going Manhattan entails forgetting friends at home to cultivate "big names" in New York, selecting highly visible prestigious summer vacation spots, joining all the best-known clubs, name dropping, and perhaps being divorced and remarried once or twice. They didn't get involved in this type of New York social scene. They avoided activities that drew society headlines, vacationed in a remote area of Canada, and returned to visit their families in Ohio whenever possible. They had very good friends in New York and elsewhere, of course, but Ed moved up the Wall Street ladder of success on his own merits without going Manhattan.

The diversity and impact of Ed Kennedy's enthusiastic support of higher education in several areas of the country led to his nomination by Ohio University for the CASE Volunteer of the Year award. In introducing him at the Washington affair, Ohio University President Charles J. Ping explained that he had been a "counselor and benefactor" to other institutions as well as the one from which he had graduated. Among those were Hiram College, Juniata College, Ohio Northern University, Hampden-Sydney College, Utah Southern University, Findlay College, The University of New Mexico, and Cottey College. "Edwin and Ruth Kennedy built wisely and well when it was bricks and mortar they gave, but most of all they invested in people—distinguished faculty and hundreds upon hundreds of students in a crisis of need," said Dr. Ping.

Congratulatory letters from President Reagan and Vice President Bush commended Kennedy's "extraordinary efforts on behalf of public and private higher education" and the "generosity, wise counsel, and exemplary character that have made a difference in the lives of generations of Americans." Secretary of Education William J. Bennett described the impact of Kennedy's thoughtfulness as being "international in scope" because he had "aided students from foreign lands as well as American students in helping them reach their goals of quality higher education."

Edwin Kennedy's life as an investment banker, private entrepreneur, sportsman, and philanthropist was noteworthy and exciting—daring in a generally conservative financial setting, conservative in the generally liberal field of education, happy, sad, sometimes bizarre, nearly always interesting. His self-imposed commitments were unswerving. He could be tough in a business situation, but break into thunderous laughter at his wife's uproarious humor. He and Ruth had purchased luxury fishing camps operated as commercial enterprises in Canada and Panama. They were welcomed as good friends into Navajo hogans in the American Southwest, and had been made honorary members of Africa's Hausa Tribe in northern Nigeria.

But as he stood before guests at the black-tie gala in Washington, his hair parted in the middle as always, his eyes revealing a smile of appreciation through dark-rimmed glasses, the five-feet-eight, svelte honoree still bore an astonishing resemblance to high school debater Edwin Kennedy, whose senior photograph, accompanied by the words, "He hath a head to contrive, a tongue to persuade, and a hand to execute," appeared in the 1922 yearbook of Harding High School in Marion, Ohio.

Chapter 2 **An Early Resolve**

When my brother Edwin went to school, he would keep his shoes from getting dusty and dirty by wearing rubbers over them. But he would hide the rubbers before arriving, then retrieve them on the way home. I could tell he didn't want to stay on the farm.

—Gladys Kennedy Linville

Most boys in the rural areas of central Ohio during the early years of the twentieth century were groomed to follow their fathers into farming. Edwin Clarence Kennedy assumed the same would be true of the son who bore his first name. But he was wrong.

At an age when children ordinarily are oblivious to economic conditions, young Edwin Lust Kennedy was troubled by having been born into what he later referred to as "restricted financial circumstances." Like other youngsters in Marion County's Scott Township, Edwin enjoyed childhood friendships and family fun. He joined his father in working the corn, wheat, oats, and soybean fields of the 160-acre farm and helped tend the cattle, sheep, and hogs that likewise were standard products of Buckeye State agriculture. He also accepted his fair share of daily chores, with the exception of milking cows. In later years he could not remember why he dreaded that routine phase of farm life, nor how he managed to escape it. What he did recall most vividly was the early realization that despite the pleasures of growing up in a loving family and an invigorating open-air environment, farming before the era of tractors and combines and electricity and paved country roads meant working from dawn to darkness just to stay alive. That was true, at least, on the Kennedy farm.

Tucked by retreating glaciers into a fertile edge of the midwestern central plains, Marion County would one day be considered one of the most productive agricultural sections of Ohio. Early settlements were made on the gentle rolling hills of the county's southern region, which had been reserved for payment of bounties to American Revolutionary War veterans. From there, pioneering farmers migrated northward into flatlands offering more efficient tilling and opportunities to quarry limestone underlying the rich black soil.

Many years later, Frank and Olive McCurly Kennedy moved with their two young sons from Missouri to Ohio, settling first in the northwestern corner of the state, then in the northern flatland area of Marion County, near the village of Kirkpatrick. Imprecise records indicate that one of the sons, William, later became a self-taught engineer and moved to the Canton area, where he married and raised a family. The other, Edwin Clarence Kennedy, took over the family farm, including its sizable mortgage, soon after his twentieth birthday, and the following year, on March 14, 1900, he married Emma C. Lust, the 16-year-old daughter of a prosperous farm couple.

Jacob and Rosa Lust were respected in Marion County's Grand Prairie Township for both their success in farming and his political activism. A native of Germany who had migrated to Ohio with his family when he was a child, Jacob was described by a Marion County historian as a general farmer "with particular interest in raising fine hogs," and a Democrat who "served in various offices." Those included several terms as township trustee, twenty-one years on the school board, six years on the county board of infirmary, and terms as director and clerk of his school district and assessor of the township. He and Rosa eventually became the parents of seven children, four of whom, including Emma, began housekeeping in Marion County after their marriages. Sunday family gatherings soon became a tradition, as well as the major social outlet for these

An Early Resolve

young married couples, and remained important as they began to raise families. Emma's family in effect became the closest relatives also to her husband when his parents died shortly after he was married.

Born on May 25, 1904, Edwin L. Kennedy soon looked to Helen, his older sister by two years, for companionship. When he was old enough for first grade, he joined her in walking two and a half miles to and from a one-room school house in Kirkpatrick, a difficult task made all the more trying during severe Ohio winters. Two years later their father bought them a pony named Prince and an open buggy. Delighted to be liberated from the five-mile daily walk, the children nonetheless encountered a new vexation. They had to bundle a daily lunch for Prince, harness him, and put him in a rented barn stall when they arrived at Kirkpatrick, then retrieve and harness him again for the return trip home. Furthermore, the sometimes stubborn pony wasn't always certain he had to obey the reining of an eight-year-old driver. Seventy-nine years later, that driver still remembered what changed Prince's mind:

> Prince decided one day that he didn't want to take us to school, so when he came to a wide place in the road, he turned around. We didn't have strength enough even together to prevent him from doing that, but we couldn't have abandoned him either, so he simply took us back home. Well, after that happened two or three more times, my father decided to hide on the back of the buggy. When we came to the pony's favorite turn-around spot, dad jumped off and whipped him. That ended the problem.

Housing eight grades in one small building, the Kirkpatrick school embodied characteristics endemic of a revered, yet often underrated era in American education. For nearly a century, rural one-room schools formed the backbone of educating Midwestern farm children. Some 65,000 of the small wooden or brick schools could be found in eight states, including Ohio, when Edwin and Helen Kennedy were elementary students. Most of those in Ohio were organized at township levels, but methods of establishing different types of school districts were debated regularly in the state legislature. Although movements toward consolidation into schools that could compete with those in cities were under way, they were countered by strong opposition from farm communities. Proponents of the status quo believed that teachers in the one-room schools worked with pupils as individuals, thereby training them better in the basics of reading, writing, spelling, and figuring. Many professional educators agreed, adding that bright children in lower grades could be challenged by listening to lessons being taught to older students. They noted that many leaders in business, industry, the professions, and politics had attended one-room rural schools, and that tests given to fifteen thousand students revealed no marked educational advantage in city and consolidated schools. One professional, however, explained that the tests concentrated on the rudimentary "Three Rs" and, therefore, did not reflect the important advantage of educating students in "the beauties of nature and the elementary sciences, in the rich content of geography, history, and civics, in music and art" at the larger schools. Indeed, Edwin Kennedy was to become aware of such deficiencies in his primary education. On the other hand, he benefited from having one of the remarkable teachers who were able to motivate, teach, arbitrate squabbles, and deal with petty political bickering, while serving also as counselors, nurses, and baseball umpires. These teachers, most of them women, received low salaries, but enjoyed high standing within their communities.

Jessie Daugherty, who taught all eight grades at the Kirkpatrick school, was both a skilled educator and an experienced disciplinarian. Like others in the room, young Edwin Kennedy learned to detect the danger point in her temperament when she smacked her lips—an unconscious signal for an abrupt end to mischief and a return to lessons—but he had to discover also that her governance did not end with the expiration of classes. At the end of one day's session, Edwin and three other boys rushed through the door, then whirled and held it so younger students could not get out. They had calculated correctly their strength against the smaller children, but failed to factor in the ingenuity of their teacher, who opened a back window, climbed out, ran around the building, and apprehended the guilty foursome. The whipping that followed was matched by Edwin's father that evening—a standard punishment in the Kennedy household and others of the era.

Mrs. Daugherty, however, was best remembered by Edwin as having trained her students well in basic subject matter, and being therefore the first person to have an important influence on his realization that education represented his only avenue of escape from the harsh, impoverished circumstances that seemed to have a strangle-hold on his life. It would not be an easy path, nor would fruition of his aspirations become tangible for many years to come, but an unyielding desire had been imbedded firmly in his mind and he would forever respect Mrs. Daugherty and all others who helped him make the journey.

As they progressed to higher grades and larger wooden seat-desks in Kirkpatrick School, Helen and Edwin advanced in terms of transportation to a driving horse and closed buggy. They also added a daily passenger—a girl who lived at one of the farm homes scattered sparcely through Scott Township. Then a change in school districting sentenced them once again to walking. With their new one-room school inaccessible by the dirt road leading past their home, the children followed the shortest possible route, which took them across fields, over fences, and through a woods. Finally, their parents somehow arranged to have them attend a country school in nearby Monnett, little more than a mile away but in another county, where both completed the eighth grade.

The elder Kennedy was a good father and a dedicated farmer who felt decidedly more comfortable working the soil than managing the necessary corollary business affairs. His wife was known for her good looks, good cooking, and strong will, all of which friends attributed to her German background. There had been a marked German migration directly to Marion County, and many farmers in the area, Emma's relatives among them, expressed pride in being able to retain much of their heritage without diminishing an intense loyalty to their adopted country. Excellent farmers, they considered uncompromising morality to be an essential ingredient of success. Emma Kennedy possessed such a spirit and passed it on to her children by encouraging them to always set worthwhile goals. She understood and supported her son's appetite for learning.

In 1910, the family grew to five with the birth of a second daughter, Gladys. The number of farm buildings grew also that year with completion of a new barn. Six years later, the family built a new house on the gently sloping yard in front of their home, an old structure that had been purchased with the land and was overdue for the demolition that followed. While the father worked to build most of the new house himself, his son, then twelve, drove a wagon team to and from the Millard Hunt Store in Marion, a round-trip of twenty-four miles, to haul cement blocks.

By then, young Edwin also was skilled in driving the family "Model T" Ford, which his parents had purchased when he was nine years old. He had learned to maneuver it around a pasture when he was so small that on his first attempt he was forced to stop the vehicle by running into a post when he discovered his foot could reach but not fully depress the brake pedal. An understanding father, however, permitted his son to take it out on the road as soon as he was tall enough to peer over the dashboard and push the brake pedal simultaneously.

The car enabled the family to enjoy infrequent outings such as a full-day's trip to and from Olentangy Park in Columbus, but it did not replace the horse and buggy that continued to be the only feasible mode of transportation during winter months and when warm-weather rains turned the dirt road into a mud slide.

During some rain storms, however, road conditions were comparatively minor concerns. One particularly devastating series of downpours, combined with melting snow, flooded a creek between the Kennedy barn and a pasture where sheep were grazing, at a time when Edwin's father was attending a cattle sale at the Chicago Stockyards. With water rising rapidly in the pasture, young Edwin and his mother had to move swiftly to save the herd from drowning. No amount of enticement could lure the frightened animals across the creek, so mother and child had to brace themselves against the strong current, grab each sheep by its wool, and heave it to safety. Then they drove the still-reluctant herd to the barn. When the flood finally subsided, water had risen to within two feet of the barn. Memories of the incident returned to Edwin many times in the years ahead, and while they afforded a sense of accomplishment in an emergency situation, they also reinforced the aura of constant struggle he associated with farming.

Social life at that time was limited largely to church events, infrequent visits by neighbors, and the family get-togethers. The Kennedys rarely missed a Sunday service at the small Disciples of Christ Church (later called the Christian Church) in Kirkpatrick, and accepted active roles in its social affairs. After church in warm weather, the expanding families would gather to share chicken dinners. "All the aunts, uncles, and cousins would take turns serving at their houses, and we grew so large it would take the whole summer to make the rounds," Gladys later recalled. When they finished eating, the grown-ups sat in a large circle outside the house and talked politics. "All of them were Democrats," Gladys said, "and they didn't think much of Warren G. Harding, even if he was from our county." A Republican, Harding served in the U.S. Senate for six years before being elected president by an enormous majority in 1920. He had been owner and editor of *The Marion Star* since 1884.

As Edwin grew older and increasingly aware that simply meeting each mortgage payment represented a monthly crisis for his parents, he developed an aversion toward borrowed money. It was an attitude he later described matter-of-factly—"If you can't pay for something, you can't afford it"—and it lasted his entire life. By the time he was in junior high school, he was raising and selling rabbits, helping neighboring farmers make hay, and doing whatever else could be worked into the schedule of responsibilities at home, to pay for things he wanted. The combination of those jobs and realizing the continuous financial struggle of his family reaffirmed his resolve to become well educated.

The great Meuse-Argonne offensive led by American troops was bringing an end to World War I when Edwin entered high school at Marion in September of 1918. With no secondary school in the township where he lived, he was forced to leave home at 6:30 a.m. and walk two miles to catch an interurban car at a wooden platform where it stopped about half-way between the Bucyrus and the Marion stations to pick up cans of milk placed there by area farmers. To keep his shoes clean during the long walk, Edwin wore rubbers, which he removed and hid between planks of the milk platform. "I didn't want to appear as a country bumpkin to other students," he later confessed in discomforting retrospection. "It was an excessive emotion on my part, but it seemed terribly important at the time." Each afternoon, he rushed from school to barely catch the 4:00 p.m. interurban that would take him back to the milk stop, where he recovered the rubbers and retraced the cross-country leg of his daily trek in time to help with the chores. The tight commuting schedule prompted him to estimate that he did as much running as members of the track team, and his season lasted all nine months of the school year.

For a young man who had little exposure to people, entertainment, or culture, the difficulty of making a transition from one-room country schools was intensified a few weeks after classes began when a severe epidemic of influenza swept across America. Marion High School was among many that were closed temporarily, with students given assignments they were expected to complete at home. Working on his own, with some help from his mother, Edwin quickly recognized deficiencies in certain subjects, particularly science and mathematics. These threatened to increase as the flu epidemic continued and the school closing passed from days into weeks. "I remember that it was well into November before we returned to school, because I was on a corn binder when I heard all the whistles, bells,

An Early Resolve

and sirens signal the news that the war in Europe had ended on November 11," he said later.

The influenza spread so rapidly in the fall of 1918 that medical experts predicted it could become as devastating in the United States as malaria in southeastern Asia. A bulletin of the National Research Council described the 1918 epidemic as "the most calamitous event for many generations, aside from the Great War." Even when the panic subsided, many feared that any recurrence of flu could start another epidemic, especially in the cities. Perhaps the isolation of farming, with all its drawbacks, saved members of the Kennedy family from contracting the dreaded disease.

Studying at home and having time to reflect on his new life of daily commuting convinced Edwin that he should seek another method of pursuing his high school education. His older sister, Helen, already had solved the problem by staying with their Aunt Lucy Lust, who lived in an apartment in Marion, and working for a dentist. Edwin decided to seek a similar arrangement, and the thought persisted throughout his freshman year, as he closed the gap in his knowledge of mathematics and managed to make what he called "an adjustment to what seemed to me to be a new and different world."

One of the most memorable persons in that world was a teacher of ancient history named Pansy Rauhauser. "From her I learned to think analytically," he said later, "and that was something I never forgot. What she gave me was useful throughout my subsequent life. It certainly is the heart of finance and it's useful in a great many other things as well."

Working at home the following summer gave him little opportunity to earn money for himself, but when he began his sophomore year at Marion High, his plans were in order. By postponing each day's trip home to a later interurban, he could hurry from school to Mr. Harding's newspaper plant, grab one of the first papers off the press, and beat other job seekers in searching the "want ads." The enterprising idea brought an early result in the form of employment as a delicatessen clerk. Meanwhile, he was able to rent a bedroom and get one meal a day at the home of Mr. and Mrs. Charles Rowe, whom he had known all his life. The Rowes owned the only general store in Kirkpatrick for many years before retiring and moving to Marion. "They were marvelous people," he said, "and I had always admired Mr. Rowe for giving the most beautiful prayers I had ever heard in church, even though he was not the minister."

With the promise of a new lifestyle thus fulfilled, young Edwin Kennedy set about working his way through high school, returning home only on weekends. The delicatessen job proved to be adequate, except for one major drawback. Each Friday's "Seafood Day" was preceded by a long Thursday evening session of fish cleaning. The problem was not the work itself, but the lingering aftermath of scaling and boning hundreds of fish. Scrubbing one's hands with soap and applying a cheap cologne purchased at the Five and Ten Cents Store could not erase the smell of those fish. After many Fridays of keeping his hands in his pockets during school hours, the self-conscious clerk looked for another job, which he found at the Frank Brothers Department Store.

The position of elevator operator, package wrapper, and delivery boy paid five dollars a week, enough to live on if he skipped some of his lunches. But when a post-war business collapse deflated the nation's economy in 1920, throwing three million men out of work, Frank Brothers regrettably informed their newest employee that his services could no longer be afforded. Fortunately, they gave him sufficient notice to look for another job. Without losing a day's work, he was able to find part-time employment with the Gem Pharmacy, whose owner, James Messenger, paid him seven dollars a week, eight when he also worked on a weekend. Advice and help from Messenger added another layer of background for Edwin Kennedy's later conviction that "all of us who want some sense of self fulfillment can achieve it by helping others who have problems."

Rural America suffered more than business and industrial centers in what was labeled "The Farm Depression" of the early 1920s. Despite the advent of hybrid corn and extraction of oil from soybeans, wholesale prices of farm products plunged and foreclosures began an upward spiral that would accelerate on into the next decade. Descendants of Jacob Lust predictably attributed this disaster to the newly installed Republican administration of President Harding, whose famed campaign speeches from the front porch of his home in Marion had failed to stir their local pride. Edwin Kennedy recalled that he and other students gave only passing notice to the campaign centered right in their own city, and were only mildly impressed when their school was renamed Harding High School following the election. Presidential supporters attributed the unexpected recession, hitting at a time of the anticipated "return to normalcy" advocated during the campaign, to the combination of a glutted domestic market and a sharp drop in exports. Harding himself referred to it as a period of reconstruction and readjustment. Rural opponents thought it ironic that the recession's most severe and lasting impact was on agriculture when the leader of their country had himself been born on an Ohio farm.

Whatever the reason, the timing was devastating to the Kennedy family. At the conclusion of World War I, the elder Kennedy had joined a group of farmers purchasing a grain elevator at Monnett. In the wave of economic failures, the business went bankrupt, and Edwin Clarence Kennedy never recovered financially from the loss of his large investment.

Those lean years, however, had moments of happiness. High points were the births of two more sons, Richard in 1920 and Robert in 1922. The age spread of children was described by Gladys as being somewhat like having three families. "Helen and Edwin grew up together, then I came along more or less by myself, then Dick and Bob appeared after two other sons had died in infancy, and they grew up together." Whatever struggles lay ahead, preserving a close family bond would always be a top priority of all the children and their parents. In a reversal of most families' experiences, Gladys noted, "we grew closer rather than drifting apart as the years went by."

Only the older daughter would continue to be involved with farming in later years. Helen Kennedy married Raymond Baer, and moved to a farm near Marion, where they had a daughter,

Dorene. After Baer's death ten years later, Helen married Edgar Likens, a dealer in farm products; they lived near Kirkpatrick before moving to Marion.

Studies and work consumed most of Edwin's time during his remaining years in high school, forcing him to be somewhat of a loner, and contributing to a shyness he would have to battle in the years ahead. Although he became a member of the senior debate team, he was unable to take part in activities requiring after-school participation. Yet, he enjoyed working at the pharmacy, and he observed carefully the talents of customers engaged in various professions and businesses.

By the time he was ready for graduation, Edwin already had decided he wanted to become a lawyer and join Marion's most prominent firm, Crissinger, Guthrey and Strelitz. To accomplish that, he was determined to attend Ohio Northern University, the alma mater of most Marion attorneys. This feeling was reinforced when he discovered that both of the state's U.S. senators, Frank B. Willis and Simion Fess, were Ohio Northern graduates.

An excellent student, Edwin was encouraged in his educational ambitions by his mother and by several of his favorite teachers, one of whom was the sister of President Harding. "I remember clearly that she demonstrated poetic rhythm by reading poetry to us while we marched around the room," he said. "That's good teaching."

Jobs during school months had provided just enough money for sustenance, but Edwin had saved some money by working at a stone quarry, helping pave a new highway between Bucyrus and Marion, and filling silos in the late summers. It was enough to pay tuition and begin college, but only if he could obtain part-time employment as quickly as possible.

Ohio Northern University was located in the small town of Ada, forty miles northwest of Marion. When Edwin Kennedy arrived there in the fall of 1922, his immediate objectives were to enroll as a freshman and get a job that would support him through four undergraduate years of the arts law curriculum. Part-time employment was almost nonexistent in Ada, so he accepted the only available job, as a door-to-door Fuller Brush salesman, despite what he considered "more shyness than was comfortable to live with." To his own surprise, he quickly discovered an ability to sell successfully, but the gnawing distress of knocking on the doors of strangers was overpowering. When the opportunity to become a cook in a combination restaurant and snack shop arose, he wanted it badly enough to avoid discussing his culinary qualifications. Somehow bluffing his way through what his employer apparently did not recognize as a training period, he became sufficiently adept to carry out nightly stints in the kitchen (although the first time he tried to flip, rather than simply turn an egg, it hit the ceiling).

Working at night also offered the solution to a problem Kennedy had encountered when he registered for classes. As a brush salesman he had found that daytime work, even though he had some control over its schedule, seriously limited his selection of courses. What he could not have visualized at the time was a piece of good fortune hidden in the apparent drawback of that restriction. Enrolling in a class, "Economic History of the United States," only because it was available during a reasonable non-working hour, changed the career pattern of Edwin Kennedy's life. Enthralled by the exciting classroom presentations of a dynamic professor named Wilfred E. Binkley, he abandoned all desire to become a lawyer in favor of studying economics, banking, and finance. Dr. Binkley, who afterwards received international acclaim as a lecturer and the author of authoritative books on political parties and presidential power, encouraged his young student to pursue this new ambition, but explained that he could not receive the necessary coursework at Ohio Northern.

Coincidentally, Earl Dobbins, one of Kennedy's good friends who also had been reared on a farm near Kirkpatrick and was one year ahead of him at Ohio Northern, had decided to change schools. Dobbins, who came from a prosperous family, suggested that they both transfer to Ohio Wesleyan University, which had a highly regarded department of economics. Unable to afford the tuition at Ohio Wesleyan, however,

Kennedy chose Ohio University from a list of state-supported institutions Binkley had suggested. Then he talked Dobbins into accompanying him there, arguing that they could find a place to be roommates. "Ed was a mighty persuasive fellow," Dobbins explained many years later.

The reason for Kennedy's somewhat random selection of Ohio University was not indelibly imprinted in his memory. But what he did remember clearly was Professor Binkley as another person who helped guide him toward success. The experience at Ohio Northern would someday be among myriad recollections contributing to Edwin Kennedy's self-imposed moral commitment to "discharge" what he considered "personal indebtedness" toward the people and institutions that helped him achieve the difficult task of obtaining the education that would launch him on his wide-ranging and remarkably successful career.

Chapter 3   Gaining Confidence

> *Education in its widest sense includes everything that exerts a formative influence, and causes a young person to be, at a given point, what he is.*
> —Mark Hopkins
> Educator, Theologian

Anyone who has grown up in a world of high-speed communication and transportation would have difficulty comprehending the excitement of the Chautauqua Circuit that brought entertainment, culture, intellectual discussions of current events, and a touch of religion to American communities during twenty-eight years of the early twentieth century.

The traveling summer programs began in 1904 as an extension of what had originated thirty years earlier as a training center for Sunday School teachers on the shores of Lake Chautauqua, New York. The beauty of the lake and its surrounding hills had enhanced the popularity of "The Chautauqua" as it evolved rapidly into a center for general educational entertainment and summer outings. By the end of the nineteenth century, speakers, singers, and actors across the country were competing for summer engagements that drew thousands of visitors to the center, bringing it a fame that overshadowed the purpose for which it had been planned. Yet, its location in the southwestern tip of the state made it virtually inaccessible for millions of others who could only read of its allure in newspapers, general magazines, and the monthly *Chautauquan*, which had a circulation rivaling those of other national publications. It was left to an Iowa talent broker named Keith Vawter to sell the idea of developing a circuit that would spread the programs from the guiding "Mother Chautauqua" to other areas.

Although the movement, referred to by President Theodore Roosevelt as "the most American thing in America," spread from coast to coast, the Middle West became known as the "Chautauqua belt." Separate circuits emerged, each with a metropolitan hub, but booking its week-long tent shows in smaller cities and towns. One section of the Redpath Circuit, based in Columbus, Ohio, covered all of that state and West Virginia, and parts of Kentucky, bringing to those areas such celebrities as humorist and World War I correspondent Irvin S. Cobb, celebrated political orator William Jennings Bryan, opera singer Madame Schumann Heink, Arctic explorer Vilhjalmur Stefansson, evangelist Billy Sunday, author-playwright Edna Ferber, journalist Walter Lippmann, senators, musicians, comedians, magicians, and scores of theatrical and motion picture personalities.

In its peak year of 1924, nearly five hundred Chautauquas were presented in Ohio alone, and a national tally revealed that more then 10 percent of the American population attended the popular programs offering professional billings in more than nine thousand communities. A reporter who attended several Redpath performances explained that the familiar "brownish-tinted tent—whether in Chillicothe, Cuyahoga Falls, Mt. Victory, or any of the remaining 137 places on the circuit—with all its appurtenances, posters, folding chairs, and platform properties, makes the circus tent resemble a deserted wigwam." Although the typical show remained in one location for five to seven days, depending on the size of the community and the extent of financial backing, a flow of individual acts on one-day stands moved from town to town. Logistics of this arrangement required outstanding management, cooperation of all participants, and a great deal of luck, particularly with railroad schedules, on which the entire operation depended. One lecturer showed a reporter his 1923 contract calling for ninety-one appearances in ninety-one days at ninety-one towns.

"Season" tickets entitled holders to attend all afternoon and evening sessions at a price of two or three dollars, compared to fifty cents for individual events. An advance contract signed by the city and ordinarily backed by bankers, merchants, and civic organizations, guaranteed a minimum number of sales.

Anticipation of "Chautauqua Week" was stimulated when an advance publicity agent arrived to work with the guarantors and promote the coming attraction. A few days later a three-man set-up crew and a "junior girl," all college students, would follow. While the young men pitched the huge tent in a meadow or large vacant lot near Main Street, set up fifteen hundred folding chairs, and put the platform together, the young woman sold season tickets and organized activities for children. After performers began arriving, often to be met by town dignitaries and high school bands, the set-up crews helped them with luggage and props, then maintained and guarded the tent and its belongings. The junior girl worked with the children each morning and sold individual performance tickets in the afternoons and evenings.

Being selected as a set-up crew member in the summer of 1923 brought two valuable benefits for Edwin Kennedy. Most important, it assured him of earning money for tuition at Ohio University. Second, although he did not fully realize it at the time, the camaraderie he enjoyed within his own unit and with others whose paths he would cross during summer Chautauqua seasons, along with the opportunity to meet a wide variety of celebrated entertainers, would greatly broaden his limited interpersonal and cultural background. "I heard *Faust* so often that first summer that I almost memorized the entire opera," he recalled.

At the end of each week, crew members took down the tent, chairs, and platform, loaded it all onto a box car, along with cots that would serve as their beds, and rode on to the next location. Thus, during the summer months before entering Ohio University as a sophomore, Kennedy became familiar with more towns than he had visited in the previous nineteen years of his life, and became acquainted with nationally known personalities, whose names he carefully recorded. He also received the promise of joining a crew the following year.

When Edwin Kennedy and Earl Dobbins enrolled at Ohio University in September 1923, they rented a room together at the home of Mrs. Bessie "Ma" Shepard at the foot of Mulberry Street hill, near the campus in Athens. Mrs. Shepard, whose husband had been killed in a train accident, rented rooms to support herself and her four young sons. To supplement money he had saved from the Chautauqua job, Kennedy worked every day at the Men's Union Boarding Club cafeteria in the basement of the Agriculture Building and sought whatever part-time tasks became available from time to time.

Under the leadership of President Elmer B. Bryan, Ohio University recently had resumed a building program interrupted by World War I. At the same time, curricula were being broadened, with emphasis on areas of study that would attract more men and help overcome an imbalance of sixty percent women among 1,573 students, a situation that had developed after the highly publicized establishment of a state normal college for teacher training at the university. With that same objective in mind, the university was about to complete a new men's gymnasium as a first step in strengthening the physical education department and encouraging sports in general. A campaign had been launched the previous year to raise $300,000 by subscription from university graduates and friends for construction of an Alumni Memorial Auditorium, and plans were being made for an engineering building and a new university-operated elementary school for student teaching. The latter would release an older training school building for other uses (it was remodeled to house the School of Music).

Located in the forested hill country of Southeastern Ohio, the university had been established in 1804 as the first institution of higher learning in the Northwest Territory. Almost exclusively a residential university, with commuting unfeasible from distant population centers, it was an integral part of Athens, a county-seat city of 6,500 people. Although most coeds lived in three large dormitories and ten cottages, there was no dormitory available to men; consequently men's housing was limited to community homes and ten fraternity houses.

(Sorority women were not yet permitted to have individual houses, and their meetings were held in West Wing, later renamed McGuffey Hall.)

As an entering sophomore in the School of Commerce, which was part of the College of Liberal Arts, Edwin Kennedy avoided the requirement of wearing a green-and-white freshman cap known as a "dink," and such first-year hazing as parading down Court Street clad in pajamas, learning freshman yells, and singing a school song whenever ordered to do so by an upperclassman. During his first year on campus, he earned a grade-point average of 3.66 based on a 4.00 scale, receiving no grade below "B" and setting a pace he would maintain throughout his college career. Focused always on a future in finance, he carefully structured a collegiate pattern that varied only in terms of living quarters and extracurricular interests.

In the fall of 1924, Earl Dobbins's parents retired from farming in Marion County and moved to Athens, where they rented a house in order to be near their son during his last year in college. Earl moved in with them, but insisted that Edwin Kennedy continue to be his roommate. Two other students also rented rooms there, providing an atmosphere not unlike that in the home of "Ma" Shepard. Kennedy would share the Dobbins home until the family moved back to Marion County after Earl's graduation in June 1925.

Taking part in intercollegiate debate proved to be an enjoyable extension of the interest Kennedy had developed in high school. And it seemed logical that the same penchant for controversial argumentation should lead also to membership in an organization that was gaining a high degree of notoriety across the country. Established in New York City, the League for Industrial Democracy published newsletters and pamphlets and organized local chapters to promote "education for a new social order based on production for use and not for profit." Socialist leader Norman Thomas, a native of Marion, Ohio, resigned his associate editorship of the *Nation* to direct activities of the League. Labor leaders, college students, social workers, and professors crowded New York meetings to hear such speakers as Bertrand Russell, socialist author-philosopher, and Dr. Wesley C. Mitchell, president of the American Economic Association. Student and faculty chapters on campuses of most major universities sponsored speeches and seminars led by men billed as "intellectual observers of the capitalistic system."

Paul Blanchard, field secretary for the League and hailed as "the world's greatest college trotter," spent most of his time visiting campuses. Speaking at Ohio University on January 25, 1924, Blanchard charged "industrialism" with creating a situation in which "sixty percent of the wealth is in possession of two percent of the people," resulting in conditions that "deny human freedom" and cause "great poverty." Following the impassioned speech, several students, including Edwin Kennedy, organized a new chapter that soon held roundtable discussions on social questions and relevance of higher education to the labor movement. Their impact was sufficient to bring Blanchard back the following year to address combined classes in sociology and a campus-wide convocation; the student newspaper reported that "Twenty-six new members joined the League that day." Students were elated when a headline in the *Columbus Dispatch* announced a state legislator's suggestion that "Socialism at Ohio University should be investigated."

In retrospect, Kennedy laughingly remembered the thrill of learning that the chapter's message was being heard. "We didn't really know exactly what we were for or against, and all we did was get together and talk, but we felt important in being classified in Columbus as dangerous people," he said. "We stood against making profits, which, of course was what we were going to school to learn to do, but most of the things we considered liberal would one day become ultra-conservative."

Still feeling a need to further combat the shyness stemming from the social impairment of his restricted background, Kennedy joined a local fraternity, Gamma Sigma, where he made many lasting friendships. While he was an undergraduate, the group became affiliated with a national fraternity, Theta Chi.

Belonging to a fraternity, viewed from the vantage of later years, might have seemed incongruous with struggling to meet college expenses, but in 1925 it was considered important to social growth. "Either you wore a fraternity emblem and had a good time, or you did not have an emblem and had your life confined to classes and a very few social events," wrote a researcher of that era. Indeed, at the Theta Chi installation banquet attended by university administrators and faculty, as well as some three hundred other guests, President Bryan expressed his belief in Greek organizations as a part of university life, adding, "There is no more real spiritual need at Ohio University than the establishment of more fraternities and sororities."

Despite having worked a second summer with the Redpath Chautauqua circuit and continuing his student jobs, Kennedy encountered increased problems in meeting expenses by the second semester of his junior year. For the first time since he began his college education, he admitted to total discouragement, and when he went home for Easter vacation in 1925 he told his parents he was going to drop out of school because there was no money to continue. Before the end of that vacation, however, someone in his church told him about an organization called the Teachout Foundation. That information led to another critical milestone in his quest for a college degree.

Albert R. Teachout was a successful Cleveland businessman who was active in both the Christian Church and as a trustee of his alma mater, Hiram College, which was affiliated with that church. "The more he prospered, the more he gave," reported a writer in *World Call* magazine. A soft-spoken man who had been born on a farm, Teachout made millions in the sash and door manufacturing business and other diversified interests. He was described by a friend and writer as a dependable and thorough man who believed in supporting institutions that would benefit large numbers of young people, and providing financial contributions "which others may find pleasure in enlarging." Among his many philanthropic ventures was permanent funding of the foundation bearing his name. Annual income from the endowment helped finance religious programs he had supported personally before his death in 1922, and provided cash scholarships for deserving Christian students.

By applying through his church in Kirkpatrick, Edwin Kennedy received a fifty-dollar Teachout scholarship—perhaps a pittance by later standards, but in 1925 a sum sufficient to support his return to Ohio University for the remainder of the spring semester. When he received the check in the mail, with the envelope postmarked "Hiram, Ohio," Kennedy assumed the Teachout Foundation was part of Hiram College. "That check was the most important thing in my life at the time," he recalled, "and I vowed that if I could ever repay Hiram College, I would do so, and that I would also pass on to others the priceless help given to me by the foundation." Nearly four decades later Kennedy would discover that the Teachout Foundation was unrelated to Hiram College; the letter had been mailed from that location, presumedly by a member of the Foundation who happened to be visiting the campus. But by then his support of Hiram was well underway.

It is an interesting coincidence that Kennedy's later philosophy of philanthropy would parallel that of the man who made it possible for him to receive the scholarship he would remember for the rest of his life.

In the summer of 1925, Kennedy returned to the Chautauqua Circuit, this time as a crew captain. Although he again enjoyed the experience, he was bothered by the loud profanity being used by his set-up crew, particularly because the tent always was pitched near homes, and youngsters gathered to watch the action. Realizing that young men away from home, some of them for the first time, were "prone to use considerable profanity," and that it was prevalent throughout the organization, he nevertheless put a stop to it within his unit. Afterwards he learned that letters of appreciation were sent to Redpath headquarters in Columbus from citizens of several communities. He was commended for the action, but more importantly, he had discovered a natural ability to influence attitudes in a way that avoided resentment by men working under his supervision.

With the beginning of his senior year at Ohio University, Kennedy moved into the Theta Chi fraternity house where he cleaned bathrooms in exchange for receiving a free room.

Enrollment at the university was continuing to increase, and the 250 students beginning their final year were expected to set a Commencement record the following June. Edwin Kennedy had hoped to be in that group, but the depletion of funds again would dictate a change of plans. Realizing he would need to find another means of completing his undergraduate studies, he enrolled in three courses within the College of Education, in addition to those in his major area of interest, and in February 1926, he accepted a position as eighth-grade teacher at the village of Tuppers Plains, twenty miles southeast of Athens. The remaining four credit hours needed to complete his A.B. would have to be earned through correspondence study.

Kennedy always considered himself to be a member of the Class of 1926. So did the many friends who regarded him as a classmate. But completing the necessary correspondence courses extended beyond that time, so the granting of his degree actually took place in 1927. It was a technicality that mattered only in the keeping of records. His final 3.629 grade-point average placed him in the top 10 percent of either class, with eligibilty to become a member of Phi Beta Kappa.

Pondering possible routes toward the future he visualized in finance, Kennedy concluded that an undergraduate liberal arts degree emphasizing economics still fell short of the preparation he would need. A master's degree from Ohio State University in Columbus seemed appropriate as an intermediate goal, but the usual roadblock—a lack of funds—made it necessary to map a somewhat circuitous means of getting there. Teaching could provide the answer. Motivated by a happy experience at Tuppers Plains, he calculated that a couple of years at a larger school should provide ample opportunity to settle debts and save money for graduate studies. In the fall of 1926 he accepted a position as history teacher at Washington Junior High School in Niles, Ohio, a steel town near Youngstown. His salary was $1,400 for the school year.

Although he did not lose sight of his primary target, Kennedy enjoyed his temporary career of teaching. "I loved working with children and I also loved history," he said. With a few exceptions such as fending off physical threats from the rather large eighth-grade son of a steelworker, he viewed the variety of experiences as "interesting and rewarding." Being accepted into the social life at Niles proved to be equally pleasant for a young man who had dated regularly but seldom seriously during college days. He had been engaged once at Ohio University, and almost became engaged again in Niles, but each time the tunnel-vision view toward his intended career interfered with romance. While teaching at Niles, he spent many evenings studying business courses in Youngstown.

At the end of the school year, Kennedy was invited to return to Washington Junior High School in the fall. During the summer interim, he rejoined Chautauqua. Although many recollections of the Redpath summers became clouded in later years, he remembered specific details of one incident that took place on an August evening in 1927:

> Following a final performance in Findlay, Ohio, we loaded everything into a box car as usual and moved by rail toward a city in West Virginia. But the infamous Detroit, Toledo and Ironton Railroad stranded us overnight in Ashland, Kentucky. That didn't bother us. We just went over and visited another group that happened to be there. Our paths often crossed, so we knew college students from other units of the circuit. This time I met a new Junior Girl named Ruth Zimmerman, who was a student at Ohio University. Well, since we traveled in our working clothes, I suddenly found myself trying to hide a hole in the seat of my pants, so our meeting was brief. Nothing historic. But I remembered her.

After completing a second year of teaching, Kennedy had saved enough money to buy a "Model T" Ford and enroll in the Graduate School of Business at Ohio State, beginning in the fall of 1928. He had established a good record at Niles and made friendships that would be preserved through correspondence and exchange visits in the years ahead, but nothing could divert him from his master plan.

Also a successful veteran of Chautauqua's Redpath circuit by then, he was promoted for his last summer with the organization to the prestigious role of advance publicity agent. And it was in that capacity that he again met Ruth Zimmerman, this time at Tiffin, Ohio.

Edwin had been working with guarantors and promoting publicity for several days when Ruth arrived in Tiffin to sell tickets and begin training children for the traditional "Kids' Circus" that would close the week's program. A talented piano player, she would help also with acts that required musical accompaniment.

A close friendship blossomed that summer. Edwin learned that Ruth would return to Ohio University in the fall, and told her of his intention to enter graduate school at Ohio State. With Athens just seventy-five miles from Columbus, he suggested, it seemed logical to continue their relationship during the months ahead. She agreed, and when the last Redpath tent was lowered and folded for winter storage, the two planned to meet next in Athens.

Tent Chautauqua faded with the rise of radio and talking pictures, disappearing in 1932. It had spread awareness, culture and entertainment over a wide swath of the country, and with the advent of good highways, increasing numbers of Americans made the trek to Chautauqua Lake, where the summer programs continued to flourish. Some communities along the circuits claimed their civic personalities had been forever improved by the spirit of the movement. Others reacted less enthusiastically, but the prevailing feeling was positive. To Edwin Kennedy, who broadened his vision, earned money for college, and met his future wife on the Redpath circuit, "Chautauqua" had gained high standing among the major influences on his life.

Chapter 4   **Family Ties**

> *The family is the only preserving and healing power counteracting any historical, intellectual, or spiritual crisis no matter of what depth.*
> —*Ruth Nanda Anshen*
> *The Family:Its Function 1959*

Church bells at Massillon, Ohio, had already begun ringing in the new century when Ruth DeWeese Zimmerman was born, moments before midnight on December 31, 1900. For many years afterward, "Cy" and Sadie Zimmerman enjoyed telling of hearing the bells and realizing that similar sounds, along with flashing lights and shrieking whistles in Cleveland, Washington, and other Eastern Time Zone cities were heralding the birth of the twentieth century while they themselves greeted the arrival of their third daughter. The account of those concurrent events, in fact, remained a favorite family story even after the daughter arbitrarily and permanently changed the observed date of her birth.

Cyrus W. Zimmerman had been born in 1857 and reared on a farm near the tiny village of Beach City, twelve miles south of Massillon. For several years after graduating from high school, he combined studies at normal schools with teaching, eventually receiving a degree from Delaware (Ohio) College. Moving to Massillon to accept a teaching position with the public school system, he married Sadie DeWeese, who had grown up in the nearby city of Canton.

During a career involving a variety of business activities, Zimmerman was best remembered for opening a business college in 1889. Beginning with only one full-time student in a small rented building, Massillon Business College and Normal School enjoyed an immediate growth reported in the March 27, 1891 issue of a Massillon newspaper, *The Gleaner:*

> The school has grown, not only in numbers, but in interest as well, until this winter the enrollment is over two hundred, with an average daily attendance of seventy-five, with five regular teachers in charge. Persistent effort, backed by a determination to succeed, has accomplished much, and Massillon today has a business college that is not only a credit to the Principal and corps of teachers, but to the community as well. Too much praise cannot be given Professor Zimmerman for the efficiency of this school.

Four children were born to Cyrus and Sadie Zimmerman, Helen in 1891, Edna in 1897, Ruth in 1900, and John in 1908. All attended school in Massillon, but the entire family spent each summer at the Beach City farm, operated by Cy's brother, Albert. Family reminiscence often centered on those summers, including stories of Ruth and John hiding behind trees that lined a long driveway to the farm house, and making sounds of owls and other nocturnal creatures when their older sisters' boyfriends came to call. Cyrus, who never earned much money as an educator and salesman, worked the farm alongside his brother during the summer months.

The gumption and determination of Cyrus and Sadie Zimmerman, said by family and friends to have been passed on to their children, appeared early in their youngest daughter. Although no documentation exists, a story passed through family channels and never disputed by Ruth concerns an incident said to have started when the doorbell rang on June 30, 1913. When Ruth's mother opened the door, she faced a delivery boy who said he had birthday flowers for her daughter. "You are mistaken," Mrs. Zimmerman exclaimed, "none of my daughters has a birthday today." At that point, twelve-year-old Ruth came bounding down the stairs to declare, "Yes, this is my birthday. I changed it and ordered the flowers." Explaining that the proximity of her actual birthday to Christmas cut down on parties and presents ("My presents always say Merry Christmas and Happy Birthday"), she made the pronouncement that remained in effect from that day forward.

Younger brother John displayed some of the same moxie many years later when he changed his last name to Carpenter as a first step in pursuing an acting career in Hollywood. When his father objected, he explained that Carpenter was merely the English translation of the German word Zimmerman. Not only did he use John Carpenter as a stage name while performing mostly small supporting roles in films and theater, he made it official through court proceedings when he entered the Army in World War II.

An excellent student at Massillon High School, Ruth Zimmerman was able to begin teaching at a one-room rural school immediately after graduation in 1919, enrolling also as a part-time freshman at Kent State Normal School (later Kent State University). While continuing her teaching during the following seven years, she attended three summer sessions at Ohio University and one at the University of Michigan. Consequently, when she enrolled at Ohio University in the fall of 1927, she already had accumulated enough credit hours to enter as a second-semester sophomore.

An English major, Ruth had a secondary interest in advanced piano classes, which she took strictly for pleasure. And although she remained in the College of Education, serving as a student assistant librarian steered her toward a liberal arts orientation emphasizing literature and social science. This emphasis received further encouragement from a colorful and revered professor, Dr. Hiram Roy Wilson, who headed the English Department.

A campus leader, Ruth was active in the Folklore Club, the Women's Sponsor Committee, YWCA, Pan Hellenic Council, dramatics, and musical productions. In her senior year she was elected president of Alpha Sigma Alpha social sorority.

Strong-willed, sometimes described as fiesty, Ruth Zimmerman nevertheless was extremely sensitive to the hardships and misfortunes of others. A member of her family noted that she "never could erase the memory of an exceptionally bright child who was killed getting off a school bus when she was teaching at a rural school in 1921."

Ruth was a person others came to for comfort and reassurance. Yet, she always chose to speak only of the happy things in her own life, dealing with unpleasant incidents without comment or outward show of emotion. The most devastating chapter in her young life was the death of her mother, at the age of sixty-three, when Ruth was twenty-four. The intense love and admiration between them had been apparent to those who knew them best; such characteristics as compassion, a sense of humor, and unwavering moral principles were said to have passed from mother to daughter. After Sadie Zimmerman died following a gall bladder attack, Ruth staunchly camouflaged what her sisters knew to be heartbreak. But she never again was able to enter the family home in Massillon.

The Zimmerman family maintained its close ties even as the children moved in different directions. Helen became a millinery designer, then married Lloyd Bletzer, who headed Noakers Ice Cream Company in Canton. Soon afterward, Bletzer joined Moores and Ross of Columbus, when it bought Noakers, beginning a series of steps in a highly successful career. Moores and Ross had two major divisions, dairy products and pharmaceutical research. Among other accomplishments, the latter group developed Similac, which became a leading infant formula. Moores and Ross then sold its pharmaceutical division to Abbott Laboratories and its dairy products division to Borden. Although Bletzer moved to Chicago as a regional manager of Borden, then to California as head of operations in that state, the pharmaceutical division sale also netted him a substantial stock interest in Abbott Laboratories, which became one of the nation's most prominent companies in terms of returns to investors. He and Helen had one daughter, Nancy Jane, who became owner of a 325-acre horse ranch near San Jose.

Ruth's sister Edna married Howard Oberlin, a mechanical engineer with Republic Steel. They lived at Lake Cable, between Massillon and Canton, and had a son, Charles, who died at the age of six. John (Zimmerman) Carpenter represented Arthur Rank Productions in the Orient for several years after World War II, then joined a Houston advertising agency. And Cyrus Zimmerman lived to the age of eighty-nine, making his home in later life with Edna, but spending two months a year with each of his other daughters.

The promises Edwin Kennedy and Ruth Zimmerman made at the close of the 1928 Chautauqua season proved to be more than fleeting summer fancies. That autumn, Edwin began a series of weekend treks along Route 33 from Columbus to Athens for dates with Ruth.

As a graduate student at Ohio State, Edwin was elated to be on the final leg of preparation for the career in finance he had envisioned for nearly seven years. He stayed at a rooming house near the campus and spent most of his time studying, except for the Saturdays spent at Ohio University. Having been away from college for two years, and lacking a few prerequisites, he struggled with accounting and foreign exchange, but had no trouble with other subjects, and quickly resumed the high overall academic standing he had held as an undergraduate. Characteristically, he attributed the exceptional qualities of individual professors as influencing his success. Dr. Charles A. Dice, a professor of banking, was "just a great teacher in every respect," Kennedy would say later. "He knew all phases of banking, and in the spring of 1929 he made the prophetic statement, 'One of these times when we least expect it, our banking system is going to collapse on us.' That is verbatim. Because of my interest in finance, he was almost a God in my judgment." Another professor, Henry Hoagland, used the Harvard case method to teach business management, and, like Dice, he continually emphasized the importance of uncompromising ethical standards. "I don't think I would have become a criminal without that influence," Kennedy later observed, "but those two men fixed firmly in my mind the value of ethical and moral conduct in business."

The only adversity in an otherwise gratifying year occurred not at the University, but at his family home near Kirkpatrick.

Driving home early one morning on the first day of spring vacation, Kennedy approached a familiar hill from which he always got the first glimpse of the family farm a half mile in the distance. When he reached the crest this time, however, he stopped and stared in disbelief. There in the distance, in front of the barn, was a pile of smouldering ashes and rubble. The house had burned to the ground during the night.

Richard Kennedy, who was nine years old, remembered the fire as leaving permanent scars on the family's life:

> I was old enough to realize the tragedy of the fire. It happened about midnight when the weather still was cold. My father had taken a kerosene lamp to the barn, where he took care of a sick calf. When he returned, he left it on the porch while he went inside, and before he could return to get it, the lamp apparently had fallen over and set the house on fire. It spread almost instantly. Mother, Robert, and I were all asleep, and we were fortunate to get out. I remember sitting on the lawn while my father tried to go back inside to save what he could. But it was impossible. All we could do was go to a neighbor's house about a quarter of a mile away and watch our house burn down. Everything was lost except the clothes we were wearing.

Along with their household possessions, the family lost virtually all records, photographs, and other memorabilia, including what Edwin had saved from high school, college, and Chautauqua. Only a few photos remained in the possession of the elder daughter, Helen, who was married and living near Marion. Gladys, a business college student in that city, had been looking forward to seeing Edwin during his vacation. "All I did, though, was cry my eyes out the entire day after the fire," she said.

While a new house was being built on the same site, the parents and their two youngest sons lived in Monnett. Unable to recover financially from the fire and the ensuing Great Depression, the family lost its farm a few years later and bounced almost frantically from one rental location to another, while the parents attempted to stabilize their lives. For a time their only income was from selling milk, and at one point during the struggle, the father temporarily lived apart from his family and sons. Richard and Robert picked potatoes to earn money for school clothes.

Then, in the mid-thirties, Rosa Lust decided to live the remainder of her life with her four children, spending three months a year with each family. Insisting that she "pay her way," the frugal matriarch gave each son and daughter ten thousand dollars from savings accumulated while she and Jacob operated their farm. With her share of that money, Emma Kennedy made a sizable down payment and negotiated a mortgage to buy a 103-acre farm on State Route 61, five miles north of Mt. Gilead in Morrow County, Ohio. Life continued to be harsh, but she made certain both younger sons graduated from high school.

Gladys Kennedy married Fred Linville, a businessman, and moved to Columbus, where they had two children, Saundra and Fred. Richard Kennedy stayed with his sister and her husband for three of the four years he attended Ohio State University (moving to a rooming house after the birth of Saundra). He was employed part-time at the university's Bureau of Research for a year and a half, then worked full night shifts as an usher and doorman at the RKO Palace Theater until he earned a business degree in 1942. After working for a short time on the family farm, he joined Hydraulic Press Company in Mt. Gilead, where he met and married June Russell. They had two daughters, Debra Lynn and Peggy Jean. Richard later became export manager for Riddell Corporation, expanding sales around the world until he barely survived an automobile accident in South Africa. After that he returned to Marion and entered the real estate business.

Robert Kennedy remained on the farm after graduating from high school in 1940. Almost immediately, he began managing operations while his father accepted a job at a grain elevator. During World War II Robert combined wheat for other farmers as well as working the family farm, and for the first time ever, the Kennedys retired their mortgage. With that accomplished,

Robert enrolled at Capital University in Columbus. Having been away from school for five years, however, he was restless to begin a career in sales, so he left Capital at the conclusion of his freshman year. Subsequently, he earned a substantial reputation as a senior salesman and sales manager for National Dairy Company, then became sales manager for Gem City Ice Cream Company in Dayton. At the age of forty-nine, he switched to a new career with Seonco Products of Cincinnati, but stayed in Dayton, working independently in accomplishing record-setting sales of air tools. He and Patricia Frederick were married in 1948 and had two children, Michael and Kay.

Robert Kennedy once said of his brother, "Family has always meant a lot to Ed. He has shown that feeling as long as I can remember." Concern for his family, indeed, dominated Edwin Kennedy's thoughts as he peered across the ruins of the farm house that cold March morning in 1929. Most painful of all was knowing there was little he could do to help at the time. In his mind, education still offered the only feasible solution to his inherited problems, and in a few months he would at last begin to find out whether or not that assumption was justified.

Chapter 5   **Tumbling Wall**

People later would speak of "before 1929" or "after 1929" as Noah's children may have spoken of the days before and after the flood.
—Joe Alex Morris
What A Year

Edwin Kennedy completed coursework for his master of business administration degree in June 1929. Time consumed in making up some deficiencies in prerequisite courses had kept him from writing the thesis needed for graduation, but living on what he termed "the thin edge financially" gave job hunting priority over remaining for summer sessions at Ohio State University. If there was any hesitancy in making this decision it was quickly quelled when a recruiter from the prestigious Standard Statistics Company offered him a position in New York City. That July he joined the financial printing organization, which later would be renamed Standard and Poors.

The financial marketplace was reaching epic proportions when Kennedy arrived in New York. Stock prices were climbing to such heights that some economists considered them overinflated. Yet, the prevailing opinion on Wall Street was that with production on an upward trend, corporate prosperity would keep pace with the costs of securities. The Dow Jones Industrial Index had begun to report a steady series of record highs, and investors were so enthusiastic one business writer claimed they didn't want to take vacations because making money in the market was more fun than going to the beach.

Kennedy's twenty-five-dollar-a-week job as a clerk, although somewhat routine, placed him near the nerve center of this financial maelstrom. Stationed with other employees at a U-shaped desk, he studied voluminous corporate reports, sifting out such pertinent data as dividends, stock spreads, and earnings that could be checked and reported in Standard's *Daily News*. For a young man being introduced to the complexities of the financial world, events of late 1929 provided a comprehensive crash course, first in unrestrained business prosperity, then the effects of the most disastrous economic turnaround in history.

In early October, Wall Street felt the first stings of panic when stock prices began to rise and fall erratically. Before investors could adjust portfolios to avoid impending losses, bidding at the New York Stock Exchange plunged so drastically on October 24, 1929, that the day became known around the world as "Black Thursday." While the Federal Reserve Board held an emergency session in Washington, D.C. and leading investment bankers gathered for a hastily organized joint meeting in the office of J. P. Morgan, thousands of bewildered investors crowded the street in front of the Exchange, all seeking information on what was happening. The following day's *Wall Street Journal* described the situation as "probably the most demoralizing condition in stock market history."

Through organized efforts of brokers, bankers, and government agencies, and with reassurance from President Herbert Hoover that "the fundamental business of the country, that is the production and distribution of commodities, is on a sound and prosperous basis," prices of securities rebounded temporarily after Black Thursday. With a Bankers' Pool committing money to buy securities and trading resuming some semblence of order, 1930 began with a general belief that faults in the system soon would be corrected and recovery would be under way by summer.

Whenever possible, Edwin Kennedy departed the daily stampede of New York finance for a weekend at Ohio University. This required traveling to Washington to catch a 5:30 a.m.

Baltimore & Ohio Railroad train to Athens. Such a schedule, he often said, was explanation enough of how much he wanted to see Ruth Zimmerman. Their last date before her mid-year graduation was documented by a society note in the January 21, 1930 issue of the campus newspaper, *The Green & White:* "A formal dance of Alpha Sigma Alpha was held Saturday night at the Hotel Berry. The grand march was led by Miss Ruth Zimmerman, sorority president, and Mr. Edwin Kennedy of New York City."

The relationship between Edwin and Ruth was becoming increasingly serious, but both believed they hadn't really been together enough to decide on marriage. The most logical solution, they agreed, would be for Ruth to get a temporary job in New York. Partly by design, but with a dash of serendipity, Ruth soon was offered a summer position, to begin in July, at the New York City Library.

In the spring of 1930, Kennedy was given additional responsibilities for analyzing corporate information, making judgments on the degrees of significance, and writing the results for Standard Statistic Company's monthly round-up section appearing in its *Daily News*. Some of this information was channeled also to Standard's annual report, which offered complete profiles on all major corporations.

Three months later—only a year after having joined the company—Kennedy was chosen as one of three employees to attend a special summer session for business executives at Harvard University. From a psychological standpoint, that honor proved to be a major turning point in his ongoing struggle to shed the insecurity still stemming from the isolation of his upbringing. This added greatly to the more obvious benefit of taking part in the six-week seminar on interpretation of financial statements (later to evolve into the world-renowned Advanced Management Program), coordinated by Dr. John C. Baker, an assistant dean of the Harvard Graduate School of Business Administration. The opportunity contained only one negative element, mildly serious at the time but humorous in retrospect. Edwin Kennedy left for Harvard just two weeks before Ruth Zimmerman arrived in New York to begin her summer job.

Studies at Harvard exceeded Kennedy's expectations: they quickly became a highlight of his early career. His enthusiasm was such that at the end of the summer session he was offered a position on the staff, further strengthening his self-confidence. Dual commitments in Gotham, however, overrode any temptation to accept the Harvard proposal. In August, he returned to New York and the woman soon to become his fiancée.

At the end of summer, Edwin and Ruth were engaged. Precarious economic conditions in New York, however, made postponement of marriage seem wise, so Ruth returned to Massillon to live with her sister, Edna, and teach at the nearby village of Brewster.

By then, both production and employment were on steady declines in the United States. The government instituted federal subsidies to bolster the former, and banned further immigration to relieve the latter. Retail sales understandably were dropping. Stocks went into another slump during the second half of the year and most heavy industries suffered setbacks from what had appeared to be minor recovery. Construction was sinking. Distressed farmers, some of whom organized futile strikes to combat falling prices by withholding produce, expressed utter hopelessness, made worse in the Great Plains states when a horrendous drought created a dust bowl in which nothing would grow. Despite a statement by the American Economic Association that recovery seemed assured in the spring of 1931, many persons were convinced opportunities in New York's financial community would continue to dwindle. Among them was Edwin Kennedy. When an offer to become an investment officer with a bank in Scranton, Pennsylvania, appeared in the winter of 1931, he accepted it.

The career change contained no dissatisfaction with the company Kennedy was leaving. He considered the experience a valuable foundation for his career, and in the years ahead he spoke of his first boss at Standard, Charles Roy Martin, as being "very important to my life." The contributions Martin made to the business community and society were "manifest," Kennedy said. "His own life was so unusual, it should be told as an inspiration to anyone, and certainly it meant a lot in helping mold aspects of my own progress through the years."

Roy Martin was an orphan from Kansas who rose from laborer to drilling contractor, first in the lead and zinc districts of Missouri, then in Kentucky oil fields, where he owned his own rig. When he still was a young man, he was so severely burned in a fire he was not expected to live. He survived, with great difficulty, however, and while thinking about his future during eight months of recovery, he decided he would go to college. With that in mind, he applied in person at the Admissions Office of Western Kentucky State College (later Western Kentucky University), where he was told that what he sought was impossible, and for a very good reason: he had never attended high school. Never easily discouraged, Martin sought and received an audience with College President Dr. H. H. Cherry, who listened attentively to the young man's appeal, asked some searching questions, then told him, "I am convinced that you really want an education, and we are going to see to it that you get the opportunity to try." Not only did Roy Martin try, he graduated in 1927 with the highest grade-point average ever achieved at Western Kentucky up to that time. Then he moved on to graduate studies at Harvard Business School and a diversified business career.

"Roy Martin knew everything about drilling, and he exposed me to the mystique of underground exploration," Kennedy said. "So in a sense I became psychologically oriented toward oil, although at that time I knew nothing specific about it."

Scranton in 1931 was a railroad center and distribution point for the anthracite-coal region of northeastern Pennsylvania. The county seat of Lackawanna County, it was the state's fourth largest city, with several textile mills and other diversified industries, all of which were suffering economically along with the rest of the nation. It also had two Catholic Colleges, St. Thomas and Marywood.

Edwin Kennedy was hired by the president of the city's Dime Bank-Lincoln Trust Company, whom he had met at Harvard, to head the investment department. A sound company, experiencing only problems with small loans, Lincoln Trust appeared to be avoiding the widespread decline in capital suffered by many banks, including some of the leaders in New York and Chicago. Within a year, however, it was caught in a new gust of fear shaking the country. Questions on the safety of banks prompted depositors to begin withdrawing their money, in small numbers at first, then in droves. Whether true or perceived, speculation led to rumors that in turn led to runs on banks, one of which was Lincoln Trust. "I never forgot the scene of worried people lined up to withdraw their money," said Kennedy, "and I always was convinced our bank could have survived if unfounded rumors hadn't set off that fatal run."

As an alternative to insolvency, Lincoln Trust was merged into the larger First National Bank of Scranton, located across the street. With no opening available to him in the combined organization, Kennedy contemplated the depressed banking situation: collapsing assets, lack of protective devices in the system, an international currency crisis, the domino effect of panic. Then he made a decision typifying the sagacity that would become a widely recognized hallmark of his business acumen. He got a job with Pennsylvania's State Department for Banking, liquidating failed banks.

Hope for economic recovery ebbed rapidly in the spring of 1932, even among business and political leaders whose reassurance was essential to a restoration of confidence. Financial markets were paralyzed, and no relief was in sight for Americans suffering individual hardships. With such a forecast, Edwin Kennedy and Ruth Zimmerman recognized the futility of waiting for a more propitious time to get married. "If the country was heading toward starvation, we preferred to starve together," Edwin said.

Edwin and Ruth were married on his birthday, May 25, 1932, at New York City's Church of the Transfiguration, better known as "The Little Church Around the Corner." After a brief honeymoon trip through New England, the newlyweds moved into the furnished lower half of a home in Scranton. Social life in 1932, the worst year of the Great Depression, was understandably limited, but Edwin and Ruth exchanged visits with other young people, and became close friends with a couple next door, Donald and Eva Shotten. That friendship never faded; Kennedy aided the Shottens in financial affairs as they became elderly, accepting power of attorney for them during the last years of their lives.

Edwin Kennedy's assignment with the state of Pennsylvania was to liquidate remaining assets of eight failed banks in the Third Realization District, which was Lackawanna County. The statewide policy stipulated that all mortgage loans, investments, and other assets were to be sold to any organization or individual that would purchase them, as quickly as possible and for whatever price could be obtained. Assessing that directive, Kennedy reasoned that dumping all assets would leave nothing for an attempted comeback by the banks. Yet he realized that some distribution must be made to the 22,000 desperate depositors who were depending on him for some kind of help.

"No description of that situation can convey how terrible it was," he said. "These people had lost everything, and you wanted to get what you could back to them. I don't mind admitting that I occasionally cried when I thought about those depositors and the helplessness they felt."

Convinced that he could create a formula combining short and long term solutions, Kennedy was able to obtain an exception to the total bail-out policy for his district. Then he set about selling portions of the eight banks' assets for distribution to depositors, while holding others for possible recovery. This called for critical judgments in determining the relative comeback potential of various investments, knowing that the results would be monitored closely in Harrisburg. The plan he devised to tilt the odds in his favor contained a factor that would direct his future to an extent he could not have envisioned at the time.

Kennedy never met James Paul, founder of the Carbondale Savings Bank, the first to fail in Lackawanna County, but he became well acquainted with the man's reputation. Before the Great Depression, the bank had been so successful Paul advertised it by printing his financial statements next to those of the First National Bank of New York, showing the superior accumulative savings in relation to invested capital (surplus) at Carbondale Savings. In the mid-twenties, Paul had become almost fanatic in supporting oil stocks, particular those of a company then known as Tidewater Oil (changed to Tidewater Associated after a merger with Associated Oil). Not only had he preached the gospel of oil investments to clients who borrowed from Carbondale Savings to acquire them, he had spread the good word throughout the county with spectacular results that quickly became apparent to Kennedy: Oil stocks represented a disproportionate percentage of assets in all eight banks under his supervision.

Already intrigued by what Roy Martin had told him about oil, Kennedy began learning as much as possible about this currently deflated industry that might hold a key to the long-range segment of his liquidation plan. With oil prices dipping as low as four cents a barrel, the market value of Tidewater's common stock had plummeted to two dollars a share, compared to forty dollars before the 1929 crash. Phillips Petroleum had dropped from thirty-six to three, and even Standard Oil of New Jersey, which persevered better than others, had gone from eighty-three to nineteen. To judge the wisdom in holding such securities for possible recovery, Kennedy subscribed to oil magazines and scoured the library for anything he could find on the subject. When he had difficulty interpreting esoteric material, he telephoned Martin, who still was employed at Standard Statistics. "I became totally fascinated by oil," he said. "I really worked at learning about it on my own, and I just couldn't get enough of it."

During a hiatus between the 1932 elections and the inauguration of Franklin D. Roosevelt—a lame duck period generally considered mishandled by both the outgoing and incoming presidents—economic conditions continued to deteriorate, as the frequency of runs on banks increased. By spring, 5,504 banks had been closed, 140 of them in Pennsylvania.

In successfully carrying out his mission, Kennedy soon discovered that the time he had to devote to the job lessened in direct proportion to the number of remaining assets in the banks he was working with. Consequently, he accepted an offer to begin teaching an evening class in finance at St. Thomas College (later named the University of Scranton). This led to an opportune concomitant: as Kennedy's liquidation duties receded, the college gradually added more courses to his teaching load, until he became nearly a full-time-equivalent member of the faculty, with the rank of associate professor.

Out of desperation, President Roosevelt invoked a four-day nationwide bank holiday by proclamation, beginning on Monday, March 6, 1933, two days after his inauguration. With the closing of all banks and savings-and-loan associations, FDR and Congress, took immediate steps to design an Emergency Banking Relief Act and in other ways lay a foundation for recovery. The most potent antidote, announced by the president after conferring with bankers, was permitting only the strong financial organizations to reopen. On the morning after the bank holiday, deposits exceeded withdrawals for the first time in many months. Although financial historians differed widely in their assessments of the holiday's worth, Kennedy considered it the "crucial event of that particular time," because it represented the start of measures needed to save the collapsing banking system.

Throughout the Bank Holiday, stock exchanges chose to suspend operations also. Believing strongly that a substantial rise in prices would follow, Kennedy invested $500 he had saved from his teacher's salary to buy several carefully selected stocks on margin. When the speculation paid off a few months later, he and Ruth collected a $5,000 profit. It was enough to finance furniture-buying sprees in New York City and a Wilkes Barre warehouse, then move into a new unfurnished apartment in Scranton. This first-ever experience for them both enabled

Edwin to discover in his wife a talent he had not known. "She had such an instinct for decorating that more than one merchant asked her where she had received her training," he said. "She was resourceful too. We bought carpeting left over from furnishing a mansion built by the owner of the Luden's Cough Drops company for less than two dollars a square yard, and it lasted for fifty years."

While the United States was recovering slowly and adjusting to a plethora of newly formed federal agencies, Kennedy completed the systematic liquidation of his eight banks. As a group, they showed a greater gain in conversion—sales proceeds compared to value at the time of closing—than the other 132 liquidated banks in Pennsylvania. Moreover, the Carbondale Savings Bank was the only one of the 140 to be liquidated with a balance to stockholders. Kennedy was commended for this achievement, which he attributed to selling Tidewater oil stock at a substantial profit.

The Great Depression had placed what appeared at first to be an obstacle in Kennedy's career path. This seeming diversion, however, would prove to be more attuned to his long-term objectives than he realized as he planned his return to New York in 1936. And before leaving Scranton, he again passed a test of dedication to that objective by turning down an offer from the president of St. Thomas College to become dean of the business school.

Chapter 6   # The Right Niche

> *Business, like politics, in a democratic organization always finds a place for the individual who can outrun the herd.*
> —Henry E. Hoagland
> Corporate Finance (1933)

The United States was emerging slowly from its economic morass when Edwin Kennedy returned to New York in February of 1936, but the financial district of that city was flustered by muddled interpretations of federal regulations. The government had empowered new agencies to oversee collective bargaining, pension programs, interstate transmission of power, the breakup of certain holding companies, and pricing of commodities, all of which affected investments. Seemingly endless changes stemming from the trial-and-error method of plugging each gap with a new federal act created a stream of uncertainties in the corporate world, reflected and often magnified on the floors of the stock exchanges. Caught in the blur of these fluctuating patterns, Kennedy became associated with two Manhattan companies, Washburn and Company and Young Management Company, in two years. "With the financial district remaining in deep depression long after the general economy had started to recover, it was difficult to find an organization where I could develop a strong sense of belonging," he said.

Home life for Edwin and Ruth Kennedy was far less confusing. Having moved from Scranton to a large rented house in Madison, New Jersey, they focused attention on a son, Edwin DeWeese, born March 15, 1936. When the home in which they lived was sold, they rented a smaller one in another part of Madison, with no disruption of the lifestyle that included commuting by train to New York City.

In searching for the most propitious means of utilizing the expertise he had begun to acquire in the oil industry, Kennedy felt he needed to gain more control over determining his future than was afforded by working for Young Management Company. To accomplish this, he organized a partnership in 1938 with A. E. "Al" Askland, an officer with Young Management, to serve as the financial planner for Mutual Associates Inc., a private organization made up of eight members of the du Pont family of Wilmington, Delaware.

The descendants of Irénée du Pont, who had emigrated from the Nemours, France at the end of the eighteenth century to found what would become an industrial dynasty in the United States, were recognized as the nation's richest and most influential family. Dubbed the Barons of the Brandywine, referring to the creek near Wilmington where the first E. I. du Pont de Nemours and Company plant was located, the family had expanded immensely in interests, as well as numbers to the extent that some close observers insisted they controlled the State of Delaware. Their ranking at or near the top of East Coast society had been further solidified with the June 1937 marriage of Ethel du Pont and Franklin D. Roosevelt, Jr., headlined by the press as a union of the House of du Pont and the White House. Mutual Associates was established as a corporation apart from the giant du Pont chemical conglomerate to build and shelter personal investments of family members.

From their cubbyhole office in New York City, Kennedy and Askland guided Mutual Associates in buying and selling securities and establishing other forms of investments. Traveling to Wilmington at least once a week for personal consultations, Kennedy also developed close friendships with members of the group.

When Al Askland died shortly after the partnership was formed, Kennedy recruited his good friend, Roy Martin, as a replacement. Martin had left Standard Statistics in 1935 and moved to Washington where, as a senior financial analyst with the Securities and Exchange Commission, he was instrumental in unraveling complexities of the Public Utility Holding Company Act.

As word of their activities spread, Kennedy and Martin were approached by a host of entrepreneurs seeking financial backing for various enterprises. "We evaluated all such proposals, rejecting most of them as unsuitable," Kennedy said, "but when we believed others contained elements of strong interest, we took the ideas to Wilmington." In this way, Mutual Associates soon had rapidly growing, highly diversified portfolios.

During the late thirties, the Du Pont group became increasingly insistent that Kennedy should move to Wilmington, until finally he had to decide whether to leave New York or change positions. "In truth, I happened to dislike Wilmington because the city had only two levels of society, the Du Ponts and the others, and the latter category wasn't considered important," he said. Consequently, in early 1940 Kennedy dissolved his association with Mutual Associates, leaving the financial counseling in the capable hands of Roy Martin (who moved to Wilmington), and joined the New York investment house of Shields & Company.

Although he thus severed formal affiliation with Mutual Associates Inc., Kennedy enjoyed continuing friendships with several members of the du Pont family, most notably Lammot du Pont Copeland and Hugh R. Sharp, Jr., both E. I. du Pont de Nemours and Company executives. The former, son of Charles and Louise du Pont Copeland, became the eleventh president of the corporation in 1962. Sharp, whose mother was the former Isabella du Pont, also became increasingly influential in corporate decision-making. Roy Martin, who remained with Mutual Associates until his retirement many years later, became so close to the Kennedy family that son Eddie called him "Uncle Roy."

Within a brief period of time, Kennedy learned that his principal interests were not compatible with those of Shields & Company, which was primarily a commission house. By then

The Right Niche

he was recognized as possessing exceptional background knowledge and investment insight regarding oil, something that had not gone unnoticed in his handling of du Pont financial matters. Among those aware of that talent was Lehman Brothers, one of the city's best-known investment banking partnerships. When he decided to leave Shields & Company, Kennedy experienced no trouble being hired by Lehman Brothers as one of New York's early specialists in the research and analysis of oil investments. Reflecting on events of the preceding twelve years as he began the new job in November 1941, Edwin Kennedy was able to tell his wife, "I am certain that I now am exactly where I belong."

In 1941, an ornamented eleven-story corner building at One William Street in Manhattan was recognized worldwide as the House of Lehman. Built in 1907 by J. & W. Seligman & Co. and purchased eleven years later by Lehman Brothers, its distinctive Italian Renaissance architecture, with facades of granite and limestone, featured a sculptured figure atop a decorative tower. A flattened corner containing an entry at the intersection of William and Stone Streets—one short block from Wall Street—produced the illusion of "flat-iron" construction, although the building was not an exact triangle.

A member of the New York Stock Exchange since 1887, Lehman Brothers had become so prominent in investment banking that few persons would envision its roots as being imbedded anywhere outside the nation's largest city. Yet, the firm traced its ancestry to a general store in Montgomery, Alabama. In 1844, twenty-two-year-old Henry Lehman emigrated from Bavaria, launching what he hoped would become a successful career by opening a combination dry goods, hardware, and grocery store in the railroad and commercial center of a productive cotton-growing region. A few years later, he was joined by brothers Mayer and Emanuel, and in 1850, the trio formed a partnership under the name of Lehman Brothers.

As the business grew, the brothers began accepting cotton as payment for merchandise purchased by area farmers, then reselling it in bulk quantities to brokers. Recognizing the disadvantage of middle-man status in this chain of transactions, they soon organized their own brokerage operation, which became so profitable they moved out of retailing. Henry Lehman died from yellow fever at the age of thirty-three while starting a branch in New Orleans, but his brothers carried on the plan of expansion. Emanuel opened a New York City office in 1858, but closed it when hostilities between the North and South became apparent. Returning to Alabama, he joined the Confederate Army when war erupted in 1861. Mayer also served the Confederacy as a fund-raising envoy of President Jefferson Davis.

At the conclusion of the Civil War in 1865, Emanuel Lehman traveled against the tidal wave of northerners rushing south to take part in reconstruction, reopening the cotton-brokerage office in New York City. After Mayer joined him three years later, Lehman Brothers grew as a commodity business, helping establish the New York Cotton Exchange and branching into trading of sugar, coffee, and grain, but dealing sparingly in securities. It remained for the next generation of the family to begin underwriting security issues in the early 1900s, often in conjunction with Goldman, Sachs. When that association was discontinued, Lehman Brothers underwrote ventures for several of the most prestigious names in American business and industry, especially those in retailing, television, and air travel. Non-family members were admitted to partnership status for the first time after World War I, as the firm rose to preeminence among the nation's investment bankers. This reputation was enhanced by a solid performance during the Great Depression, including originating the idea of direct placements with institutional investors. When investigators for President Roosevelt's "New Deal" programs studied investment trusts, several reforms suggested by Lehman Brothers became laws. A four-story annex to the company's building in 1940 was evidence of post-depression growth and a harbinger of more to come.

Robert Lehman (called "Bobbie" by friends and colleagues), a grandson of Emanuel, headed the partnership engaged in syndicating large stock issues, managing underwriting projects involving competitive bidding, organizing mergers, consulting, and other functions of investment banking. In addition, the partnership held a commanding interest in the Lehman Corporation, a diversified investment-trust company listed on the New York Stock Exchange.

With no precedent for his new position, Edwin Kennedy was assigned to Lehman Brothers' research and investing division, with the dual responsibility of servicing both the corporation and the partnership. Within a month, however, America's military entry into World War II following the December 7, 1941, Japanese attack on Pearl Harbor brought an abrupt change in the oil industry.

Mobilized for war under government control, all industry was regulated by the Office of Production Management (OPM), with price ceilings established by an Office of Price Administration (OPA). Representatives of oil companies and their trade associations were organized into a Petroleum Industry War Council (PIWC), charged with developing cooperative controls programs and sharing technical discoveries, but functioning under broad policies set by the Petroleum Administration for War (PAW), headed by Secretary of the Interior Harold Ickes. Fearing that tankers moving along the East Coast might be torpedoed, PAW received permission from the War Production Board to build a network of crude oil pipelines, the most spectacular of which was the "Big Inch," extending from Long View, Texas, to Norris City, Illinois, then on to an eastern terminus at Phoenix Junction, Pennsylvania. Completion of the 24-inch-diameter pipeline solved crude supply problems for East Coast refiners, but not the need for finished products. Consequently, a "Little Big Inch" line soon was constructed to move processed petroleum from Beaumont-Houston refineries to Norris City, from where it too was transported eastward.

The need to ration gasoline for non-essential civilian use was dictated not so much by shortages of crude oil as by transportation bottlenecks, refinery limitations, and other factors. Refineries whose principal outputs had been directed toward a motoring public switched their priorities to providing high-octane aviation fuel. Meanwhile, other military and industrial demands for oil increased spectacularly. With Japanese conquests in South Asia cutting off ninety percent of the world's rubber supply, American refineries were called on also to provide huge amounts of chemicals essential to the production of synthetic rubber.

Yet, from the perspective of oil production companies, a combination of frozen crude prices, drilling restrictions, and shortages of machinery severely reduced exploration of possible new fields—the most important factor in making investment determinations. "Understandably, nearly everything in the business of financing new production ventures was put 'on hold,' for the duration," said Kennedy, who had been a year beyond the maximum age of registration for the military draft when selective service legislation was enacted in September 1940.

Rather than reducing his activities accordingly, Kennedy responded by helping put together some projects involving the war effort, and focusing other efforts on building a strong base for the future. This meant continuing to learn as much as possible about the oil industry and the men who shaped its destiny in the United States and Canada. Gaining an early reputation for having what a friend described as "an incredibly retentive mind," Kennedy soon knew the histories and extensive current details of companies, names of executives and their families, and how individual organizations fit into the panorama of American oil operations. Shaking hands and making friendships were not mere exercises carried out for business purposes. Kennedy was truly fascinated by the personal and business interests of those he met. Many of these new acquaintances later remarked that they quickly recognized strong moral and ethical characteristics that enabled them to trust him with confidential information and to seek his advice.

The regulatory agencies relaxed drilling restrictions somewhat in 1944, resulting in modest growth of wildcatting. It was not until the summer of 1945, following the surrenders of Germany and Japan, however, that the market gradually became free of regulations and oil producers geared up for the largest peacetime demand ever experienced for their product. By June

30, 1946, when the last government wartime price controls of crude oil and refined products were dismantled, they were straining exploration and field development equipment to replenish reserves.

With the oil industry again highly competitive, Kennedy used the lead he had garnered through the war years to counsel his own company and major clients in seizing upon what he determined to be the most attractive investment opportunities. Traveling often and widely, he visited oil companies, becoming acquainted with their people, policies, and properties, then made analytical studies leading to investment decisions. "I considered myself a most fortunate individual," he said. "There were plenty of problems and extended business hours to be sure, but I was having so much fun I didn't think of it as work." Even a slight heart attack, suffered in 1948 while he was traveling West to negotiate a Union Oil purchase of Texas Pacific, slowed his pace only briefly.

One of the most flattering endorsements of Kennedy's eclecticism came from a stranger who recognized him as he exited an elevator in the building where Lehman Brothers had a Los Angeles office. "I believe you are Ed Kennedy," the man began, "and if so, I want to thank you for what you have done for me." Startled, Kennedy confirmed his identity, but denied knowledge of what he might have done. "I'm not with Lehman, but I also have an office in this building," the man explained, "and as a small stockholder in Lehman Corporation, I receive quarterly reports that include what you buy and sell in the oil industry. As soon as each one is published, I make investments by following every move you have made." Smiling broadly as he offered a friendly hand, the man added, "We're doing quite well, aren't we?"

Kennedy approached his study of oil companies with the conviction that "investing is merely a choice of risks." Most oil investors made decisions essentially in an atmosphere of ignorance, he insisted, from advice based on unsubstantiated information and gut reactions. To reduce the risk as much as possible toward the unobtainable zero level, he talked to top-ranking officials of oil companies, learning about their weaknesses as well as their strengths, and ascertaining the extent of their physical facilities, the capabilities of their personnel, and their blueprints for the future. His most specific objective was to make reasonable estimates of oil reserves. "That was the name of the game, because that would determine what would happen to the stocks in the marketplace," Kennedy explained. This was a major challenge in an era when companies carefully guarded information on the quantity of their oil reserves; many years later they would publish such figures in their annual reports, but at the time, they held close rein on information, a cautiousness that eased as Kennedy began to gain the trust of corporate leaders. In doing so, he made a gradual transition from research and analysis into full investment banking.

The first transaction steering him in that direction stemmed from a close relationship he had developed with Paul Blazer, president of Ashland Oil Company in Kentucky. Learning through another acquaintance that co-owners of a Buffalo refinery were about to resolve a disagreement by selling out, Kennedy investigated the value of the property. When the impending sale was formally announced, he was prepared to recommend that Ashland Oil purchase it. Blazer bought the refinery with very profitable results for his company.

Studying probabilities of long-range success was more important to Kennedy than linking his activities to fluctuations in the stock market. Through the partnership, he represented buyers and sellers of oil properties, put together mergers, and organized new capital ventures, involving either common stock or cash, for expansion and exploration. In other instances, he recommended that Lehman Brothers become underwriters—buying quantities of stock, then selling them publicly or privately at somewhat higher prices. "Underwriting is a thin-margin business," Kennedy said, "and, of course, that margin can be a loss if your judgment is faulty and you pay more for stock than the public will subsequently pay for it."

When unpredictable circumstances alter the most carefully drawn lines of reasoning, strong personal confidence can make the difference in surmounting what might seem in hindsight to be a mistake in judgment. One such challenge began in 1948 when Lehman Brothers signed an underwriting agreement with the Kerr-McGee Oil Company. Kennedy had followed the career of Dean A. McGee, an innovative geologist who had become head of Phillips Petroleum Company exploration at a very young age, then joined Robert S. Kerr in A & K Petroleum, later renamed Kerlyn Oil Company. When Kerr was elected governor of Oklahoma in 1942, McGee assumed operational responsibility of the company, which became Kerr-McGee Oil Industries four years later. In 1947, the company became widely known for drilling the first well "out of sight of land" off the coast of Louisiana in a joint venture with Phillips Petroleum and Stanolind Corporation. By then, Dean McGee was the recognized leader of the company, although he did not officially succeed Robert Kerr as president until 1957. Kerr never returned to active management, but he remained the largest stockholder, a director, and a strong voice in planning new undertakings, after being elected U.S. senator from Oklahoma in 1948, a position he held until his death in 1963.

As Kerr-McGee developed into a larger and more diversified company requiring substantial new capital, Kennedy persuaded Lehman Brothers to underwrite what he admitted to be a speculative investment. His justification was faith in Dean McGee, whose record he considered outstanding, and a joint agreement the new company had with Phillips Petroleum for further offshore drilling in Louisiana. Lehman successfully underwrote the sale of common stock. For his sponsorship of the underwriting, Kennedy was elected to the Kerr-McGee Board of Directors on January 15, 1949.

Elizabeth Zoernig, who had joined the company as executive secretary to Dean McGee in 1946 and later became corporate assistant secretary (the first woman officer of Kerr-McGee), remembered vividly the first time she saw Edwin Kennedy, one day before his first attendance at a board meeting:

> When I walked down the hall, I saw a man whom I didn't know sitting in one of the offices, completely surrounded by material

from our corporate files. He was diligently examining papers stacked all over a table and even on the floor. This seemed strange to me, because I knew everyone in the office building, so I quickly told Mr. McGee what was going on. He said, "Oh, that is our new director, Ed Kennedy. Go over and introduce yourself." I followed his suggestion, and we were friends from that moment on. I discovered that he had gotten some of our Kerr-McGee people to gather nearly everything available on the upcoming meeting, as well as those of past years, so he could learn as much as possible about the company. As I later found out, this wasn't a one-time occurrence. In the years that followed, he always came a day early so he could study information about everything that was to be discussed at a board meeting. He was always thorough, and he showed a tremendous interest in our operations. Many of his traits paralleled those of Mr. McGee. They had restless, inquiring minds, always searching for new ideas. They liked to create ventures that hadn't been done before. I'm sure that is why they developed such a warm rapport.

Six months after Kennedy joined the board, the United States Supreme Court handed down a decision that neither Louisiana nor Texas could grant oil leases to private companies for offshore drilling. When appeals by both states were denied, Kerr-McGee stock plunged to half the price for which Lehman had sold it.

Although his own firm already had received its profit, Kennedy was personally dismayed. But his faith in Dean McGee was unshaken. The oil company, which had expected its production future to be in offshore drilling, turned its sights toward land and went on to become highly successful. The company also resumed offshore drilling after passage and Supreme Court approval of the Submerged Lands Act of 1953, assigning state ownership within the three-mile limit and federal control beyond that boundary. Kennedy continued to represent Lehman Brothers as an investment adviser to Kerr-McGee and remained a close friend of Dean McGee, as well as a member of the company's board for forty-one years.

The development of such lasting friendships from business associations became increasingly prevalent in Kennedy's life. As a consultant to Keystone Custodian Funds of Boston, he worked with a young analyst, Ora C. Roehl, who had joined that mutual company after serving in the Office of the Secretary of the Navy in World War II. "Ed kept us well informed on what we should do about our oil investments, telephoning us regularly after his visits to companies in Texas and elsewhere," Roehl said. "Then he reached the point where he not only advised investors like Keystone, but also the oil companies themselves, and that advice didn't come cheap." Roehl went on to lead Keystone as executive vice president, then formed his own consulting organization, which had Lehman Brothers as an important account. On trips to New York, he often visited Edwin, Ruth, and Eddie in New Jersey.

Kennedy joined another friend, Robert Wilson (whose brother, Charles, was president of General Motors), in arranging for the first supply of natural gas to be transported through the Big Inch pipeline, after its landmark conversion from wartime use as the nation's longest petroleum carrier.

Successful business leaders often are able to pinpoint a single event or project that was pivotal in gaining distinction among their peers. Such a chapter in the life of Edwin Kennedy might well be entitled "Monterey." The scenario opened in 1949 with disclosure that Jergins Corporation, a small privately owned oil and gas company in California, was up for sale. Kennedy was favorably impressed with the company, but did not want to infringe on the rights of another investment banking house which had been authorized to find a buyer. That November, Kennedy headed for the annual meeting of the American Petroleum Institute in Los Angeles. As he entered the revolving door of the Biltmore Hotel, a vice president of Chase Manhattan Bank, exiting through the same door, motioned for him to come back outside, where he said, "Ed, the Jergins sale fell through." Thanking his friend, Kennedy proceeded to register for the convention, but he never attended a session. Instead, he began to work on what promised to be a very complicated situation.

Not only did A. T. Jergins blame the rival investment house for what had happened, he had soured on all investment bankers. Unable to even get on the Jergins property, Kennedy worked through the unsuccessful banking group to learn more about the Jergins holdings, the most intriguing of which was half ownership in the San Ardo oil field, known as "the biggest white elephant in California." Although a sizable field, it contained heavy viscous fuel oil for which there was almost no current demand.

Kennedy alone believed San Ardo held long-range promise. When asked what he thought could be done with such thick oil, he replied, "We might be able to extrude it for fence posts." The personal opinion he concealed, however, was that although rumblings of a possible confrontation in Korea had not yet affected fuel prices, the demand for heavy oil used in power generating plants and military-oriented factories on the West Coast should increase markedly if the controversy escalated into war.

In working with the rival investment group, which had lost any chance of dealing again with the oil-and-gas company, Kennedy learned that one of their number, Al Barton, was an excellent piano player, as was A. T. Jergins. The two sometimes had played classical music together during respites from business sessions in which Barton had learned a great deal about the Jergins company, so the oil man's sudden dislike for investment bankers did not extend to this particular friend. Gambling that he might utilize such an unusual circumstance effectively, Kennedy hired Barton as a contact representative. Consequently, while the two pianists once again played Bach fugues together, Jergins was persuaded to make a second exception to his firm stand against investment bankers, with just one small proviso: Kennedy was allowed to negotiate without being permitted to visit company properties. The story later circulated through Wall Street, enhancing Kennedy's reputation for resourcefulness. Meanwhile, Al Barton joined Lehman Brothers.

Shortly before the anticipated time of purchase, Kennedy discovered that a competitor also was preparing an offer for

Jergins. Nevertheless, when the two sealed bids were opened on December 30, 1949, the California corporation, with eight million dollars in cash and a wide assortment of properties, including half of the "white elephant," went to Lehman Brothers for $30.1 million. To finance the purchase, the firm borrowed $20 million from Chase Manhattan Bank, and raised another $10 million by selling preferred stock to Lehman Corporation, Lehman Brothers, and eight other investors. Each member of this group of ten organizations and individuals also purchased ten thousand shares of common stock at one dollar.

During the next few months, the new owners used the Jergins cash and sold an office building at Long Beach, approximately one-third of the stock of a liquefied petroleum gas (LPG) company named Petrolane, Incorporated, and more than a 30 percent interest in the electronics firm Beckman Instruments, all from the Jergins "package," reducing the loan to $14 million and paying back $5 million to investors. "Tax and legal requirements made it advisable to sell properties to reduce the loans as quickly as possible," Kennedy said, "so we actually got rid of some I would have preferred to keep."

When it became evident that Kennedy's prediction about the use of heavy viscous oil was correct, several offers were made for the interest in the San Ardo field. Within a year, it was sold to General Petroleum, a Socony Mobil Oil subsidiary, for $18 million. (Kennedy told Mobile executives this would be one of the best purchases their company would ever make. Again, his forecast proved to be accurate; Mobile's share of San Ardo eventually produced huge profits, as light crude oil became scarce, prompting refining improvements that made heavy crude increasingly valuable.) The remaining oil properties were put into an operating company named Monterey Oil, with Kennedy a member of the Board of Directors.

The value of Monterey and money accrued from the two-year series of transactions was enough to retire the Chase and preferred stock loans and retain more than $36 million for the ten common stock holders. In addition, Monterey Oil returned substantial profits during the next ten years, before it was sold to Humble Oil. Kennedy later calculated that more than $60 million of profits accrued to participants in the venture during subsequent years, and if all these accrued assets could have been retained, their value would have been something over $400 million in the early eighties.

"I looked for another Jergins for the rest of my career, as did other investment bankers, but none of us ever found one," he said. On January 1, 1952, Kennedy was elected a partner in Lehman Brothers. As such, he became one of an elite group characterized by *Fortune Magazine* as "merchants of money, intermediaries between those who want to produce goods and men seeking outlets for surplus funds."

But activities of Lehman partners extended well beyond that basic function of investment banking. In the course of an antitrust suit against Lehman Brothers and sixteen other large investment bankers that had begun in 1950 and was dismissed in 1953, the firm's attorney argued successfully that "special attitudes of Lehman Brothers form a continuity of character that it is impossible to confuse with the modes of business of the other defendant firms. The investment-banking activity of the firm is but a part of its independently conceived relation to industry." It was pointed out that in addition to raising venture capital and helping create new businesses, partners served in such capacities as counselors to business and industry, arbitragers, economic forecasters, directors, and even backers of oil wildcatters.

For several years, articles in trade magazines and general publications made reference to the Monterey Oil coup. Kennedy often was referred to as "a legend" in oil investment, and his reputation grew as a man seemingly driven to know more than anyone else about anything that caught his interest. Some clients even asked for his opinions on how their own companies were being operated.

Edwin Kennedy always was intrigued by the number of seemingly unrelated personal experiences that converged in later years. Realizing such incidents were not particularly uncommon in people's lives did not diminish his love of happenstance and coincidence. He savored each with the excitement of finding a buried treasure. Friends said his insatiable curiosity and determination to learn as much as possible about nearly everything he encountered put him in a position for more path crossings than might normally be expected, and they probably were right. But Kennedy was uninterested in giving these recurring situations meaning. He simply enjoyed them.

One of the most vivid examples had its roots in Kennedy's continuing association with Kerr-McGee Oil Industries. In its search for new energy projects to offset the loss of offshore exploration, Kerr-McGee in 1952 purchased a uranium company located in the northeast corner of Arizona, on a section of the vast Navajo Reservation. During the following two years it organized an exploration staff and built a uranium processing plant fifty miles from the mining area.

As a director and financial adviser for the company, Kennedy accompanied a regional manager of Kerr-McGee on an automobile trip in 1954 to the Lukachukai Mountains, where they were scheduled to inspect the mine and the new mill. After entering the Navajo Reservation near the border of Arizona and New Mexico, the driver made an intentional detour from the primary route to stop at a building bearing a sign, "Red Rock Trading Post." Underneath were the names of the proprietors, "Kennedy and McGee." Curiosity understandably demanded further investigation.

Inside the building, the men met one of the co-owners, Troy Kennedy, and his wife, Edith. After a brief discussion on the coincidence of names revealed no possible family connection, the conversation turned to a display of Navajo blankets. Despite an admitted lack of knowledge about the tribe or its weavings, Edwin Kennedy purchased a white Yei blanket woven by Vera Begay, the wife of a medicine man. "You didn't have to know anything about technique or tradition to recognize something that was beautiful," he explained. Edwin and Ruth Kennedy never met the McGee partner, who soon sold his trading post interest to Troy and Edith Kennedy, but the incident marked the beginning of an unexpected intimacy with the Navajo culture and a close friendship between the two Kennedy families.

In that same year, Edwin and Ruth reestablished an affiliation with their alma mater, Ohio University. And to borrow a favorite Kennedy expression, "in due course" the two divergent events of 1954 would be wed. That union, however, would be far into the future. In the mid-twentieth-century years, Kennedy's foremost concerns were for family and career.

Chapter 7 **Fate's Interventions**

> *Ruth didn't manage Ed, but she was pretty influential in many things he did and how he did them. They were very close, and they both had boundless energy. It was a partnership.*
>
> —Ora C. Roehl
> Management Consultant

On a business trip in late November 1942, slightly less than a year after he had joined Lehman Brothers, Edwin Kennedy arranged to have dinner with his wife's brother, John Carpenter, who was stationed in Texas with the Army prior to going overseas. After customary family greetings, John asked, "Where is this house you just bought, or are about to buy?" Puzzled by the question, Kennedy confessed to knowing nothing about such a house. "Oh," John replied, "I just talked to Ruth and she mentioned it."

The house Ruth Kennedy showed her husband when he returned to New Jersey was located in Short Hills, ten miles east of their small rented home in Madison. "I didn't even know she was looking for a new home," Kennedy said, "but I was only mildly surprised. We often had discussed the advantages of two strong-willed persons with a young son having more maneuvering room. We both had grown up in large houses, and this small place actually had begun to affect our attitudes toward each other. So when Ruth looked approvingly at the Short Hills house, she was sure I would like it too. And she was right. We had that kind of rapport." Although she was pressed by time to make a tentative decision before Edwin returned from his trip, Ruth managed to stall the final commitment to purchase until they could make it jointly. Nevertheless, Kennedy liked to remind his wife that he essentially had learned of their first home purchase (for $7,500) from her brother.

Although they soon had close friends in the Short Hills area, the Kennedys did not become active in civic or social clubs. They liked people, but abhorred the thought of becoming what they labeled as "joiners." Indeed, Ruth contended that too many wives promoted so much "social partying" that it affected their husband's jobs and oftentimes their health. She and Edwin did play tournament bridge, reaching a high level of success before abandoning it when they decided the enjoyment was becoming overshadowed by serious concerns and personal arguments over minutiae of the game.

Both preferred to direct their societal energies toward causes related to education. Ruth became intensely involved in the P.E.O. Sisterhood, a national philanthropic organization fostering educational opportunities for women though loans, scholarships, grants, and operation of Cottey College, a women's two-year liberal arts college in Missouri. Following initiation into the Millburn Chapter near Short Hills, Ruth held several offices, including New Jersey state president, and was instrumental in organizing two new chapters. She frequently held P.E.O. parties in the Kennedy home.

Consequently, nearly all close friendships grew from those activities and Edwin's business contacts. "Her friends in P.E.O. became my friends, and my friends through business became her friends," Edwin said.

Ruth's niece, Nancy Bletzer, admired her aunt's piano talent and remembered several pleasant visits to the Kennedy home, from the time she was in grammar school to her early teens:

> Aunt Ruth could transpose into other keys even when she was sight reading. She did that for practice. I had taken piano lessons since the age of five, so when I visited Aunt Ruth, we would play duets. I loved that. We always had a wonderful time. After we played for a while, she would turn the music upside down, and we would play it that way. That was typical of her. And it was lots of fun. I always was delighted when we did that.

Travel and business pressures set tight limits on socializing in those days of mounting responsibilities at Lehman Brothers. On most evenings, Edwin returned from Manhattan carrying two brief cases stuffed with material. After dinner, he sat in his favorite chair, going over papers, often bouncing ideas off Ruth, whose opinions he greatly respected, until he dozed off just before midnight. Ruth then would wake him so they could go to bed. Whether by physiological make-up or determined self discipline, Edwin was among those rare individuals able to garner seemingly unlimited energy from just a few hours' sleep.

The couple shared strong religious beliefs, but attended a Lutheran Church only sporadically. Ruth supported Silent Unity, a Missouri-based religious organization providing printed devotionals and group prayers to members around the world. She sometimes telephoned this "church invisible" to receive prayers in times of anxiety.

The most alarming predicament the couple faced surfaced gradually in the mid-forties as they realized their eight-year-old son was suffering from health problems that seemed to defy diagnosis. As his condition worsened, the parents became increasingly desperate to find a solution. Learning of their frustration, an officer in Kennecott Copper Corporation recommended that they contact Dr. Harry Eberhardt, who, he insisted, "performed miracles for my wife" at Hahnemann Hospital in Philadelphia.

Edwin and Ruth immediately took their son to Dr. Eberhardt. "We became certain very quickly that we had indeed found a performer of miracles," Edwin said. For the first time, Eddie was diagnosed as having a combination of physical problems, the most serious of which were an unusual form of colitis and an allergy to wheat products. Dr. Eberhardt assured them the condition could be overcome through treatment, a special diet, and being outdoors as much as possible. In time, the latter advice not only contributed to the total recovery of young Eddie Kennedy, it also induced a major change in the lifestyle of his father, adding the new dimension of "outdoorsman." Father and son began fishing together often, and, within a few years both became avid anglers. Then they added hunting to their vacation itineraries and became avid hunters.

Following his mild heart attack in 1948, Kennedy went to see Dr. Eberhardt, who had him tested thoroughly, told him his heart was not damaged, but said a digestive system problem would lead to angina if left untreated. Cells generating hydrochloric acid necessary for digesting proteins were not working. After less than two years of following a medication and diet routine prescribed by the physician, the cells were coaxed back to activity, and the problem never recurred.

When an Eberhardt Foundation was formed in Philadelphia, Kennedy became a regular financial contributor. Later he became president of the medical research organization's board.

As Edwin Kennedy's parents approached old age, they admitted reluctantly that they no longer could live comfortably in the isolation of their Ohio farm home, which did not have modern facilities. Certainly, it was impossible to work the farm after their youngest son, Robert, moved away to launch his business career following World War II. Like many other families, the five Kennedy siblings faced the problem of determining feasible arrangements that would assure comfort without completely disrupting their parents' way of life. Their solution was to sell the farm, add money of their own to the proceeds, and build a small house for their parents in the nearby town of Galion, Ohio. In addition, they established a fund to provide living expenses. The plan worked well, and the elder Kennedys expressed contentment and appreciation, although Robert recalled, "We could tell they often missed living on a farm, after spending all of their previous years in the country."

Kennedy visited his parents, brothers, and sisters occasionally when making business trips through the Midwest. He also saw brother Richard frequently in New York, after the latter entered the export business. Despite the sixteen-year age difference, Richard bore a strong resemblance to his older brother. "When I went into the Lehman Brothers building, everyone there immediately knew whom I was looking for," Richard said.

Ruth's father, Cyrus Zimmerman, who had spent two months a year at Short Hills as part of his rotation among his children, died in 1946. Edwin's father died five years later. Tragically, Gladys Kennedy Linville's husband also died in 1951—after suffering a heart attack at the age of forty-nine—leaving his widow with two children, Saundra, eleven, and Fred, seven, in Columbus, Ohio.

After the funeral of his brother-in-law, Kennedy stayed with his sister and her children for several days. For many years afterwards, he stopped to see them often. His nephew would subsequently explain the importance of those visits:

> After my father passed away, Uncle Edwin took extra interest in our family, and every visit became a special event for us. Whenever he came to Columbus, he took us to the Mills Cafeteria, a downtown landmark, and that was a big event for us, because in those days before fast food restaurants, people didn't go out much to eat. He always told me to get everything I wanted, and my mother says that the amount of food I could put away under such circumstances became a regular subject of family conversation.

The Linville children often listened when their mother questioned "Uncle Edwin" about his current business activities. Consequently, when Fred's fourth-grade teacher asked him what he wanted to be when he grew up, he answered, "The president of Kerr-McGee Corporation." This response was transmitted from the teacher to Gladys to Kennedy, and when Fred was selected the following year as one of a group of fifth graders to visit Washington, D.C., he received an unexpected surprise.

Relating what had taken place in the classroom, Kennedy informed Senator Robert Kerr that his nephew would be visiting the capital, and suggested that the senator might want to meet the future president of his company. An agreeable Senator Kerr made elaborate arrangements, and when Fred arrived in Washington, he was taken, somewhat reluctantly, to lunch at the Senate dining room, where he was seated with the senator from Oklahoma and two aides. "Contrary to my reputation at Mills Cafeteria, I only ordered a toasted cheese sandwich," Fred remembered later, "because I was so overwhelmed, that was all I could think of." After lunch, a photographer arrived to take a picture of the senator and his young friend, which appeared without explanation in *The Columbus Dispatch*. Puzzled friends at Indianola Elementary School never were told the true story. "It was the kind of exciting event you never forget, and the mystery made it even more fun," explained Fred.

Saundra remembered that her Uncle Edwin "played somewhat of a protective role" with the family. "I think I always knew that if things didn't go well in those difficult times, he would be there to help," she said.

Meanwhile, Kennedy's commitment to outdoor sports, begun as therapy for his son, became a new-found passion. None of his family or friends was surprised. "He never did anything half way," commented Gladys, and I can't imagine anyone who has ever known him disagreeing with that opinion." Soon after the advice from Dr. Eberhardt, Kennedy rented a summer cottage on Lake Erskine in northern New Jersey, and in January of 1949 he purchased the property. By then, both he and his son were such devoted outdoorsmen that the family obtained permission the following year to have Eddie excused from school long enough for a fall deer and duck hunting expedition in Canada. Leaving Ruth in the St. Lawrence River town of Gananoque, father and son went with a guide to a remote, heavily forested region of Ontario, setting up camp on a shore of Calabogie Lake, seventy-five miles west of Ottawa. That night, however, an unexpected heavy snow storm, followed by freezing rain, left the ground covered with a heavy crust that made deer hunting impossible. "Every time you took a step the crunch was loud enough to alert the game," Kennedy said.

Waiting unsuccessfully for weather conditions to change, father and son used their time to walk around the lake, speculating facetiously on where they would like to own land. The game became more intriguing when they discovered survey stakes that proved to have been set by the descendant of an old land-owning company, who intended to sell lots. By the time they gave up the idea of hunting and returned to Gananoque for

Ruth, fourteen-year-old Eddie had become serious in suggesting that they purchase land on the lake.

"I didn't pay much attention to him at the time," Kennedy said, "but when I got back to the office in New York and my secretary reported persistent attempts to reach me by phone, I began to think that having such a place to build a retreat might be a good idea." The ensuing decision to buy three lots was followed by another visit to Calabogie Lake and the beginning of further purchases that eventually swelled the Kennedy property to a twenty-two acre tract with sixteen hundred feet of lake frontage.

Ruth Kennedy, although not enthusiastic about outdoor sports, enjoyed architecture and decorating enough to design a lodge that the Kennedy family would love and treasure for the next thirty-five years. Built of logs from the surrounding forest, the lodge was dominated by a stone fireplace covering one entire wall of the great room, exposed rafter beams, and a twenty-four-pane picture window overlooking the lake. Workers also fashioned walls, floors, cabinets, doors, an extraordinary log staircase leading to a sleeping loft, and furniture, all designed by Ruth to reflect rustic Canadian living, from lumber found in that area. Local artisans hand-crafted heavy duty hinges, door handles, and even locks. The Kennedys repeatedly turned down requests to feature the lodge in *Architectural Forum* in later years for security reasons, because it usually was unoccupied during winter months.

Total isolation from the business world during vacations actually was unrealistic for someone in financial banking, where a balance between gaining or losing large sums of money could be tipped by a single non-deferable decision. Being readily available for routine communication, on the other hand, could negate the physical and mental reconstitutional benefits of relaxing at a lake. Through no effort of his own, Kennedy discovered an ideal compromise in the telephone system servicing his Calabogie lodge. "When it rained, you could hardly hear even local calls," he said, "and long-distance calls posed a variety of problems in any kind of weather." This was verified on the first vacation at the lodge, in a conversation described by Kennedy:

> One of our senior partners called me on a matter of some importance, but we could barely hear each other over the ramshackle telephone line. So we had to communicate through the operator. I would say something to her, and she would give him the message. Then he would make a reply, which the operator relayed on to me. After a few of these exchanges, his relayed message was that he wanted to hang up and get a better connection. My answer to him, through the operator, was, "There is no better line; this is it." Later, the privately owned telephone company was bought by the Bell System, and the line was repaired to the extent that we could communicate relatively well. That was fine, because colleagues at Lehman Brothers by then had become well accustomed to telephoning the lodge only when reaching me was critical.

Ruth enjoyed picnicking, reading, sitting on the large dock, playing canasta, cooking, and walking through the woods as much as her husband and son liked the boating, fishing, and water skiing that occupied most of their time at Calabogie Lake. The lodge also offered opportunities for regular summer reunions with family members. Nieces and nephews on both sides of the family learned to water ski there, and even those who did not consider themselves "outdoors persons" gained a measure of skill in fresh-water fishing. "We had wonderful times at Calabogie," Fred Linville said.

Having attuned their lifestyles to changing patterns of personal and business maturation for more than twenty years, Edwin and Ruth were beginning to channel their affairs toward more permanent objectives. The lodge was one tangible example. More important was a new home they were designing to satisfy the comforts and specific needs they envisioned for the rest of their lives. When it was constructed on thirty-three wooded acres purchased in 1954 at New Vernon, New Jersey, the majestic two-story, Corinthian-columned home at the end of a long tree-lined driveway reflected the Kennedys' interests both in the future and the past. Its furnishings included the "Luden" carpet, a dining room suite, and other reminders of their first buying spree in 1933, and the recently purchased Navajo blanket that represented the beginning of what would become a widely acclaimed collection. The expansive grounds enabled Edwin to satisfy a long-held desire of being surrounded by dogwood trees. Ruth was more interested in enjoying the grand piano and organ that became focal points of the main living room.

But even before the house was completed, Edwin and Ruth Kennedy decided they also were approaching the time to follow through on contemplated plans for sharing their good fortune with others through support of education. Inducement to move promptly in that direction had arrived as a form letter from Ohio University to all alumni, announcing a 1954 Sesquicentennial Scholarship Fund campaign. That letter "immediately activated a commitment I had made to myself when the Teachout Foundation loaned me fifty dollars for my junior year," said Kennedy.

Chapter 8   # A New Dimension

Philanthropy is almost the only virtue that is sufficiently appreciated by mankind.
—*Henry David Thoreau*

Ohio University Alumni Secretary Clark E. Williams did not recognize the caller's name when he answered the telephone in his Cutler Hall office. Williams, who grew up in Athens and graduated from Ohio University in 1921, took pride in astounding friends with his recollection of alumni names. But "Edwin L. Kennedy" was not entered in his celebrated memory bank.

More embarrassing was the fact that Williams could not comprehend what Kennedy suggested, beyond his intention to make a significant contribution to the 1954 Sesquicentennial Scholarship Fund. What Kennedy proposed to do was transfer personally owned oil company stock into an Ohio University account he was opening at Lehman Brothers. After these transactions, Kennedy explained, the university could obtain money for the scholarship drive by instructing Lehman Brothers to sell the securities. Having transmitted this message and relieved the alumni secretary's conscience by explaining he had not contacted his alma mater since graduation, Kennedy hung up the phone. Confused but responsive, Williams gathered hastily-scratched-out notes and hurried to the first-floor office of President John C. Baker. A former associate dean of Harvard Business School should understand the language of Wall Street.

Dr. Baker had left Harvard in 1945 to accept what he considered the challenge of "creating an intellectual climate leading to better scholarship for the whole student body, not for just a few outstanding students," at Ohio's oldest university. With a swarm of World War II veterans scheduled to enroll at that time, he had taken emergency measures to expand facilities, beginning with the addition of Quonset and barracks housing units, offices, and classrooms that would be transformed into permanent buildings as funding became available. But the foremost intent of his presidency was to raise overall academic standards. As a prelude to that crusade, the new president had appointed faculty committees to examine and improve teaching, organized student evaluation groups, encouraged increased research and writing, and, in January of 1946, established an Ohio University Fund, Inc., to be financed by private contributions for programs beyond the restraints of state appropriations.

An initial drive that year raised $35,000, which Baker considered a modest but encouraging start. When 1947 campaign proceeds plunged to $2,000, however, the president realized he had not adequately imparted to alumni and friends that support of the fund was intended to be ongoing. Unaccustomed to being asked for contributions, most had assumed the 1946 drive was a one-time effort. Consequently, during this first stage of evolution from the fund to what would become the Ohio University Foundation, it took several years just to bring annual income to the level of the first year's drive.

In his attempt to rally continuing alumni support, the president was astonished to encounter refusals from several persons he expected to be leaders in such an effort. This, he discovered, was related to the auditorium fund-raising campaign of the late twenties. Although construction of Memorial Auditorium had been completed in 1928 after a number of delays, the university had sued subscribers who became unable to honor pledges. Discrepancies existed in determining whether or not this legal action had extended into the Great Depression years, but there was no question about bitter memories creating a barrier to Dr. Baker's plans.

Another obstacle was the university's relative obscurity compared to similar institutions in primary circulation areas of the state's metropolitan newspapers. Nearly all graduates had moved to locations outside sparsely populated Southeastern Ohio, many eventually supporting colleges and universities near their homes. Some even told Baker they essentially remembered Southeastern Ohio as an area made infamous by the large volume of moonshine liquor flowing generously from coal mining towns to the campus when they were students in Prohibition years of the twenties and early thirties. "Having retained such an impression, they weren't certain they wanted their children to go where all that had taken place," Baker said. Despite loyalties from the few alumni living near the campus and from other citizens of Athens, President Baker realized special action was needed to spark broader interest in the University's future. The upcoming sesquicentennial offered such an opportunity.

Only dues-paying members of the Alumni Association, which represented a small minority of graduates, received informational mailings from the university at that time. Consequently, President Baker told Alumni Secretary Williams, "Let's widen the scope you have with the association; get together all the names you can uncover so we can send literature to everyone who was ever here for a year or more." After searching University records meticulously, Williams compiled a comprehensive list that included names of former students who had not been contacted for many years. Among them were Edwin and Ruth Kennedy.

In early 1953, Baker charged a committee, headed by Professor Albert C. Gubitz as executive director, with raising scholarship money, most of which was expected to come from a coast-to-coast alumni campaign. The goal of $150,000 was considered appropriate for completion by June commencement of 1954, the University's sesquicentennial year. After securing publicity and initial "pump-priming" contributions from selected wealthy patrons of the University—a basic technique of fund raising—and prior to establishing local splinter groups to carry out its campaign, the committee sent a form letter to everyone on the new alumni roster, describing its intention of raising $1,000 for each year of the University's history.

As Clark Williams expected, John Baker immediately recognized that Edwin Kennedy had suggested a tax-favorable method of contributing to the scholarship fund. Reaching Kennedy by telephone a few minutes later, the university president gave assurance that he realized the significance of his intended gift and method of making the donation. "I'm giving you authority over the phone to sell the securities, and you will get a telegram right away," Baker said. The resulting gift of $7,000 was the largest of the campaign.

"That was how Ed Kennedy came into the university's orbit," Baker would recall. "He had been completely forgotten. Nobody at the university knew anything about him. But here was one of those rare individuals who responded generously to a letter, even though no one had previously been in touch with him."

Partly out of curiosity to meet such a person, Baker set up a campaign luncheon with Kennedy and several other alumni in New York City. When they were alone after the meal, Kennedy asked, "Who set this goal of $150,000? It is positively undignified." Unaccustomed to such candor, the university president answered just as frankly that he had made the decision because he dared not gamble on a larger goal in his initial attempt to win back alumni support. He told Kennedy about repercussions from the auditorium campaign that had been launched while he, Kennedy, was a student, and why he therefore had chosen to downplay promotion of long-term pledges. "I didn't want to reopen that old wound," Baker asserted. "Besides, I'm banking on this being only a beginning for support we'll be seeking in the years ahead."

On his next trip East, Baker accepted an invitation to join Edwin and Ruth for dinner at their home in New Jersey. Early in their conversation, Kennedy characteristically was delighted to discover that Baker had been the Harvard assistant dean who talked Standard Statistics Company into sending three employees to the summer management program in 1930. Sensing an immediate rapport, the three dinner companions discussed many topics pertaining to education, including specific plans for Ohio University. The Sesquicentennial Scholarship Fund had appealed to the Kennedys because its purpose was raising money to help needy students, and they agreed with Baker's premise that it was "essential to get alumni feeling a new day has arrived for Ohio University."

In early 1954, the Kennedys made their first trip to Athens since Ruth's graduation twenty-four years earlier. That weekend was spent talking with Baker and his wife Elizabeth, Trustee Fred H. Johnson (a lifelong vigorous supporter of the University who was serving as general chairman of the nationwide campaign), Clark Williams, some of their former professors, and students they met while wandering around the campus. "I believe it was then we were inspired to remain forever active as a team in discharging what we considered our moral responsibility to pass educational opportunities on to others," Kennedy said.

At the June 13, 1954 commencement, Fred Johnson announced that the Sesquicentennial Scholarship Fund campaign had reached $364,724, nearly two and a half times its goal. At other weekend events, Edwin Kennedy received an Alumni Certificate of Merit for achievements in investment banking, and was named to the National Alumni Association Board of Directors. Elected president of the association's New York City chapter soon afterward, he became instrumental in revitalizing what once had been an active organization, personally supervising compilation of an area alumni directory and working out organizational details to divide the chapter into sections based on geographic locations. Even after turning the presidential gavel over to a successor in 1956, he remained an active member of the board, which also included band leader Sammy Kaye, actor Bill McCutcheon, stage and film producer-director Tad Danielewski, and Richard O. Linke, owner of a personal management firm representing Andy Griffith and other entertainment personalities. That June, Kennedy was elected national president of the Alumni Association, and during two terms in office, he led the way in establishing a financial framework that put the organization on a self-sustaining basis for the first time.

As the Kennedys' involvement in university affairs deepened, so did their close personal relationship with Baker. The couple was hosted by the president and his wife, Elizabeth, on visits to the campus. Baker, who made frequent trips to New York City, was an occasional guest at dinners given by Lehman Brothers as forums for discussions on current economic concerns.

After one such dinner, Kennedy told his friend that he and Ruth had become interested in doing something that would help stimulate scholarly endeavors and good teaching. "Although they sought and received my advice on specific ideas," Baker said later, "it was their suggestion, not mine, that soon led to establishment of Distinguished Professor Awards at Ohio University. As time went on, I realized it was typical of them to initiate philanthropic ideas, rather than respond to pleas and pressures from proponents of various causes. I learned also that they did everything together. I became greatly impressed by this, as well as by the sincerity of their interest in good education. There was nothing superficial about it."

The program to reward outstanding teaching was funded anonymously by the Kennedys on a year-to-year basis, beginning in the spring of 1959. Recipients, selected by Baker and a committee named by the Faculty Advisory Council, received cash awards and six-month leaves of absence with pay to pursue academic projects of their choosing. To reinforce their intention of making the award "a truly important incentive," the donors stipulated that emphasis should be placed on good teaching at the undergraduate, not the graduate level. After establishing a candidate's teaching excellence, other contributions like research, publishing, and scientific or artistic accomplishment would be considered. If no member of the faculty appeared to merit the award in a given year, no award was to be made. However, there was no restriction on the number of awards that could be made in one year. "We hope the awards will enable gifted teachers to pursue excellence wherever it leads them, then bring its fruits back to enrich and leaven the larger community of scholars of the University," Kennedy said in a convocation speech.

Appointed to the board of the Ohio University Fund (later renamed the Ohio University Foundation) that spring, Kennedy was elected president at his first meeting in June. By then, President Baker also had recommended that Ohio Governor Michael V. DiSalle consider Kennedy for membership on the Ohio University Board of Trustees, succeeding Harvey B. Jordon, vice president of U.S. Steel Corporation, whose term expired in May.

Baker's recommendation actually was the latest step in an effort he had begun a year early. What transpired during ensuing months exemplified the extraordinary prestige—recognized, though never adequately explained—that large numbers of successful Americans place on being trustees of colleges and universities. Institutions benefit from this phenomenon by gaining access to experienced managerial minds, but the politics of selections do not always work in their favor. This is particularly true when candidates seek nominations for other than altruistic reasons.

Kennedy, who never looked upon directorships as prized *honorary* positions, nevertheless acknowledged that such attitudes were not uncommon. It had taken strong persuasion by John Baker to obtain Kennedy's approval in 1958 for the recommendation that Ohio Governor C. William O'Neill appoint him to the Board of Trustees. Although the governor accepted Baker's reasoning that Kennedy's proven interest in education and expertise in financial management would be great assets to the university, he feared the appointment of an out-of-state resident could jeopardize his bid for reelection. With several Ohio lawyers and others maneuvering for the trustee appointment, a team of young advisers had warned O'Neill that naming "an outsider," even though he was an Ohio University alumnus and a good Republican, would be politically unwise.

The governor's close friendship with Baker notwithstanding, the matter at best would have to remain in limbo until after the November election.

The controversy was resolved by voters when Democrat DiSalle, who had been defeated by O'Neill in 1956, turned the tables in 1958. The next summer, the new governor studied Baker's recommendation and appointed Kennedy to a seven-year term on the Board of Trustees without even asking about his politics. Years later, Kennedy and DiSalle became good friends. Interestingly, O'Neill, who returned to his law practice in Columbus and Marietta and lectured at Bethany College before re-entering politics as an Ohio Supreme Court judge, eventually told Kennedy he regretted listening to his advisers' opposition to the appointment.

Baker, who had written two books on corporation executives and many articles on higher education, was critical of board members who "are there for the glory and contribute nothing," but believed that "sooner or later a standard among trustees is recognized, and anyone sounding a sour note is squeezed out." He classified Edwin Kennedy and others on the Ohio University board at that time as a group of independent thinkers who studied and debated issues before endorsing plans presented to them by the administration. "You don't put programs into practice without endorsement from such a group, so their input has a significant impact on the lives of many young people," he said.

Kennedy compared his role as a trustee with similar positions he held on corporate boards: "The principal objective is to make a contribution to the solution of problems that arise regularly in such things as management and finances; and when the time arrives to select a new president, the board is charged with that most critical of all responsibilities."

Such a time, indeed, was arriving at Ohio University. At a regular campus-wide faculty meeting on May 24, 1960, Baker announced his decision to retire at the conclusion of the approaching academic year. This was in keeping with trustee action, stemming from his own recommendation made in 1948, to set the retirement age for administrators at sixty-five. "Mrs. Baker and I are not retiring because of poor health, unhappiness, lack of opportunity, nor the lure of distant fields which might seem greener," he said. "We are both well and happy and believe that greater opportunity lies ahead for Ohio University than we ever dreamed when we came here in 1945. This is merely breaking the news of my age."

Enrollment under Baker's leadership had grown from 1,500 to more than 8,000, with 2,500 other students attending classes on recently established branch campuses in Lancaster, Zanesville, Portsmouth, Chillicothe, Ironton, and Martins Ferry. Doctoral programs had been inaugurated in four academic areas, and every college in the University had added at least one major classroom building. These structures, along with fourteen dormitories, a student center (later named for Baker), a Health Center, physical education buildings, and several auxiliary structures, had altered the campus profile. Monomoy Theater at Chatham, Massachusetts, purchased by Elizabeth Baker in 1958 for annual nonprofit lease to the university, offered fine arts students and faculty summer experience in the highly competitive Cape Cod theatrical district.

After being appointed by President Dwight D. Eisenhower to serve as chairman of the United States delegation to the United Nations Economic and Social Council (UNESCO) at 1953 and 1955 summer meetings in Geneva, Baker had encouraged faculty members to become more aware of international responsibilities as educators. Many of them subsequently helped plan and staff two teacher-training centers in Nigeria. Both of the centers, organized and managed by Ohio University, were opened in 1958, after the Western Nigeria Ministry of Education appealed to the United States for educational assistance. Funding was obtained through a contract between the university and the State Department's International Cooperation Administration. In an early report on the project, Professor LaVern L. Krantz, who served as chief of party for the faculty group, noted, "It is interesting to sit among strangers and hear them discuss your country, its strengths, its weaknesses, and their attitudes toward it. Only then does the universality of the need to understand other people before you can make them understand you drive itself home." Such observations reinforced Baker's insistence that "education must serve the world."

During Baker's final year at the university, Edwin and Ruth Kennedy pondered how they might structure their next contribution to honor the accomplishments of their friend, while reaffirming their own feelings about the responsibilities of education, intensified since the October 1957 launch of the Soviet Union's Sputnik I satellite. In a January 31, 1961 letter to Trustee Chairman Fred Johnson, the Kennedys wrote:

> American education has been a vital factor in the evolution of our way of life. The influence of education has been immense and its contributions indispensable. Still, these words inadequately indicate the role of the American educational process in the years ahead. It seems probable that the outcome of the Cold War will be determined not so much by military action as by the ability of our educational system effectively to influence and form our character, our attitudes, and our national purpose in the decades that may pass before the Cold War is concluded.

The plan Edwin and Ruth Kennedy devised, announced at a trustee-sponsored "Baker Day" convocation on November 17, 1961, provided the largest single gift in the 157-year history of Ohio University. Known as the John C. Baker Fund, the endowment included permanent funding for the Distinguished Professor Award, with the remainder of the income left to the discretion of the university. The donors asked only that it be used "in the spirit of the man whose name it bears, whose contribution to the University and American education can best be described as a constant search for ways to attain advancing standards of excellence."

The Kennedys preferred not to name the amount of the endowment, but it later was revealed to be in excess of $1.5 million, a figure that would continue to grow in later years as further contributions were added. Among the uses of its funds were annual series of Edwin and Ruth Kennedy Lectures, bringing internationally known speakers to the campus, and grants for a wide variety of faculty-student research projects, awarded through competitive proposals from all areas of the university.

Although Edwin and Ruth Kennedy were motivated by a desire to help deserving students and provide an academic boost to their alma mater, they also were pioneering a change in existing general attitudes toward private contributions to publicly supported institutions. The concept of such private and corporate backing became widespread in the following years, and some specific examples could be traced directly to Kennedy's influence. Financial Consultant Ora Roehl arranged a client-sponsored lectureship, patterned after the Ohio University program, at the University of Minnesota. Entrepreneur Walter R. Davis, who never attended college, became one of the most important patrons, as well as a trustee of the University of North Carolina, where one of the nation's leading libraries was named in his honor. Charles Roy Martin became the number one benefactor of Western Kentucky University's College Heights Foundation.

At the request of Ohio University trustees, John Baker remained president through 1961 while a search was made for his successor. After several months of recommendations and interviews, a committee of trustees and faculty members again selected an associate dean of Harvard Business School as its first choice. Vernon R. Alden and his wife, Marion, had visited the campus in the spring of 1961, met with trustees and faculty members, and indicated an interest in the position, although they were spending that summer in Japan. Alden's next contact was a telephone call from John Baker, who invited him to a meeting at the home of Edwin and Ruth Kennedy. It was a visit the thirty-eight-year-old candidate never forgot:

> Ed picked me up at Newark Airport, and on the way to his home in New Vernon, we had a flat tire, which I changed. When we arrived, I was surprised to see Gordon Bush (a trustee and head of the search committee), John Baker, and Fred Johnson, waiting for me. They asked me about Japan, and we talked about various other things until Ed said, "Let's stop the chit chat; we are gathered

here to formally offer you the presidency of Ohio University." Unbeknownst to me, Ruth was waiting in the dining room with a tray of champagne glasses. I said that Marion and I were impressed with the University, but we really needed to think further about such an important change in our lives, and I also wanted to discuss it with Harvard Business School Dean Donald David, who was a friend and mentor. When Ruth heard that, she burst into the room and said, "Well, let's have some champagne anyway." That broke the tension, and about ten days later, I did accept the position.

Vernon Alden began his duties as president on January 1, 1962 and was inaugurated officially four months later. Both Edwin and Ruth Kennedy attended the outdoor inauguration on the "college green," followed by a formal banquet that attracted 550 guests.

While the Kennedys were becoming active in affairs of Ohio University in the fifties, they also began a chain of largesse at Hiram College. The first link with the liberal arts college located in the northeastern Ohio village of Hiram was formed when their son, Eddie, enrolled as a freshman in 1954. Eddie's choice of Hiram, made after visiting several other colleges and universities, was largely coincidental to his father's associating it with the Teachout Foundation that had given him the critical fifty-dollar scholarship thirty years earlier.

During Eddie's first term as a student, he unintentionally stirred painful memories by telling his parents about financial struggles some student friends were having to remain in school. Edwin and Ruth immediately began contributing money earmarked for student loans, asking that the gesture be listed anonymously while their son was enrolled. After a serious automobile accident forced Eddie to withdraw from school, his parents made a sizable donation of Monterey Oil stock as the base for a low-interest-rate Kennedy Loan Fund, which grew into a $1 million endowment. This led to other large financial contributions that would place Edwin and Ruth among the most prominent benefactors of the college in the following decade.

In 1956, Kennedy began another long association with Hiram when he accepted an appointment to the Board of Trustees. "The transition from the Loan Fund to other involvement in Hiram affairs was natural," Kennedy commented later, "and it was skillfully nurtured by Paul Fall [then president of Hiram College] and his successors."

Chapter 9   # The Lehman Mystique

> *I get tired of people who think investment banking is accounting; banking is imagination.*
> —Frank J. Manheim
> Lehman Brothers Partner
> and former college professor
> 1966

One of the most sacrosanct traditions of Lehman Brothers through the years was the luncheon meeting beginning promptly at 1 p.m. each Monday. Outsiders perceived correctly that many major decisions were consummated there in the eighth floor dining room, but only the partners and a coterie of tuxedoed waiters were in attendance. Travel schedules ordinarily precluded the appearance of all partners—seventeen in the late fifties—so topics were selected in accordance with primary interests of those seated around the large walnut dining table.

At the head of the table, President Robert Lehman presided over the informal discussions that disregarded protocol. Never pretending to possess an intellectual bent, the only partner bearing the Lehman name nevertheless was an articulate master at channeling discussions among the group Edwin Kennedy described as "a rambunctious bunch of entrepreneurs." True, the partners functioned independently, each in his own area of expertise and all with equal status, at least on the organizational chart. "Sometimes," Kennedy said with a smile, "a motion carried when Bobbie Lehman was the only person who voted for it." More often, when discussions progressed to the point where a policy decision was needed on how the partnership should proceed on a specific venture such as underwriting a new issue, the majority vote was honored. Recommendations by the partner closest to a given issue were afforded the greatest weight in any deliberation, but the group believed strongly in what it termed "pooled judgments."

A variety of service departments helped keep partners aware of worldwide occurrences that might affect the investment banking business, as well as providing information directly to Lehman clients. Primary among these were the Industrial, Economics, and Investment Advisory Departments, which included lawyers, engineers, accountants, and other specialists. Strict rules were enforced by the partnership to make certain no employee could profit personally from insider information.

Most securities were moved through some six hundred independent broker-dealers throughout the country. None of the partners was considered to be a "trader" at that time. All were investment bankers, a designation covering the wide range from consulting to organizing mergers and new issues.

Kennedy headed an oil department staff that included ten persons trained in geology and petroleum engineering. He also worked closely with senior partner Monroe Gutman, who had been manager of the Lehman Corporation since its inception in 1929. "I had considered Monroe an important mentor during my early years with the firm," Kennedy said. "He had extraordinary judgment, even in areas where he had no specific experience." In 1957, the corporation's assets totaled $211 million, making it the largest closed-end investment trust controlled by a banking house, and forty percent of that amount was in oil properties.

When Ohio University selected Kennedy for honorary membership in Beta Gamma Sigma business honor society, he answered a request for a job description in a letter dated March 14, 1958:

> One of my functions is to translate technical information into what I call the vulgar end result—money. The banking function has not superseded investment activity, rather it has developed as the investment function expanded. My department is responsible for the management of a huge amount of investments in oil

through the Lehman Corporation, a soon-to-be-launched open-end investment fund to be called The One William Street Fund, a very large investment counsel service, firm funds, partner and family funds, and special arrangements with institutions. Our banking activity includes underwriting, setting up special ventures, a considerable number of directorships, and a great amount of consulting work. In the last half dozen years, we have purchased about $500 million worth of oil properties, mostly on a fee basis for the accounts of others. We do a great deal of valuation of oil properties for tax reasons or other purposes, work out reorganizations, and advise on mergers. I have just concluded an arrangement with an oil company whereby we will aid in formulation of managerial policy.

At the height of his career, Kennedy continued to avoid company politics, preferring to maintain a low profile in concentrating on the oil and gas business. He enjoyed working closely with other partners and employees on individual matters, but shunned general committee memberships and administrative positions dealing with overall management of the firm.

Kennedy's fifth-floor office, bridging the entrance corner, mirrored his personality and interests. A large room with leather furniture and a deep-red decor patterned after a room he admired in the famed Folger Shakespeare Library in Washington, D.C., it was described by a colleague as having a "friendly, clubby atmosphere." Turret-shaped corner bookcases displayed geological samples, books on energy, and small bottles of petroleum. Stuffed birds lined the walls. In the center of the room, a huge desk invariably was piled high with analysis reports, memos, letters, and notes. On one occasion, a visiting client who had profited substantially from recommended oil investments glanced at the clutter and said, "Ed, I will pay you for any piece of paper on that desk."

The story was told that Kennedy had first occupied a similar office, albeit somewhat smaller, on the tenth floor. When the Oil Department was moved to the fifth floor, he had the earlier room re-created in such precise detail that another partner remarked, "When Ed moved, his entire office moved with him."

In visiting Western and Southwestern oil fields, Kennedy's regular modus operandi was to catch a Friday night train from New York, study voluminous publications, reports, and documents during the weekend cross-country trip, and arrive at his destination primed for consultation with production company CEOs, whom he came to know on a first-name basis. "Success in those days was based essentially on how successful these companies were in finding oil," he noted. "To build a good banking relationship, you had to know your client well enough to tell him honestly and exactly how you thought he should be handling his financing."

Kennedy became an adviser and close friend of Charles Murphy, Jr., who headed a family-owned business in El Dorado, Arkansas. Building on a strong financial foundation his father had developed in farming, lumbering, and some oil activities, the younger Murphy had started a small production company in 1950, while also managing other family interests. Through visits to Lehman Brothers, he became acquainted with Kennedy, who subsequently supervised investment banking negotiations for a public offering of Murphy Oil Corporation stock in 1956. Soon afterward, Kennedy accepted an invitation to join the Murphy board, beginning a relationship that lasted for many years. As the company grew into an international oil enterprise, Kennedy played a strong supportive role in its development, as reported by Murphy:

> Ed was a very effective director. He worked at it, attending all our board meetings and insisting on seeing for himself what was happening at our refineries and principal oil fields. I went with him on those trips, so we traveled together on airplanes and driving cars from one field station to another, sometimes spending nights right there at the drilling and production facilities. That drew our friendship even closer.
>
> We talked a great deal about philosophy, as well as just the petroleum industry in general and Murphy Oil in particular. I had known him even before that time as a person of intellectual and philosophical bent, but I began to comprehend through those travels together that here was a man of sound personal instincts and

great concern for his fellow man, although not on a do-gooder basis. He wanted people to improve themselves through education.

Influenced by Kennedy, Murphy later established an Institute of Political Economy at Tulane University, not simply providing the funding, but also working with faculty members and administrators in determining texts and teaching methods deemed most attuned to business life in "the real world."

As the investment banker for Husky Oil Company, located in Cody, Wyoming, Kennedy enjoyed a personal friendship with the founder and CEO, Glenn E. Nielson, who also was a national leader in the Church of Jesus Christ of Latter-day Saints (Mormons). Nielson gave his friend a large aluminum briefcase, which became another recognized Kennedy trademark for the remainder of his career. When oil shale appeared to be a possible new source of production, Nielson wanted to buy a section or two of shale land as protection against sudden competition. Already knowing where such a tract was available, and approving of the plan, Kennedy immediately arranged a purchase at a very low price. "All the ventures in which Ed was involved turned out to be advantageous to the growth of Husky," Nielson said.

Kennedy enjoyed a similar friendship with Christopher Chenery, an oil patch genius who founded an entire group of profitable companies. After several projects in which Lehman Brothers served as bankers, he was invited to be on the board of one Chenery gas and oil company, Southern Production.

Yet, Kennedy learned from an incident in the mid-fifties that closeness, while holding a key to success, could sometimes camouflage peril. Lehman Brothers had invested in a company that reached anticipated production levels, but seemed unable to convert that success into a correspondingly sound financial pattern. Kennedy and a fellow partner, Monroe Gutman, discussed the situation at length, as they did on many matters, but they could not pinpoint the problem. Finally, after a period of self-evaluation, Kennedy detected what proved to unravel the puzzle. He had come to know and like the president of the company so well, he had failed to analyze top management with his usual objectivity. It never happened again.

As an adviser to Sinclair Oil, Kennedy was asked to take part in a series of deliberations between management and representatives of a subsidiary stockholder group suing the corporation over alleged irregularities in operation of properties in Venezuela. His role was to provide operational facts surrounding the issue, without giving his opinion on legalities. At the final session, when it had become evident his information had demolished the opposition's case, the suit was dropped. Pete LaVan, attorney for the subsidiary stockholders, quickly gathered his papers and headed for the door, pausing briefly to confront Kennedy, who still was seated at the conference table.

"Mr. Kennedy," Lavan said, "the next time I'm involved in something with you, I hope you will be on my side."

"Mr. Lavan," Kennedy replied, "if you'll pay more attention to the facts, I'll be glad to be on your side."

When Sinclair later initiated discussions to buy Southern Production from Christopher Chenery, Kennedy was placed in the untenable position of being closely allied to both companies. Resigning immediately from the Southern board, he nevertheless was able to maintain relations with the two organizations in other matters.

Kennedy's travels in the fifties also took him into Canada, where his name became recognized throughout the oil industry. Exploration in that country, which had brought only sporadic production and brief notice since the turn of the century, had burst suddenly into the headlines with dramatic strikes of oil and gas in Western provinces during the late forties. Most producers burned off the gas, which they considered an annoying by-product, as they moved rapidly to expand oil drilling. In the early fifties, however, a flamboyant millionaire Texas oil man named Clint Murchison, a close friend of President Dwight D. Eisenhower, conceived the idea of exploring specifically for natural gas and building a pipeline that could deliver it from

Alberta, across Northern Ontario, to the more populated industrial areas of Eastern Canada. With that in mind, he called on another friend, Ed Kennedy, in New York.

The two men had come to know each other through Kennedy's involvement with Delhi Oil, a Dallas production company Murchison had owned since 1948. Kennedy had organized several underwriting projects for Delhi, working closely with its chief geologist, Frank Schultz, who headed operations, and with Murchison, the chairman and CEO. This escalation throughout the Southwest in the early fifties had elevated Delhi to a prominent position in Murchison's business empire. It also had cemented Kennedy's friendship with both Murchison and Schultz. The three worked together in forming a subsidiary, Canadian Delhi, to manage the Alberta exploration, and TransCanada PipeLine Limited, created with the hope of transporting the gas.

Murchison and Kennedy conducted their private meeting at the Waldorf-Astoria Hotel, and although they often had brainstormed the idea of a pipeline linking the western gas fields to the eastern marketplace, the time had come to discuss specifics. The concept was revolutionary—a pipeline would be the nation's largest undertaking since construction of the Trans-Canada Railroads—but by the end of the afternoon, the two agreed that Murchison should launch the project, with Lehman Brothers underwriting the American financing. The indomitable Texan then revealed his scheme to the Canadian government and applied for the necessary permits.

Several other companies, most notably Western Pipelines Limited, were at that time requesting permission to pipe gas to United States markets, serving customers in Manitoba and Saskatchewan along the way. Murchison's idea had both the appeal of keeping Canadian gas entirely within Canadian borders and the support of eastern metropolitan areas, but with Western Pipelines amending its plans on several occasions, the competitive proposals generated heated political infighting that stoked long bureaucratic delays. Finally, Minister of Trade and Commerce Clarence D. Howe ruled that the all-Canadian route was the only plan the government would approve. That improved the odds, but did not squelch the politicizing. Eventually the Canadian government decided that TransCanada could begin the ambitious project in 1956, but only as a joint venture with Western Pipelines. By then, Murchison had become so disgruntled by red tape he turned all responsibility over to Schultz.

Two years later, on October 10, 1958, the world's largest natural gas pipeline, stretching 2,200 miles beneath ninety-nine rivers, six lakes, forests, farmlands, streams, highways, railways, and the formidable Canadian Shield, from the border of Alberta and Saskatchewan to Montreal, was completed, on time and under budget. Kennedy had played a behind-the-scenes role all the way from feasibility studies through enormous problems of private financing to completion of construction.

Meanwhile, Kennedy was serving as financial adviser to Home Oil Corporation, a Calgary-based oil and gas production company headed by Robert A. Brown, Jr., whose father had drilled the first significant Western Canada oil well in 1936. Growing rapidly under the leadership of CEO Brown and Executive Vice President Robert Campbell, Home Oil began buying pipeline interests from major oil companies that had helped finance its construction. "Although Ed represented some majors, he was more active with those we classified as 'independents,' and he was really good at dealing with the giants," Campbell said. "Part of the reason was that he enjoyed doing it so much." Within a few years, Home Oil became the most prominent independent in Canada, with the largest equity share—28 percent—in TransCanada PipeLine. Brown, Campbell, and Schultz all became members of the TransCanada board, and Kennedy later joined them, succeeding Lehman Brothers colleague John Fell, who had served on the board from the time the pipeline was being built until his death soon after its completion.

TransCanada eventually reached sales exceeding $3 billion a year, with pipelines in Canada and the United States making it the second largest natural gas carrier in the world.

While the pipeline was being planned and constructed, Lehman Brothers, largely through Kennedy's efforts, also became a leading participant in forming four new Canadian production companies: Sunlite Oil, Banff Oil, Canada Oil Lands, and Prairie Oil Royalties. Sunlite was organized soon after the discovery of oil in Canada's Arctic Islands; Kennedy described it as being "moderately successful," even though exploration in the remote islands never reached expectations. Banff, formed to explore a vast segment of the Western Canada oilpatch, became successful, albeit without achieving an expected bonanza. "You hope for a home run, and we came close a couple of times," Kennedy mused, "and although we didn't quite get it, we did all right." Afterwards, Kennedy negotiated Banff's sale to a large French company, which used it as an entre into Canadian exploration.

Lehman Brothers participated as investment bankers in organizing Prairie Oil Royalties and Canada Oil Lands, and although Kennedy helped manage the latter for a brief period, he sold his investment interest after it made a reasonable gain.

In addition to becoming a director of both Sunlite and Banff as well as TransCanada PipeLine, Kennedy increased his role in the steady growth of Home Oil Company. Typically, he often accompanied Campbell on visits to production sites in the Arctic Islands, within four hundred miles of the North Pole. On some of these occasions, Campbell noted, when their small airplane landed on a frozen lake for a mid-summer visit, "Ed chopped a hole in the ice and dropped in a line to see if he could pull out a fish, before moving ahead with business." There was plenty of time, Campbell said, because daylight lasted twenty-four hours a day.

A December 1957 *Fortune* magazine article, "The Bustling House of Lehman," reflected the firm's benefits from oil and gas ventures in the United States and Canada:

> Lehman Brothers has achieved the largest postwar growth of any Wall Street house, and has been one of the biggest profit mak-

ers—many believe the biggest—in the business.... All told, Lehman has probably done more than $1 billion of financing for the oil industry since 1946, and handled the purchase of oil properties for some companies to the tune of $400 million to $500 million.... The oil department, the firm's most successful field of activity in recent years, is headed by Edwin L. Kennedy ... (who) has given Lehman as a sponsor of oil properties, a prestige unrivaled in the Street."

Competing firms soon began moving more vigorously into the oil investment arena. None of these organizations, however, disputed Kennedy's first-place ranking among oil company analysts.

As his department continued to grow, Kennedy looked for a possible understudy who shared his passion for the oil and gas business and had a proven track record in dealing successfully with other people. Knowledge of investment banking was secondary, he reasoned; the right man could acquire that. Investigating possible candidates in his usual thorough manner, Kennedy selected James W. Glanville, an engineer with Humble Oil Company in Houston, Texas. A graduate of Rice University who earned a master's degree at the California Institute of Technology, Glanville had done some work in finance and property acquisition for Humble during eleven years with the company, but basically, he was an engineer.

At a luncheon meeting to discuss the possible career change, Glanville expressed strong interest in the position, but a reluctance to leave his home state of Texas prompted him to proffer what he assumed would be unacceptable conditions for the move. "Fine," Kennedy replied without hesitation, "we'll see you Monday." The tongue-in-cheek suggestion of a time frame was made with such an earnest expression, a startled Glanville at first thought it was serious. Yet, it wasn't long before he, his wife, and three young children settled into their new home near New York.

"I had an oil background, but I didn't really know much about investment banking," Glanville recalled several years later, "but Ed was my mentor, and he was incredibly gracious in letting me make mistakes while I was learning. He and his wife also went out of their way to help our family adjust to this new life, and they continued to treat us that way through the years. Moreover, Ed clearly was responsible for my being made a partner in 1961, less than two years after I joined the firm."

The sale of Monterey Oil to Humble and complicated negotiations for an acquisition of Plymouth Oil Company by Marathon were among the first important transactions the two men arranged together. Glanville's observations on that period provide further insight into the Kennedy personality:

> I learned a great deal from Ed, not only about the mechanics of the business, but about personal integrity and the importance of client relationships. You learned from Ed because you saw these things working. He had strong views, and he could be tough. But I never saw him out of control. I never saw him wave his arms or shout, but when you knew him well enough, you could tell when he wasn't pleased.
>
> Ed didn't have a lot of patience for persons who contributed nothing but suggestions after the fact, although he didn't show his feelings outwardly. I remember that after we sold a Canadian gas property to Mobil, with a substantial profit to Lehman Brothers, one of the partners suggested that we could have negotiated a higher price. Ed didn't like that. He took real exception to anyone who didn't know much about the subject looking at it in hindsight.

Since America had moved from a net exporter to an importer of petroleum in the mid-fifties, quotas had been set on imports. At the same time, diminishing success in domestic exploration had produced a substantial drop in oil reserves. By 1962 eight participating nations in the Organization of Petroleum Exporting Countries (OPEC)—Iran, Iraq, Venezuela, Kuwait, Saudi Arabia, Qatar, Libya, and Indonesia—accounted for 90 percent of world oil exports. Oil stock prices fluctuated with headlines announcing OPEC intentions to maintain high wellhead prices (more than half of the profits went to governments of those countries) alternating with contentions by some American observers that a world oil glut was about to depress prices.

Kennedy acknowledged that short-range fluctuations would continue with "periods of pause and readjustment," and that the extraordinary upsweep of oil security prices following World War II could not be expected to return, but he believed such investments would be favorable in the sixties. Studying industrial capabilities and marketing trends should enable security buyers "with courage and analytical skills" to add or subtract from positions as changing moods of the financial world produced these fluctuations. "Optimism will, as it has in the past, overreach itself and pessimism will, as it has in the past, be overdramatized," Kennedy told a group of security analysts. "Emotional outbursts in oil stocks either way should be taken as warnings. Don't let the stock market do your thinking for you. Do it yourself."

With that expressed philosophy, Kennedy primed the Lehman Oil Department for an era of industrial diversification and acquisition. "Mergers of companies, along with sales and purchases of oil properties, spread like a disease in the sixties," he said. Many of these were handled by Lehman. Kennedy summarized this outlook in a 1962 statistical report:

> Since 1952 there have been thirty-one production-emphasis companies listed on the New York Stock Exchange either continuously throughout the period or for a portion of it. Of this total, fifteen, or 45 percent, have sold out and gone out of business. Seven of the fifteen sell-outs have taken place in the past year, or are currently underway. Sixteen remain in business, but, of these, eight have sought to break the Gordian knot arising from being oriented to domestic exploration and production by either going abroad in a meaningful and significant way, by diversifying into non-production activities, or in some cases by doing both. About 75 percent of all the producing or production-emphasis companies listed on the Stock Exchange for the past ten years have either sold out or have materially reoriented the pattern of their operations. Only eight, or 26 percent of the total number, are operating without significant change in the way they seek to profit and keep their stockholders happy. If one were to add to the number of sell-outs the number currently subject to rumor in the gossip canyons of

Wall Street, it would indeed add up to a very high proportion of the total thirty-one.

The earnings trend of the eight producing-emphasis companies that have gone abroad or moved into non-producing activities is interesting when related to the nine producing companies that have not materially changed their operations. The aggregate net income of the eight companies in 1960, as reported, showed an increase of 48 percent over the aggregate of the same group in 1952. During the same years of comparison, the eight companies that have not materially changed operations increased only 6.5 percent. A complete analysis of the causes of this marked difference in performance undoubtedly would show that many factors unrelated to diversification entered into the comparison. Still, the implication is clear that diversification into foreign areas and into non-producing activity has been a substantial factor in this relative performance.

Despite his feeling that "as the stern realities of competition descend on us, everybody is getting into everybody else's business," Kennedy was not uncomfortable in accommodating himself to change. "As a banker," he said, "I have very well-developed instincts for a client's self-preservation." He insisted, however, that diversification would be most likely to succeed when based on extensive research, and he could cite examples where failure to do so had led to hasty, ill-conceived action, with disastrous results.

Kennedy tempered comments on the subject, however, by making distinctions between "geographical diversification" (such as moving exploration and marketing operations abroad), expansion into such logical fields as petrochemicals and coal or uranium mining, and conglomerate flings into totally unrelated arenas. He advised the oil industry not to follow the latter path, simply because their management skills were not geared to success in so many areas. Years later, such examples as Exxon's ill-fated entry into the electrical equipment business and Standard Oil of Ohio's attempt to manage a copper company added testimony to his contention.

Yet, Kennedy indicated by word and example that caution was not akin to reluctance. Indeed, he had helped Murphy Corporation move aggressively into foreign marketing and production when careful analysis indicated a reasonable opportunity to reach its objective of becoming a flexible, medium-sized company. "While long-range planning is a part of the daily routine of this management," Kennedy said, "it is quick to shift emphasis as industry conditions change." In spite of recent difficulties within the oil industry, Murphy earnings had increased by 25 percent in three years.

Similarly, Kerr-McGee was broadening its scope in the early sixties to include energy sources other than hydrocarbons and uranium, but only with careful planning and guidance from experienced consultants. "Even then, the headaches have been many, and there still are quite a few around," Kennedy said, "but a significant proportion of increased total profits will be coming from activity not in the company's picture a few years ago." He referred to such operations as the mining of potash and coal, which related to the company's expertise in the exploration of mineral reserves.

Obviously not opposed to diversification, Kennedy nevertheless did not envision it as changing the oil industry's outlook significantly. Utilization of energy was certain to grow in step with population, business, and the worldwide standard of living, he reasoned. In presenting this opinion to a group of engineers at a gathering in New York, he concluded, "I should think the oil industry in general might more fruitfully dedicate its skill to the maintenance of its position in the energy market, and the making of profits therefrom, than to push into other fields of activity."

Throughout his career, Ed Kennedy considered "the ability to remain dispassionate enough to advise against our own interest when that seemed best for a client" an invaluable ingredient of "the Lehman mystique." Because of that belief, he received great satisfaction from an incident which took place long after he retired from participation in Lehman affairs: During the forties, both friendship and a business relationship had grown between Kennedy and a young independent Tulsa oil operator who was a client of the Lehman Investment Advisory Department. Early in the next decade, the man had solicited Kennedy's opinion about going public with his privately owned company. After analyzing what he had come to know about the man and his company, Kennedy advised him to remain private, although handling a public stock offering would have brought a sizable profit to Lehman Brothers. Having lost contact after retiring from Lehman, Kennedy was surprised in April 1992 to receive a telephone call from the man, whose company still was privately owned. Without explaining what had reminded him of the advice he had received forty years previously, the man told Kennedy, "I just called to thank you again for one of the most important things ever done for me."

Chapter 10   A Hard-Core Philosophy

> *When I think of Ed Kennedy, many specific incidents of boards relying heavily on his advice blend into an overall memory of his deep insight. He seemed to know everyone in the oil industry.*
>
> —Erwin Millimet
> Retired New York Attorney
> Former Director and Legal
> Counsel to Tosco

Serving as an occasional spokesman for the energy-investment business in the sixties came with the territory of achieving status. But experience as a debater, knowledge of his subject matter, and confidence in his own judgments could not totally erase Edwin Kennedy's uneasiness in speech-making. Those who listened did not detect a shyness to which he still confessed, but speaking in front of an audience was much different for him than expressing his thoughts in meetings of peer groups or private conversations. In fact, he insisted, it was "downright painful." To help ease that pain, he studied for each address as if it were the thesis he never found time to prepare at Ohio State University.

"Just as with everything else, when Ed prepares a speech, he works and digs and gets absolutely involved in the preparation," observed his friend and confidant, John Baker. A trustee at Juniata College in Pennsylvania, Baker was assigned the difficult task of getting Kennedy to speak on energy at a meeting of Juniata Valley businessmen. Accepting the invitation only because of its source, Kennedy spent numerous hours assimilating his personal expertise and in-depth research into what Baker termed "a masterful speech" entitled "Energy Comes of Age." Juniata owned some coal fields at a time when everyone wanted to get into the coal business, Baker said, "and if trustees had followed Ed's advice, Juniata would have become wealthy." The college printed the speech, and when partners at Lehman Brothers read it, they had it reprinted in a high-quality booklet.

Yet, that speech might never have been delivered. Baker laughed heartily in recalling what had happened when he visited Edwin and Ruth in New Vernon to proffer the invitation:

> I mentioned that the meeting would be a stag affair. Ruth, who bristled at that chauvinistic idea, told me that if the president of Juniata didn't invite her to the program, her husband wouldn't be there either. Well, I immediately telephoned President Ellis, who explained that they never had women at those particular affairs. I told him that if he knew Ruth Kennedy, he would make arrangements to change that policy. He did just that, also inviting his own wife, and the stag concept was dropped forever.

Wherever the Kennedys appeared between 1961 and 1963, people seemed to wonder if they were, perchance, related to the president of the United States, and in travels abroad, they found the shared surname almost guaranteed superior accommodations at hotels. "When I telephoned for reservations, there always was a pause, during which time I knew what the clerk was thinking," Kennedy said, "so we never had a problem, even if it was a last-minute request." In the United States, the question became so inevitable that Ruth could anticipate what was coming before the sentence was completed. Frequently, depending on the person and the circumstance, the resulting opening conversation would follow a standard pattern:

"Oh, are you part of the . . . ?"

"Yes, we are part of the Kennedy family, but not the one you think."

As time passed, Ruth often shortened her response by simply saying, "No relation." Either way, the exchange rarely failed to draw a hearty laugh from Edwin. He didn't mind the mistaken assumption that he might be a relative of John Fitzgerald Kennedy, but years later he shuddered with displeasure when erroneously referred to as "Edward Kennedy."

One of the most satisfying personal and business relationships of Edwin Kennedy's career began in 1960, when he met Walter R. Davis, a tall, deep-voiced Midland, Texas, oil man. A self-made millionaire who had dropped out of high school in Chatham, Virginia, to become a long-distance truck driver, Davis had joined a nationwide trucking company owned by Californian Fred Rumley, later moving to its West Coast headquarters. After advancing from driver through a series of management positions, Davis had received financial backing from Rumley to form Western Oil Transportation, a Midland-based enterprise trucking crude from small producing wells to the pipelines of major oil companies. Beginning with six vehicles in 1952, Western Oil had spurted to leviathan proportions, with trucks and its own pipelines crossing the Southwest. Meanwhile, in 1957, Davis and Rumley had formed Permian Corporation to purchase a large share of the oil being moved by their transportation unit.

Davis had an aversion to borrowing money. This had not interfered with development of Western Oil, nor the early progress of Permian, because mushrooming profits had easily covered the costs of expansion. In the early sixties, however, he decided Permian should go public to finance a large extension of the pipeline network, which was less profitable, but more secure than a fleet of trucks. Rumley did not agree, but rather than oppose the move, he sold his share of the business, valued at $20 million, to employees for a combined $1 million, thereby making each of them wealthy. The extraordinary gesture was characteristic of Rumley, to whom wealth was never very important. He once advised Davis, "If you have your hat paid for, and your roof doesn't leak, and you don't need to look at prices on the menu, what difference does it make whether you have a hundred million dollars or a hundred dollars? Everything is okay."

Before his departure, Rumley recommended that if Davis insisted on going public, he should contact Lehman Brothers to arrange financing. Davis, who recalled his friend as adding, "Their oil people have an impeccable record of being honorable," accepted the suggestion. After visits by Lehman partner Steven DeBrul, questions on underwriting the venture arose within the banking firm. DeBrul was confident enough, however, to commit personal money to the financing. Kennedy scrutinized the proposal and agreed to join him, thereby prompting Robert Lehman and other senior partners to do the same. Kennedy then took the lead in consummating the private, rather than public offering of Permian stock, and Davis himself was among the buyers.

In future dealings, Davis worked directly with Kennedy, sometimes in New York—although the big Texan harbored a strong dislike for that city—more often in Midland, and sometimes at other locations. Davis considered Kennedy a man "sincerely interested in seeing our company prosper, not just in fees he could charge." Kennedy described Davis as "a caring man with a golden touch," specifying such coups as paying one million dollars for an old refinery that was about to be closed, "just to protect the jobs of long-time employees," then selling it later for about fifteen times that amount when a gasoline crisis emerged.

Following construction financed by the stock offering and other projects partially funded through Lehman Brothers, Permian became the largest independent crude oil purchaser in the country, with five hundred trucks and five hundred miles of pipelines covering the mid-continent region. Kennedy served as a board member for a short time, before negotiating a 1965 merger of the company into Occidental Oil, headed by the controversial Armand Hammer. Davis, who had earned the high respect of Chairman and Chief Executive Officer Hammer, was elected president and chief operating officer of Occidental. "Walter Davis is the smartest truck driver I've ever met," said Kennedy.

Three years later, concerns over some methods of Armand Hammer prompted the Lehman Brothers board to consider dropping Occidental as a client. Late one Friday afternoon, Bobbie Lehman asked Kennedy, who by then knew the Occidental CEO very well, to assess the situation and provide a candid recommendation.

"Let me think about it over the weekend, before giving an answer," Kennedy replied.

On Monday, Kennedy offered his typically analytical evaluation: "Armand is aging noticeably, and Walter Davis has been designated as his successor. If something should happen to Armand in the not-too-distant future, and Walter should take his place as CEO, we would have made a serious mistake by dropping the account." Although his friendship with Hammer had waned, because of differences in business philosophies, Kennedy suggested continuing the relationship, at least for awhile, but with the caveat that Lehman Brothers should "observe it carefully as we go along." The board accepted that advice.

On Wall Street, Edwin Kennedy often was referred to as "a professional director." Although he disliked the term, he conceded its basis in fact. During the most active years of his career, he served on the boards of directors of fourteen energy-related companies, for varying lengths of time and with varying degrees of involvement. In doing so, he followed a general, though unwritten policy of Lehman Brothers to have partners and associates sit on boards of client companies. A report in the mid-sixties showed Lehman representation on boards of more than one hundred large corporations.

In some instances, Kennedy was elected to boards following his leadership in arranging financing for expansions or acquisitions. In others, such as Sunlite and Banff, he was active in forming the companies. Occasionally, board membership was based strictly on his reputation, as in the case of Columbian Carbon Company, later sold to Cities Service.

Kennedy viewed the role of a director as bearing responsibility to many constituencies—customers, employees, investors, governments, and the general public—and he vigorously opposed "any attitudes or actions of management or directors that may be promotional to market action of the stocks of the corporations they serve." What he labeled his "hard-core working philosophy" for board membership was recounted in opening statements of a chapter he wrote for a Dow Jones Irwin Incorporated *Chief Executive's Handbook:*

When I first accepted membership on boards of directors, I formulated certain rules to apply to such membership. I believe they have served me well; I pass them on in the hope they may be of help to others. These basic principles have been:

1. Accept an invitation to join a corporation as a director only when you are really convinced that the management is of good character and subscribes to a code of high ethical standards.

2. Regardless of the circumstances which cause the invitation to be given, I was, and I am convinced that a board member must, without pause and without reservation, represent all stockholders. Membership in a board of directors where views on corporate problems or policies are shaped by the attitudes of a single or a special-interest stockholder are not compatible with the basic thesis of corporate democracy. Furthermore, a narrow special-interest representation that dominates a corporation's affairs may lead to unwarranted risks in the field of directors' liability.

3. I assumed, and I take it as unarguable that one must not serve on a board unless one is both able to and committed to give sufficient time to become a knowledgeable director. Absences from directors' meetings should be minimal. Maintaining a position as a knowledgeable director involves much more time and work than merely attending meetings.

4. A board member should have a direct ownership of sufficient stock of the corporation to give him a meaningful personal stake in the board decisions in which he participates. A meaningful, personal stake does not necessarily mean a large number of shares. We know able directors who do not have great personal wealth for whom ownership of 100 shares meets the requirement, and we know of others for whom a much larger position does not meet the requirement. Ownership should be more than a token one as measured, not by the number of shares owned, but in relation to the director's total financial picture.

5. A board member, clearly, must keep himself continuously informed about the problems, trends, and managerial performance of the company with which he is associated as a director. He avoids getting into the area of operating decisions except as management

may inform him while considering broad matters of policy. His most important function is evaluation of managerial performance. He performs his duties in a background that presumes his general support of management. But his support of management is not automatic or rubber-stamp. It comes from independent thinking and analysis. When a director's judgment, carefully determined, differs too often on major issues from that of management, the director must reassess the situation to determine whether he is misplaced in his director's position or whether management should be strengthened. This may pose a hard decision; if so, I believe it should be faced and made.

In later years, Kennedy regretted not accepting an invitation to join the board of a reinsurance company, the first of many such organizations he advised on oil-stock investments. When Fidelity Funds, Tri-Continental, Prudential, and other institutional investors were building portfolios, they regularly retained Kennedy to counsel them on trends in the oil business and suggest specific stock purchases most apt to maximize returns. "Ed definitely was the most important investment banking person in oil, and, more importantly, the most prominent oil analyst in the fifties and sixties," said Charles Maxwell, who joined C. J. Lawrence Incorporated, a member firm of the New York Stock Exchange, as an oil analyst in 1968. Maxwell, who had worked in production, refining, transportation, and marketing with Mobil Oil for twelve years, later became a five-time winner of an Institutional Investor poll, which selected the top oil analyst of the year. "The poll didn't exist in Ed's day, or he would have won it every year," Maxwell said.

Because Kennedy liked to share ideas with influential leaders, he became active in the Economic Club of New York. He was astounded to discover the organization, whose members were top executive officers of major business and industrial firms, had serious financial problems. After one occasion on which he and others used their own money to keep the club solvent, he managed to overcome its problems and establish a satisfactory financial structure. Dinner meetings featured talks by such celebrated foreign heads of state as Nikita Khrushchev,

Harold Wilson, and Menachem Begin, as well as top-ranking United States political and economic figures.

Despite the demonstrated performance of America's first nuclear plants, energy in the sixties continued to depend on four primary sources: coal, oil, natural gas, and water power. The latter, which provided only four percent of the supply, had approached its saturation point in the United States; there remained relatively few favorable sites not already harnessed for hydroelectric generation. The other three sources were nonrenewable. With consumption increasing at an even greater rate than the population explosion and widespread public apprehension threatening the proliferation of nuclear energy, many industry analysts feared that a resource limitation was in sight. Edwin Kennedy did not agree.

"Technology, the great multiplier, has reached a point of break-through which assures an ample supply at costs which will support our advancing standard of living," he told a business group. "This assurance is qualified only by the reservation that this nation keep the essential components of a venture-capitalism economy. We refer not alone to the structure of this system, but even more to the intangibles that make it work—competition and incentives stimulating free men in a free society. I do not look upon our present proved energy resources as a single warehouse that sooner or later will be emptied. Rather, I believe technology will find the key to newer warehouses as required, and, in all probability, in advance of need."

Aside from the nuclear energy capabilities already being exploited, Kennedy had become vitally interested in the potential of the "warehouse" of oil shale. The richest known zone of this mixture of organic and inorganic matter was the so-called Mahogany Ledge spanning parts of Wyoming, Utah, and Colorado, where a small, struggling company, The Oil Shale Corporation, hoped to mine the shale and produce refinery feed stock through a process known as hydrogenation. After being asked to help salvage the venture in 1960, Kennedy had delayed his answer for a year, while his staff made a study to estimate when the United States would lose its self-sufficiency in oil. With the study indicating 1969 (it missed by less than a year), he agreed to become a member of the board and help guide the company's progress.

"My only serious mistake was assuming that when we needed the necessary backing it would be there," Kennedy recalled later. "Boy, was I wrong." As the company continued to struggle, always on the edge of failure, other Lehman partners asked Kennedy why he stayed with it. "Because the national interest requires it," he replied.

At one board meeting, when collapse seemed certain, Kennedy told fellow directors, "It is normal at a time like this when a crisis is approaching to say, 'Let George do it.' Well, I want to remind you that the only available Georges are those in this room. So I'll begin by putting in $100,000." Others quickly raised the ante to $500,000—all of which eventually was repaid—and the company was saved.

A second rescue was effected when Kennedy explained the problem to Oren Atkins, CEO of Ashland Oil Company who was visiting the Lehman Oil Department. By the time Atkins left Kennedy's office, he had pledged $500,000 to purchase 100,000 shares of Oil Shale stock.

More recently, when bankruptcy again seemed imminent, Kennedy was instrumental in obtaining support from the Standard Oil Company of Ohio and Cleveland Cliffs Iron Company, a leading mining concern, each of which thereby owned one-third interest in both the oil shale reserves and the development operations. The Oil Shale Corporation (known thereafter by the acronym Tosco), Sohio, and Cleveland Cliffs then made plans to build a thousand-ton-a-day demonstration plant in Colorado, through a jointly-owned Colony Development Corporation.

Needing capital to fund its share of such a project, Tosco turned again to Kennedy, who brought in two French government oil companies as investors. The pilot plant proved successful, producing eight hundred barrels of oil daily, but development costs were high. During the financing, Kennedy worked closely with Morton M. Winston, an attorney who had been hired to assist Tosco at its inception. In 1967, Winston joined the corporation as executive vice president.

For reasons never quite clear, Sohio and Cleveland Cliffs suddenly withdrew from support of development—an option permitted in the agreement—but kept their interests in the oil shale reserves. "No one thought Tosco could survive that blow," Winston said, "but they didn't know Ed Kennedy."

In desperation, Winston and Tosco President Hein I. Koolsbergen agreed to a "rights offer" by the two French companies, effectively enabling them to take over all, or at least the controlling interest in Tosco, which was their stated intention. They gave Tosco a bank guarantee of $3.5 million to continue in business. This was to be repaid with a securities offering for which they were guarantors. If they bought all the stock, their purchase would simply cancel Tosco's notes, and they would own the company. When they asked Winston to suggest a fair price, he answered, "Four or five dollars would seem appropriate, but it doesn't matter, because you will end up owning the company, and all the money you pay for the stock will be right there. You are virtually buying the company for three and a half million dollars." Nevertheless, representatives of the French firms studied Tosco and determined that the stock should be worth only ninety cents a share. For bookkeeping purposes, they insisted that an offering be set at an even dollar.

"Through all this," Winston said, "Ed Kennedy was standing by and watching. He said if they set the price at a dollar, they would not be able to buy the company."

Winston passed the warning on to the French management groups, but they remained adamant, and a week later, the offer became effective. "We never said anything except the truth, but our guardian angel must have been looking over us," Winston said. "Ed saved us without leaving his office. Within forty-eight hours after he began telephoning friends who had been watching Tosco, the price went up to four dollars, and every share was sold. We ended up retaining control, with ownership dispersed in friendly hands."

Kennedy became Tosco's "central adviser and most influential director," Winston said, and chaired a meeting at Lehman Brothers in which Atlantic Richfield Corporation (Arco) agreed to purchase the Sohio and Cleveland Cliffs interests in the oil shale properties. Soon afterward, Arco moved its main office from New York to Los Angeles, and Tosco went there also, to be near its new partner. Ironically, however, an Arco drilling team was the first to strike oil on Alaska's North Slope in 1968, sparking the rush to Prudhoe Bay. That softened its interest in synthetics.

Tosco never had an income from oil shale, but it wobbled through a period when American industry vacillated fancifully in its attempts to determine the feasibility of that source of energy, before establishing firm footing in refining. Despite the series of setbacks in its formative years, Tosco would, in fact, rise to a position of 117 on the Fortune 500 list. That chapter in the lives of Tosco, Lehman Brothers, and Edwin Kennedy would become a highlight of the seventies.

Colleagues and competitors alike attributed Kennedy's ability to muster investors on short notice to what John Baker termed "lasting friendships based on an unwavering integrity that was considered somewhat uncommon even in those days on Wall Street." The Tosco stock placement was but one example. In 1967, Kennedy had just committed Lehman Brothers to underwriting a large common stock offering for Kerr-McGee when war erupted in the Middle East. "I walked the floor on that one, because investors just stopped everything until they could determine what was going to happen," Kennedy recalled. To solve the problem, he telephoned Lammot du Pont Copeland (whom he always referred to by the nickname "Motsy"), assuring him that the investment was sound. Copeland made an immediate large commitment, paving the way for a successful offering.

Kennedy continued his friendship also with Hugh Sharp, who had become a du Pont director, and on several occasions assisted him in working to improve that company's position in obtaining natural gas, an important raw material for its manufacturing processes.

Interestingly, Kennedy gained his prominence without dealing with some of the world's largest petroleum dynasties. Lehman Brothers received very little business from Standard Oil companies, whose close ties to Morgan Stanley & Company dated back to joint interests of J.P. Morgan, or from Gulf Oil, which had a similar connection with The First Boston Corporation, through the Andrew W. Mellon family.

In 1969, Robert Lehman died. Bobbie, as he was most often called, had led the company for forty-four years with what one close observer described as "an iron fist within a white glove." No successor had been groomed for the position, which would pass for the first time outside the family, but the independent nature of partners was sufficient to conceal any internal problem that might be brewing. Clients were largely unconcerned with a pending transition in the firm's leadership.

Grade schooler Kennedy and Prince.

Harding High School Senior Edwin Kennedy, 1922.

A pair of Eds. Father and son in 1944.

Cyrus Zimmerman and children in the forties: Helen and John, seated, Ruth and Edna behind them.

From left at formal affair in the late eighties: Ed Kennedy, Christa Cook, Ora Roehl, Susanne Cook, Jeff Cook, Patty Kennedy.

Ruth Kennedy uses her preferred style of breaking ground in 1967 for construction of a student center at Hiram College.

Hiram President Elmer Jagow with the Kennedys at Center dedication in 1969.

Kerr-McGee President Dean McGee, left, and board member Kennedy talk with mine engineer Bob Lane at an underground potash facility in 1966.

Ed and Ruth respond to an off-camera remark on the deck of an observatory funded by the Kennedys at Hiram's biology field station in 1970.

Parents Edwin Clarence and Emma Lust Kennedy, 1947.

Ed chats with Arnold Toynbee after the world renowned historian delivered a Kennedy Lecture at Ohio University.

Scranton bank liquidator Kennedy in 1933.

A daily ritual in his Lehman Brothers office.

Ruth in conversation with Elizabeth and John Baker.

Ruth and Ed Kennedy in 1962.

Receiving an honorary Doctor of Laws degree from Ohio University President Vernon R. Alden, June 1965.

With Marion and Vernon Alden at 1990 reception.

With Claire and Charles Ping at podium.

Award recipients Kennedy and Laurel Lee Schaefer at Ohio University 1971 Homecoming. Young admirer of the newly named Miss America is unidentified.

Ruth's niece, Nancy Bletzer, sole remaining descendent of the Zimmerman family.

Kennedy Sports & Recreation Center at Juniata College.

Chapter 11   # Contrasting Personalities

Happy is the house that shelters a friend.
—*Ralph Waldo Emerson*

The near-zero weather at Vaux Hall, New Jersey undoubtedly had much to do with the slack business in Emil Ott's butcher shop on a snowy January morning in 1960. Making some use of this uncustomary quiet, the popular German-emigrant butcher was taking time to read an overseas letter from his niece, Christa Teichmann.

Born in 1938, at the time Adolf Hitler's Nazi regime had annexed Austria and was preparing to invade Poland, Christa had grown up in the village of Wildbad, located in Germany's Black Forest region. Following graduation from high school, she had worked with her Aunt Paula, who owned a hotel. Now she was excited about an invitation to join two close friends on an extended trip to the United States. Explaining in the letter that the other girls were seeking American sponsors who would offer them employment in or near New York, she wondered if her uncle "could be so kind as to look around to see if I might also get a job in that area." She did not consider the fact that she spoke no English to be a deterrent.

As he was finishing the letter, Ott looked up to greet a regular customer who was entering the shop. After exchanging a few words about the weather, and even before discussing the

Contrasting Personalities   117

subject of meat, he asked, "Mrs. Kennedy, would you be interested in hiring my niece from Germany for a little while?"

"Sure," Ruth Kennedy replied. "Who is she?"

Christa, Ott explained, was one of seven children born to William and Klara Teichmann. In her early childhood, she never had an opportunity to know her father, an Army officer serving on several fighting fronts throughout World War II. After he was captured by invading American forces she did not even know whether he was dead or alive until he returned following the armistice in 1945. By then she lived with her aunt at the hotel, and although she saw her family nearly every day, she never experienced a true father-daughter relationship.

When she received the invitation to live and work with Ruth and Edwin Kennedy, Christa began making arrangements that included overcoming two principal obstacles. One of these— opposition from both parents—she could resolve with unrelenting determination, which she was prepared to assert. The other, also a reflection of her independent nature, was more complex. By committing themselves to a full year's employment with American sponsors, her friends were able to leave the country immediately. Unwilling to give such a guarantee, Christa stayed behind to struggle through a tangle of bureaucratic procedures leading to the coveted "green card" that would enable her to work without restrictions in another country. By the time she reached that goal, Edwin Kennedy was growing skeptical of the idea. Nevertheless, he was not a person to renege, and in April, Christa arrived in New York aboard the passenger liner Bremen. She was met by another aunt and uncle who had moved to the United States, and lived in Plainfield, New Jersey.

Two days later, Christa's relatives drove her to the Kennedy home in what still was a sparsely developed area of New Vernon. Arriving at the large home at the end of the long tree-lined driveway and meeting Ruth Kennedy was an experience Christa always remembered distinctly:

> I couldn't speak any English and Mrs. Kennedy couldn't speak any German. There were no other homes in sight, and there were

no signs of life other than Mrs. Kennedy—not even a dog or cat. Coming from a large family and from the hotel business, where I was used to being with people from morning until night, I felt totally isolated. I remember looking up at that big house and across the yard, then telling my aunt to explain in English that I was terribly sorry, but I couldn't stay there. She obviously said something to that effect, then translated Mrs. Kennedy's suggestion that I try it for six months, with no commitment. In the candid way that I later found to be typical of her, she added that her husband didn't really think it would work out, but she didn't agree with him. So I decided that in all fairness, I should stay for at least two or three weeks. As it turned out, she and her husband took me into their lives, and I soon decided to remain with them the entire year.

The import of Christa's reception into the Kennedy home was heightened by the coincidence that two days before her arrival, Eddie, who was serving with the Coast Guard at Cape May, New Jersey, announced his marriage to Margaret Johnson, following a whirlwind courtship.

Christa and Ruth worked together in cooking, cleaning, and shopping. "Once in a while she would decide we should just stop whatever we were doing and go out to lunch together," Christa said. "Everything she did, I did, and whenever the Kennedys went on a vacation, whether to the Bahamas, Florida, or their lodge in Canada, they took me along." Wanting to "Americanize" Christa's name, Ruth called her Christine, a name that was adopted also by Edwin and family friends whom she subsequently met. Christa called Ruth and Edwin "Missy" and "Mr. Kennedy."

Both Kennedys soon considered their attractive young visitor a member of the family. Showing exceptional poise for her age, she radiated joy and enthusiasm for life. And as she learned English, with Ruth's assistance, she developed an effervescent style of speech made all the more intriguing by its thick German accent. The forthrightness with which she spoke might have been attributed to her mentor, had it not been so much in evidence before she came to America. "Whatever the reasons, the two women certainly shared a lot of personality traits," observed a

Contrasting Personalities

smiling Edwin Kennedy, who claimed he always felt "outnumbered two to one" on controversial subjects.

At five-feet-five, Christa was just two inches shorter than Ruth. Although they both had high cheekbones, which might be traced to their similar Teutonic ancestries, they bore little resemblance to each other. Nevertheless, the fact that they were together most of the time led many persons to mistakenly identify them as mother and daughter, until they heard Christa speak.

Both German friends who preceded Christa to the United States were stranded in unhappy jobs at homes on Long Island, restlessly marking time until the end of their one-year commitments. Consequently, they were invited to the Kennedy home for a weekend. When she received a Saturday-morning telephone call that they had arrived at the Madison train station, Christa, who had not yet obtained an American driver's license, was unable to find Ruth. She did spot Edwin, however, who was working in the yard. Unshaven, and wearing old, torn trousers as was his wont while engaged in his favorite weekend pastime ("I feel comfortable that way"), he agreed to drive Christa to the station and get her friends. Not understanding the German conversation on the return trip, he remained silent, then resumed his yard work when they arrived. At that point, one of the girls asked Christa, "Doesn't Mr. Kennedy object when the gardener goes around looking like that?" The question, along with the girl's startled reaction to Christa's answer, "That *is* Mr. Kennedy," became a family joke that lasted, and possibly even improved over the years.

The German friends returned regularly for similar visits, which became antidotes to a loneliness Christa often experienced, despite her overall contentment and the affection she was beginning to feel for Ruth and Edwin. When their responsibilities to sponsors ended in 1961, one of the girls married a New Yorker, and the other returned to Germany. Christa, on the other hand, decided to remain at her housekeeping job with the Kennedys for a second year. Then, in early April 1962, motivated by homesickness and a promise to her family, she returned to her homeland and the hotel business.

Crista's departure left a void that was lamentable to Edwin, whose business affairs occupied most of his waking hours, devastating to Ruth, whose daily companion had become the equivalent of a daughter. Yet, neither Kennedy was prone to brooding, and there were many other interests that needed tending. Among them was the arrival of their first grandson, Danny, born April 16, 1962, and the news that their son was being transferred to a Coast Guard station on Lake Michigan. Following his discharge that summer, Eddie moved his family to Ohio, while he resumed class work at Hiram College, then transferred to Kent State University.

After finishing his undergraduate studies at Kent State, Eddie Kennedy purchased a long-established family lumber business in Canada. Moving there with his wife and son, he built a home near the family lodge on Calabogie Lake, which was within commuting distance of his company operations.

The thick, red-covered appointment book in which Edwin Kennedy kept his traveling agenda was stuffed perennially with an overlapping assortment of business, family, and university engagements. As before, Kennedy rarely attended an Ohio University board meeting without scheduling a side trip to visit his widowed sister, Gladys Linville, and her two children in Columbus. In the early sixties, Saundra Linville was completing a degree in nursing at Ohio State University, and her brother, Fred, was an offensive guard and defensive tackle on the North High School football team. Typically, Kennedy managed to manipulate entries in his red book to be in the stands when his nephew had an outstanding senior year on the team. He also spoke so fondly of his own alma mater that Fred was persuaded to enter Ohio University after graduating from high school.

Although he liked Athens and the university, Fred had grown up near the Ohio State campus, and an allegiance gained during those years was compelling. Deciding to transfer there at the beginning of his sophomore year, but having difficulty knowing how to explain it in a letter to his uncle, Fred made a trip he long remembered:

> Knowing how Uncle Ed felt about Ohio University, I thought the only fair way to inform him of my decision would be face-to-face. So I borrowed my mother's car, much to her chagrin, and drove to New York. Uncle Ed was very busy, and he had just made last-minute arrangements for an unexpected business trip, but he took time out to talk with me. Well, I nervously led up to the main purpose of my visit, and even before I got to the core of what I wanted to say, I could tell he knew exactly what it would be. I never determined what he really felt, but he quickly put me at ease, and everything was fine. When I received my business degree from Ohio State three years later, Uncle Ed was there to shake my hand and wish me well.

With most members of the Kennedy families living in central and southwestern Ohio, Edwin organized occasional gatherings in Columbus on weekends coinciding with Ohio State football games. When possible, he also drove to Galion to see his mother, before she died in 1966 at the age of eighty-three.

Kennedy rarely missed a Board of Trustees meeting at either Ohio University or Hiram College, but an important business trip to the Southwest interfered with the latter group's regular spring session in 1962. Apologizing in advance to Hiram President Paul Sharp (who had succeeded Paul Fall in 1957), Kennedy had flown to Kansas, spending a day in the gas fields of a client company, then had gone on to Dallas that night, arriving at a hotel in time to eat a late dinner, go over papers until midnight, then get the usual few hours' sleep needed to revitalize him for an early morning appointment. Less than an hour after he had fallen asleep, however, he was awakened by a telephone call from President Sharp.

Only an emergency would necessitate getting the hotel number from a reluctant Ruth Kennedy and placing the call at such an early hour, Sharp explained, but it was imperative that his friend attend the meeting in Cleveland that evening. Conversations with other board members indicated that a significant project would surely be scuttled without the persuasive influence of Kennedy.

The project to which the president referred was construction of what the college labeled a physical education center and Kennedy called a gymnasium. Kennedy and Sharp had agreed to the need for such a building, and some money had been raised for it, but conservative members of the board did not think it was sufficient to plunge ahead into what they feared would be a failed effort.

Declining at first on the basis of his upcoming meeting in Dallas and the difficulty in booking a last-minute flight, Kennedy wavered under Sharp's pleas on behalf of the college, then succumbed to the pressure of loyalty. Shortly after dawn, he cancelled the day's appointments and made what proved to be difficult hop-scotching flights to Cleveland. Exhausted, he arrived in time for dinner and the ensuing meeting.

As anticipated, several members of the board, all of whom Kennedy respected, offered reasons for tabling the building project. Although agreeing it was a vital segment of the overall physical growth plan for the college, they reiterated fears that failure could be harmful to long-range fund-raising. While they talked, President Sharp glanced hopefully at Kennedy, who remained silent. It was not until ten o'clock, when he thought everything had been said in support of the view against moving ahead, that Kennedy entered the conversation. During the next half hour, it became evident that some opinions were changing, but the vote would be close. Finally, Kennedy offered a summation: "We agree that this step forward is vitally needed; I assure you that if we commit to it, we will find ways to do it." At that point, a member of what had been the loyal opposition arose and announced, "I have to leave now, but I'll give my vote to Ed Kennedy." That was enough to seal the positive decision, leading to a successful campaign and construction of the physical education center.

After hurrying back to Dallas to complete his mission for Lehman Brothers, Kennedy returned home, where his wife already

Contrasting Personalities

was making plans for them to attend the first in a series of Ohio University's Edwin and Ruth Kennedy Lectures on Major Issues in American Life.

The university had integrated the series, established as part of the Kennedy-financed John C. Baker Fund endowment, into social science studies, but the lectures were presented for the benefit of all students, faculty, and citizens of the Athens community. Dr. Roy Fairfield, associate professor of government and coordinator of the initial 1962–63 series, wrote in a program preface, "The presence of such a distinguished group of thinkers adds immeasurably to the intellectual ferment which is so central in the life of any university."

The first speaker was Dr. Charles Frankel, an energetic humanist whose nine books and regularly published articles in leading magazines dealt with survival, progress, and fulfillment of man. Among others scheduled for the initial series were historian Arnold Toynbee, anthropologist Margaret Mead, and United States Supreme Court Justice William O. Douglas.

Kennedy considered Toynbee's lecture on "the shaping of civilizations by challenges and responses of creative leaders" the most memorable he ever heard, and claimed that the famed English historian's observations influenced him in making decisions affecting both his business and his personal life. Such a reaction was consistent with comments of several colleagues who acknowledged Kennedy's uncommon sense for assessing the lessons of history. "Whether in oil ventures or other undertakings," said one, "Ed seems to recognize patterns from the past that have the probability of repeating themselves in the future, and he uses that insight to get ahead of other persons."

Although Christa Teichmann had what she described as "some trouble adjusting again to the stiffness of life in Germany" after returning to that country, she had no difficulty resuming work at the hotel, and was happy to enjoy her family and her favorite sport of skiing. Frequent telephone calls from Ruth Kennedy kept her informed of events in New Vernon, but Christa intended to remain in her native country.

Early in the summer of 1962, Ruth and Ed visited Christa, asking her to accompany them on a tour of Europe. "I just can't do that, because my family is counting on me," she replied, "but I will visit you later this year when our tourist season is over."

Encouraged by other friends from America who stopped by the hotel during the remainder of the year, and by continued telephone calls from Ruth, Christa rejoined the Kennedys soon after Christmas. Two weeks later, however, her father died, and she returned home for the funeral. "My mother felt certain I would stay that time," she recalled, "but I made the very difficult decision to go against the wishes of my family and resume my extended visit at New Vernon."

Through friendship with a young woman she met when both were enrolled in classes at a school in Morristown, Christa began attending a church group called Young Life. Because this provided the first opportunity to associate regularly with Americans her own age, church became an important influence in her social, as well as her religious life. It also led to a relationship that would at last squelch her ambivalence in determining which country should become her permanent home.

Jeffrey Cook was an employee of Western Electric Company in his home town of Lincoln Park, New Jersey, twenty-five miles north of New Vernon, when he met Christa at a Young Life program. A tall, soft-spoken young man with a quick-trigger flair for enlivening conversations by injecting subtle "one-liners," he was well informed on many subjects and interested in obtaining a college education. After dating for a year, Christa and Jeff became engaged, and on December 19, 1964, they were married, with Edwin Kennedy giving the bride away.

The young couple's plans called for Jeff to obtain an undergraduate degree at King's College in Briar Cliff Manor, New York, then make a career change. Knowing this, Ruth suggested that they move into a wing of the Kennedy home, where they could be together on weekends and Christa could stay while her husband attended classes. The arrangement worked well.

Contrasting Personalities

Ruth and Christa again became inseparable companions. Christa joined Ruth's favorite organization, P.E.O., later serving as an officer. Parties for the group, continuing to be held at the Kennedy home, reached such proportions that automobiles filled the long driveway and its circular terminus around a cluster of trees and shrubs near the entrance.

Christa, like other friends and relatives, was enchanted by the lack of pretense and unpredictability that made her "American mother" what one artistic acquaintance described as "an original edition." Ruth had a passion for wearing fur coats, but was thrifty in other personal considerations. Recalling many shopping trips with Ruth, Christa said, "She would drive through parking lots searching for meters with time left on them until I insisted we stop at the next open spot and put in a quarter of our own." Although she often bought expensive gifts for others, Ruth usually preferred selecting less expensive things for herself. When Ruth needed a blue blazer for a western trip with Edwin and Eddie, she led Christa to the budget department at Lord and Taylor's. But Christa put her foot down:

> I said, "For heaven's sake, will you get out of this budget department and go upstairs to the designer department!" Responding only because I was scolding her, she did finally follow me upstairs, but she complained all the way, saying something like, "There you go, wanting me to spend all that money when I don't need a designer blazer." Holding my ground, I replied, "You have to look good. If I had your money, what would I care how much I spent for a blazer?" Her answer to that was, "Just think how this money would help a young person who doesn't have enough to go to college, and here I am spending it on a blazer." She and her husband had an obsession about that; education was number one with them.

When Ruth bought the blazer—or anything else, for that matter—she paid cash. Although the use of credit was fundamental to investment banking, the Kennedys disavowed it in private life. Neither Edwin nor Ruth held a credit card of any kind. Both acknowledged that this probably was a holdover from having started married life at the depth of the Great Depression, but they didn't believe such a minor eccentricity merited examination. Certainly, they had little need for an oil company credit card. Edwin had installed a five-hundred-gallon gasoline tank and service pump in his back yard, as well as two fuel oil tanks with a total capacity of four thousand gallons—enough to heat his house for a year. Not only did he buy both the gasoline and fuel oil directly from distributors, but he also used his knowledge of the markets to negotiate the prices of truck-load lots.

Ruth had a down-to-earth nature that wealth never changed. Persons who knew her best characterized her as "a real lady," who never had to work at it. "The thing that impressed me most," said Walter Davis, "was that she combined dignity with saying exactly what she meant. I love people like that; you don't have to be concerned with what their hidden objective might be." Niece Nancy Bletzer who had moved from Chicago to California but continued to visit the Kennedys at their Canadian lodge and New Jersey home, recalled with special pleasure a late afternoon trip she and Ruth made to New York City:

> We were supposed to meet Uncle Ed at Grand Central Station, then go to dinner and the theater. It was a wonderful occasion for me. Both Aunt Ruth and I got all dressed up for it. Unfortunately, our time of arrival was at rush hour, when the station was a total bedlam. Aunt Ruth said, "We'll never find my husband unless we take extreme measures." With that, she got up on a bench and began looking over the crowd. I was amazed. There she was, wearing a wonderful new hat with a veil, a sable coat, and diamonds, standing on a bench in Grand Central Station and whistling through her fingers—something she did very well. Well, Uncle Ed parted the seas of people like a steamship in rushing to us and asking, "What in the world are you doing?" He got her off that bench in a hurry, while she replied, "Well, you found us, didn't you?" He mumbled something about losing a necklace that way, but we all laughed together and went on to dinner at a very nice restaurant.

The contrasting personalities of Edwin and Ruth seemed to compliment each other. "She always was more outgoing than he," Christa Cook explained, "but neither seemed to dominate the other, and their strong love was obvious in their actions and expressions." Vernon Alden, then president of Ohio University, noted similar characteristics during Kennedy visits to the campus:

> Ed would sit in the living room of our home during trustee receptions, sucking contemplatively on his white-bowled pipe, his head tilted slightly downward, nodding occasionally as he digested what was being discussed, while Ruth would be expressing her reactions with energetic talk, including liberal dashes of humor. When Ed said something, it usually reflected a profound thought he had been putting together from the conversation. He never was garrulous.

At commencement weekend activities in June 1963, Ruth Kennedy received an Alumni Certificate of Merit for her service to Ohio University, "both on and off the campus." Mentioning that Edwin had received a similar Certificate nine years earlier, Alden noted that the presentation marked only the second time a husband-and-wife team had been so honored. Edwin and Ruth shared ideas on family, business, and philanthropies, and remaining in conversations with the Cooks at the breakfast table long after the meal was finished became a Sunday ritual.

Edwin and his son, Eddie, still hunted and fished together whenever possible, going after Kodiak bears in Alaska, black bears, wild boars, and wild turkeys in Tennessee, a variety of fish and game in Ontario, Quebec, and Labrador, and large animals in Africa. The younger Kennedy's fishing expertise, indeed, became such that he made several world-record catches. One of these, witnessed by a proud father, was an eighteen-and-a-half-pound lake trout landed on a two-pound-test line in Canada. Another was a 125-pound sailfish, caught with a fly rod and minimum-sized tippet.

Ruth was not interested in shooting—although she did accompany her husband on a "camera safari" in Africa. She did, however, enjoy fishing, and shared her husband's enthusiasm when he decided to purchase Arctic Star Lodge, a commercial fishing camp on Canada's Great Slave Lake in 1966. They sold the camp six years later.

At no time was the diversification of Edwin and Ruth Kennedy's lives more evident than in the late sixties, when the indispensable red appointment book resembled a world atlas. Having received an honorary doctorate from Ohio University in 1965, then serving for a year as chairman of the Board of Trustees, Edwin was reappointed to a second nine-year trustee term by Ohio Governor James A. Rhodes. Soon afterward, Kennedy was invited to represent the trustees at the dedication of a new Advanced Teachers College in Kano, Nigeria.

Kennedy had been supportive of Ohio University's teacher-training projects in Africa's most populous nation since they were organized in 1958. Success of the initial venture in Western Nigeria had led to a series of further contracts, through the United States International Cooperation Administration (ICA), for similar educational assistance programs in the Northern Region city of Kano. When the Northern Nigerian Ministry of Education sought to move into a higher phase of training with the creation of an entirely new college, Ohio University again had been called upon to develop curricula, prepare staff members, and supervise the equipping of buildings. Representatives of the university's College of Education also had provided technical advice in the design of buildings, but responsibility for construction had been shared by ICA and the Nigerian government. Groundbreaking had occurred in 1965, and on January 17, 1967, the eight-building Advanced Teachers College at Kano officially was presented by United States Ambassador to Nigeria Elbert G. Mathews, "on behalf of the government and the people of the United States," to Northern Nigeria Military Governor Hassan Usman Katsina. In attendance at the formal ceremony were high-ranking officials of both nations, Ohio University President and Mrs. Vernon Alden, Mr. and Mrs. Edwin Kennedy, and Dr. Russell A. Milliken, director of the Ohio University Center for International Programs.

The following day, Edwin and Ruth remained in Kano for a late afternoon program to be held in their honor. After touring the city and surrounding area during the morning and afternoon, they returned to the campus promptly at five o'clock, as instructed, curious to know what the occasion would entail. Some Nigerian members of the Kano College faculty who had attended Ohio University recently as part of the training program knew Edwin in his role of university trustee, and both he and Ruth had met others at campus social events in previous years. One of those persons they now recognized as Albert Ogunsola, who greeted them as they arrived for the program.

After a welcome by another Ohio University graduate, C. G. Kele, who asked the Kennedys to "convey our gratitude to friends at the university in particular and the United States in general" for the college, "which will serve as an edifice of international cooperation and understanding," Edwin and Ruth discovered the principal reason for the special program. Costumed appropriately, they were inducted ceremoniously into the Hausa Tribe of Northern Nigeria. One of the nation's leading tribes, Hausa has been known through history for its high level of art, literature, and cultural activities, all of which scholars have studied for centuries. The Kennedy's were surprised to discover that despite this reputation, no Nigerian artifacts had been obtained by Ohio University. Consequently, they donated $10,000 for such purchases. This provided the beginning of a collection that attracted other contributions for what later became a permanent display in the Ohio University library.

Having become reacquainted with Albert Ogunsola and witnessing how he was using his American education to help improve educational opportunities and living conditions in his native country, Edwin and Ruth quietly provided money for the young Nigerian to return to Ohio University, with his wife, to earn a Ph.D.

On October 25, 1967, a daughter was born to Christa and Jeff Cook. Although they named her Susanne, Edwin and Ruth gave her the nickname "Sugar," which they alone used from that day forward. Christa, in turn, thenceforth referred to the Kennedys as "Oma" and "Opa," German for grandmother and grandfather. Five months later, on March 28, 1968, Eddie and Margaret had their second child, Patty, born in Canada. Edwin and Ruth were delighted to have two new granddaughters, and by then their "parental" relationship with Christa was such that any other reference to Susanne would have seemed unnatural. "They thought of us as their own family," Christa said, "and the feeling was mutual." That June, Jeff Cook received his B.A. from King's College and accepted a position as claims adjuster with the Commercial Union Company, first in East Orange, then in West Orange, New Jersey, commuting each day from New Vernon.

In 1968, the Kennedys bought a second fishing camp, this one a plush resort on the west coast of Panama, thirty miles north of the Colombian border. Purchased from the estate of a Texas oil man who had developed it as an attraction for wealthy vacationers, the Tropic Star Lodge faced an offshore reef surrounded by what was listed among the world's best fishing waters. The reef itself had been discovered in the 1920s by American novelist Zane Grey. A zealous fisherman, as well as one of the nation's most popular adventure writers, Grey came upon the area while exploring Pacific bays in Central America. Finding that an unusual confluence of "a tide-rip that set in from the open sea" and the "offshore current" formed "a foaming, eddying, dimpling, rippling triangular pool" attracting large numbers of record-sized fish, he reportedly kept the exact location secret for many years to enjoy it as a private fishing ground until choosing finally to share it with the public.

A hill-top home, known as "The Palace" and occupied by the Kennedys when they were in residence, was accessible by tram. Luxurious guest cottages formed a pattern around it at a lower level. The waterfront was lined with piers and facilities to maintain and repair expensive boats from which serious anglers pitted their skills against the maneuvers of sailfish, marlin, and smaller aquatic varieties inhabiting the deep Pacific coastal waters. "I used to stand and look out over the bay and all the fishing boats there during a sunset and think it must be paradise," Christa recalled fondly.

The Kennedys spent more time than they originally intended at Tropic Star Lodge, partly because Ruth became a popular hostess for regular visitors from around the world. Her joy of decorating, supervising food preparation, and personal hospitality became added attractions. Many guests scheduled visits when they knew Ruth and Edwin would be there. That included nearly all Christmas holidays and as often as Edwin could squeeze Panama into his traveling agenda during the fishing season of December to May. Each guest family was provided a personal maid, boat, and captain.

With the Tropic Star complex serving as one of the magnets attracting money into the area, government officials considered it valuable to the general economy, which was flourishing in 1968. Partially for that reason, but more pointedly because their attorney in Panama was the grandson of a former president, the Kennedys' widening social circle soon encompassed important Panamanian politicians, among them the chief justice of the Supreme Court. Such connections were extremely interesting, and certainly not harmful to business. Ironically, they also would one day trigger Edwin Kennedy's timely decision to sell the property, but that would not occur until he and his family enjoyed it for nearly a decade.

During the first stage of its 1,650-mile flow through the southern region of Africa to the Indian Ocean, the Zambeze River forms a boundary between Zambia and Zimbabwe. It was in this area that Edwin and Eddie Kennedy chose to end the first day's hunt of an early 1969 safari by spending the night on the Zambia side of the great river. From the camp they shared with only a guide and native trackers, they could look across the wide expanse of water and reflect on what they hoped to encounter the next day. But as he lay in bed that night, the elder Kennedy could think only of a recent telephone conversation with his friend, John Baker, former president of Ohio University and long-time trustee of his own alma mater, Juniata College. Kennedy had received an honorary doctor of humane letters from Juniata in June 1968, and although he had rejected several "feelers" to join the college's board during the past few years, Baker had reported that trustees had finally elected him to membership anyway, pending his acceptance. Again, Kennedy had deferred, citing deep involvement in an exceptionally large number of business and volunteer ventures. Baker would never press him, he knew, but a feeling of guilt nagged at his conscience as he lay in a tent on the Zambeze shore. "John is seventy-four years old," Kennedy told himself. "If something happens to him without my granting what I know he wants, I will never forgive myself." Then he arose, turned on a flashlight, and penned a letter of acceptance to the Juniata Board of Trustees.

Within a year, Kennedy had carefully studied the fiscal and physical needs of Juniata and detected an over-abundance of deferred maintenance, something not previously recognized by the group. One building, he discovered, was about to be condemned and closed. Within a short period of time, the board instituted what proved to be a successful method of long-range financing for repairs and renovations. "Ed, you just can't become involved in a school without seeing its problems and becoming a participant in forming solutions," Ruth observed. But, as always, she approved of what he was doing.

(In 1992, when he was ninety-six, Baker expressed amusement that his "old age" twenty-three years earlier had been a factor in Kennedy's decision to join the Juniata board. "I'm surprised Ed hadn't checked my ancestry," the former Ohio University president said, referring to his friend's reputation for thoroughness.)

At Hiram College, where Elmer Jagow had become president in late 1966, a biology field station was being completed and plans were underway for a meeting/activities center, long sought by both students and faculty. Edwin and Ruth Kennedy supported both projects.

Through the leadership of Dr. James H. Barrow, professor of biology, the Hiram College Field Station was established in 1967 to encourage students in original research involving plants and animals, particularly birds. Wooded areas of the 126-acre site two miles from the Village of Hiram, containing one of the largest stands of virgin beech trees in North America, were inhabited by free-ranging animals. Grain produced in crop fields assured a steady growth in animal population, and abundant wild-growing plants were available for botany students to study.

Paul Frohring, a retired Chagrin Falls, Ohio, businessman and a Hiram trustee, had financed purchase of the first portion of property—a former dairy containing several outbuildings—and subsequent renovation of farm buildings, to begin the project. A major Hiram benefactor, Frohring had been an officer of SMA Corporation and later the founder and president of General Bio Chemicals Company, one of the earliest producers of penicillin.

To enhance the facility, Dr. Barrow envisioned an observatory overlooking the largest of several ponds where indigenous and migrating waterfowl could be studied and photographed:

> My dream was to at least get a pre-fabricated building of some sort out there. And I remember talking to Ruth Kennedy about it when she first came to see what we were starting. We talked about what we hoped to do with the station, and she got into deep conversations with some of the students. Then she disappeared. When she returned, Ed was with her. She was convinced that the station would provide these students with what she called "an important phase of intellectual growth," so she said, "Ed, I want them to have an observation building." That's all it took. We got the building. Furthermore, Ruth's interest was so genuine, I think it provided a great motivation for the students who were there that day, and for others who came later.

Funded by the Kennedys, the modernistic two-story Nature Observation Building soon became a focal point of the field station, and whenever the couple returned to Hiram, usually in conjunction with a board meeting, Ruth drove to the site to talk with students. Barrow recalled that she rarely had time to change from the "elegant dresses" she wore to luncheons for trustees' wives, but never seemed to be concerned about that when she became absorbed in a student project. On one occasion, an ornithology student told her about an unusual sparrow nest in a distant field. "May I see it?" she asked. "Of course," the student answered, and the two tromped off across a stubble field together. "That wasn't an exceptional example at all," Barrow said. "It was typical."

Mark Wilson, a Hiram undergraduate involved in early stages of the field station development, remembered what he called "several pleasurable relationships with the Kennedys," and the "spontaneous excitement Ruth conveyed in sharing our interests." He too had seen her "walk through the muck with us, high heels and all," and observed that "we had fun because we had a chance to demonstrate what we were doing and explain our feelings about it as well." Wilson went on to the kind of distinguished career the Kennedy's intended their largesse to help inspire. After graduating in 1972, he attended Pennsylvania State University, studied animals in Kenya and on an island off the coast of Georgia, received a doctorate from Harvard University, spent four more years in West Africa, then joined the Yale University Medical School faculty.

Professor Barrow would later recall Ruth's intense involvement with students on the Kennedy visits to the Hiram campus and at the field station. "It was interesting to note that Ruth became so enthralled working with the students that she and her husband usually had to rush to make their plane connections," he said. "I even remember one time that they missed. Yet, Ed understood. In fact, he thought it was wonderful. She got away with murder in that respect."

As the biology field station grew, and a laboratory financed by Paul Frohring was constructed near the entrance, the comprehensive facility became one of the college's major attractions for scientific-minded students interested in liberal arts educations. To expand field research opportunities and special classes in a different geographic milieu, the college added a supplemental Northwoods Field Station twelve miles from Lake Superior on the Upper Peninsula of Michigan. Six sleeping cabins and a main lodge, financed by the Kennedys, were designed and built by Hiram students and faculty on the eighteen-acre tract.

Even prior to the sixties, a student union building was considered pivotal to Hiram's long-range blueprint for growth. The college never had a place where students, faculty, staff, and campus visitors could meet for recreation, social and cultural functions, and relaxation. Students made periodic appeals for such a facility, but funds understandably were channeled to more immediate concerns, stranding their plans on the drawing board. As a trustee, Edwin Kennedy agreed with the need and recognized that a campaign to energize the project required a very substantial jump start. Although he and his wife still considered what they called "bricks and mortar support" a secondary means of aiding higher education, they decided to back the student center effort at Hiram with an anonymous donation of $600,000, well beyond the minimum for launching a campaign.

Bolstered by a $500,000 federal loan from the U.S. Department of Housing and Urban Development in the fall of 1966, the center concept reached top-priority ranking within President Jagow's new administration. An announcement from the President revealed the identity of the major donors, and a committee composed of administrators, faculty members, and students began a study of centers at other colleges for recommendations to architects. When one person suggested a modernistic outside design, however, the Kennedys uncharacteristically exercised a power of donors' veto. "I dislike benefactors who impose their will on details, but I felt compelled to do it in that situation," Edwin said with obvious conviction. "It had to be Georgian, and that was that." He and Ruth did, however, assure the committee that there would be no further interference, and when their preference for the interior was redesigned, they offered no complaint.

Ruth Kennedy was invited to turn the first shovelful of earth at the long-awaited groundbreaking ceremony on October 7, 1967. Gratefully accepting the honor, she requested, however, that the traditional gesture be made with a bulldozer, rather than a shovel. A congenial President Jagow was happy to make such arrangements, and with cameramen recording the event, Ruth climbed aboard a yellow Caterpillar bulldozer, received brief instructions from a grinning operator, then took over the controls to scoop up a huge bite of soil. As a result, what might otherwise have been considered a routine program by members of the media received extensive pictorial coverage throughout the state.

After the groundbreaking, Ruth told an appreciative audience that she enjoyed the experience so much, she would like to take up "Caterpillar driving" if the investment banking business should go sour. At the same program, Edwin announced that he and his wife were pledging another $150,000, contingent upon a similar amount being raised from other sources, bringing their total to $750,000, more than half of the $1.4 million construction cost.

Despite protests from both Kennedys, the building was named in their honor. Groundfloor lounge and game rooms were designed for "casual living." On the first floor, the main entrance led to a spacious lounge furnished with formal furniture. Surrounding it were dining, conference, and music rooms, and student government offices. A ballroom-auditorium, art gallery, and other dining areas dominated the top floor.

Completed in February of 1969, the Edwin and Ruth Kennedy Center was put into use immediately, although the dedication was scheduled for May 16. Edwin had observed various stages of construction, but his wife saw the building for the first time at the dedication. President Jagow recalled his conversation with her as they walked to the new building in the center of the campus:

> During the three years I had known the Kennedys, I always had been amused by the succinct way Ruth responded to recurring inquiries on whether her husband might be related to the Massachusetts Kennedys. She did it with two brief words. So as we approached the new building, I pointed to the large-lettered name "Kennedy Center" above the entrance pillars and apologized to Ruth that we did not have room to include in parentheses, "no relation."

Edwin and Ruth were pleased when Hiram's student newspaper referred to the center as "the living room of the campus," and by the manner in which students treated its furnishings at a time when campus protests were breaking out elsewhere in the form of destructive demonstrations. The Center's first director, Gene Young, shared that feeling. Admittedly concerned when he first saw the plush furniture in the formal lounge, he later exclaimed, "The students never abused the privilege of using the room."

The wave of destructive activism engulfing colleges and universities puzzled Kennedy, although he was well aware of the impact wrought by the Vietnam War and civil rights issues. Martin Luther King had been assassinated little more than a month before the Kennedy Center dedication. Student strikes had closed some schools for months. Anti-war demonstrations inflamed campuses. At Kennedy's own alma mater, rioting students had thrown iron bolts through windows of the president's home. "It was a time of indiscriminate protest," Kennedy lamented, "and it was difficult for me even in retrospect to recognize that protestors said and did all those things."

At Ohio University, a new president, Claude R. Sowle, former dean of the University of Cincinnati College of Law, began his duties on August 1, 1969, succeeding Vernon Alden, who resigned to become chairman of the Boston Company. "The times were nearly impossible for anyone coming into such a position, particularly at a public institution where everything—even trustees meetings—had to be open," Kennedy said, "and I think Claude Sowle handled most of it well under constant pressure."

Despite this degree of discouragement with what was happening across the country, Kennedy remained supportive and active at Ohio University and the other schools in which he had special interests. In an address at Findlay College, where he received an honorary doctor of business administration degree, Kennedy explained, "We do not believe there is likely to be a permanent answer to the plethora of problems that beset this country and the world, except the slow-moving responses from more and more education everywhere, and with ever increasing standards of excellence. Therefore, it is fitting and proper that we who are enjoying full and productive lives from the bounties of our democratic society and our venture capital system should have keen interests in quality education."

Chapter 12 **Preserving a Culture**

> *Of all the modes of expression of a given culture, visual art is the most distinguishing feature by which that culture may be identified.*
>
> —Frederick J. Dockstader
> *The Song of the Loom*

Mystery shrouds the origin of Navajo weaving and silversmithing, just as it veils the genesis of the largest remaining tribe of Native Americans in the United States.

Historians and archaeologists agree that the Navajo Nation probably emerged from a larger group of Athapascan-speaking Indians who crossed the Bering Strait, then wandered slowly southward from the tip of North America before settling into the red canyons and majestic mountains encompassing what now is northeastern Arizona, with some spill-over into New Mexico and Utah, perhaps as early as 1000 A.D. Primarily hunters and farmers, they soon became recognized also as marauders by the more peaceful cliff-dwelling Pueblo people who often let Navajo raiders take their crops rather than face the ferocity of war parties.

There is evidence that Navajo weavers learned basic skills from Pueblo captives. This influence became more pronounced in the late 1600s when Pueblos willingly fled to Navajo land as an escape from attacking Spaniards who had entered the area in search of gold. Though the invaders were driven off for several years after claiming the land as their own, they eventually returned as conquerors.

During a period beginning with the eighteenth century, Navajos began to develop their own style of weaving, using knowledge gained from the Pueblos and wool from churro sheep, introduced to them primarily as a source of mutton by the Spanish intruders, who also gave the tribe its name. The Navajos, however, continued for many years to call themselves *Dineh,* meaning *The People.*

Whereas among the Pueblos the men were the weavers, using cotton for their fabrics, the Navajos preferred to have their women master the art, utilizing wool from their rapidly growing flocks of sheep. The long churro wool fibers were stronger, easier to spin, and more receptive to dyes than cotton. These advantages, coupled with a Navajo talent for improving previously established techniques, soon yielded textile handiwork superior to that of their Pueblo teachers.

When U.S. troops drove the Spaniards out of disputed territory north of the Rio Grande during the Mexican War of 1846–48, all the Navajo Nation gained was a new enemy. At first considering themselves allies of the U.S., they soon learned that the "bluecoats" were to be stationed at a permanent fort to make way for settlement by whites.

Navajo warriors responded with such ferocity that U.S. forces headed by Col. Kit Carson diverted attention from the Civil War to subdue them. In less than a year, the tribe was defeated, its crops and livestock destroyed or stolen, its spirit broken. Prodded by army escorts, a column of 9,000 dejected Navajo men, women, and children trekked 350 miles to Bosque Redondo (round grove), a small grassy oasis amidst a cactus-infested wasteland in southern New Mexico. There, a fenced-in compound near the remote military post of Fort Sumner offered bare survival for five years.

Finally, in 1868, after signing a treaty agreeing never again to make war on Americans, Mexicans, or other Indians, the disheartened tribe was returned to its sacred homeland in the Lukachukai Mountain Range of what had since been organized as the Arizona Territory. Under terms of the treaty, the Navajo

Nation was guaranteed 5,500 square miles as a reservation, farm implements, and a new flock of sheep. Unfortunately from the standpoint of weaving, however, the government soon forced a gradual change from churro sheep to breeds that produced more meat, at the sacrifice of superior wool. Over a period of time, the churros, once so abundant on the reservation, almost disappeared. Meanwhile, as the Navajo population grew, the reservation boundaries were stretched until they encompassed 25,000 square miles.

During their exile at Bosque Redondo, the Navajo men may have learned the rudiments of silversmithing from nearby Mexicans who came to visit them or, in many instances, seized young members of the Navajo families as slaves, releasing them after the 1868 treaty. Some accounts identify earlier trading with white trappers and itinerant Spanish silversmiths as the tribe's initial exposure to that art.

Whatever the origin of this first step, documentation of major strides in creating exquisite Navajo jewelry began with the return to the Arizona Territory reservation. While the women combined shepherding chores with weaving, the men turned their attention to agriculture and silversmithing. In time, Navajo weavings and jewelry developed into distinctive art forms that retain their identifying qualities today. Turquoise, abundantly available from New Mexico mines, provided additional material for Navajo artisans, its brilliant blue-green texture complementing the silver settings and ornamentation.

The opportunity for far-reaching acclaim, as well as a new prosperity from weavings and jewelry, came to the Navajo Nation in the form of traders, who began entering the reservation in 1875. In contrast to agents of the government's Indian Bureau, who exploited the tribe and attempted to "civilize" the "redskins" by destroying their traditions, independent traders were friendly barterers. They learned elementary forms of the complicated Navajo language. Trading posts became centers for exchanging rugs, blankets, and jewelry for food and supplies.

As the nation's railroad network spread, traders increased the distribution of Native American creations across the U.S. They helped obtain raw materials and often provided advances of money or food, payable when a work of art was completed. The trader interpreted government decrees and explained Indian beliefs to white politicians. Most important, he became a permanent part of the sprawling Navajo community, a person who trusted them and could be trusted in return.

Although artistry provides a valuable mirror of any culture, the relationship between Native Americans and their art is particularly meaningful, because it is involved in their everyday lives. Within the Navajo culture, the tribe's art, religion, and lifestyles become inseparable in maintaining an all-important balance with nature. Disrupting this harmony is to invite sickness and evil, the Navajos believe.

If some misfortune does occur, exorcising evil and curing illness is accomplished by medicine men who blend religious chants and the drawing of sand paintings into healing ceremonies, sometimes lasting as long as nine days. This ability to contact Navajo gods is passed along orally through the generations, with both the chants and the designs of sand paintings retained in each medicine man's memory.

For many years, strict adherence to this tradition was inviolate. Sand paintings containing sacred figures of the chants were destroyed as part of the ceremony. It was not until the early twentieth century that a medicine man named Hosteen Klah managed to break the taboo in favor of preserving designs of the sand paintings on woven rugs. He passed this new tradition on to his nieces, who became the first and among the best to duplicate the ceremonial designs in their weavings.

Chant Weaves emerging from the looms of Navajo women since that time highlight the most important art period in Navajo history. Whereas the value of art objects often is equated with age, modern examples of Chant Weaves are of higher quality and more interpretive of the culture than those of earlier eras. Native Americans, who resent having their cultures permanently imbedded in the distant past, confirm the suggestion that the modern weavings are more truly representative of their culture and traditions.

As in nearly all their endeavors, Edwin and Ruth Kennedy shared a passion for collecting these Navajo treasures. After Edwin's first exposure at the Red Rock Trading Post in 1954, he returned whenever Kerr-McGee held a board meeting in the area of its uranium interests. One of those meetings was scheduled to coincide with an intertribal ceremonial, which Kennedy and other directors attended in the spring of 1957. While there, Senator Kerr introduced Kennedy to Tobe Turpen, a leading Navajo art dealer from Gallop, New Mexico. In the years ahead, Edwin combined trips to Red Rock and Gallop, making purchases from Troy Kennedy and Tobe Turpen. When possible, Ruth accompanied him.

During the sixties the Kennedys concentrated on collecting textiles, purchasing jewelry only for their own use. As their interest grew and they became more aware of the exquisite artistry of Navajo, Hopi, and Zuni jewelry makers, however, that segment of their collection also became significant. "The Hopis in particular did some very innovative things," Kennedy observed. "Their designs and craftsmanship were amazing." An enterprising dealer named Tom Buffalo made annual cross-country treks to visit Kennedy at his New York office. "Tom would appear with a couple of suitcases full of beautiful silver and gold jewelry, as well as a few blankets," said Kennedy. "They were high priced, but also high quality, so I usually bought them. On one occasion, the dealer who had sold a bracelet to Tom, who in turn sold it to me at a decent profit, tried to buy it back at a price well above what I had paid for it."

Yet, the most exciting element of collecting was being able to accumulate complete chants with the sand paintings woven into the blankets, and to meet the Navajo women who made them. Edwin and Ruth extended their quests to other dealers in Farmington and Albuquerque, New Mexico, but their closest relationships remained with Tobe Turpen and Troy Kennedy. Turpen later recalled how the friendships blossomed:

> Everyone in my trading company got to know Ed's taste. He was our best customer for top-quality textiles. As he began to fill

out his collection, he asked us to watch for certain things—always the best available. We did that, and he usually bought what we held for him, because we became close enough to know what he wanted. Fortunately, he also knew Troy Kennedy, who had access to some very good weavers. Troy could get them to weave into chants top quality rugs to Ed's specifications. That is difficult to do. It is hard to get a Navajo woman to weave a rug for a specific customer. I don't know why, but they prefer to weave what they want and bring it in to you.

It was inevitable that Edwin Kennedy would meet another dealer, Gilbert Maxwell, a former Chicago businessman who moved to New Mexico and became the largest wholesaler of Navajo textiles in the Southwest. Also a serious collector of Navajo art, Maxwell was helping develop a museum for the University of New Mexico Department of Anthropology in the late sixties. As a friendship between the two men deepened, Kennedy became increasingly interested in the New Mexico project, donating what the museum director assessed as "some very important Navajo textiles."

When the museum outgrew its allotted space in a university building, Gilbert Maxwell and his wife, Dorothy, were instrumental in helping acquire a separate structure, which subsequently was named in their honor. Edwin and Ruth Kennedy made a large cash contribution of an undisclosed amount to finance a display area for some of their contemporary Navajo blankets, which they donated to the university when the new Maxwell Museum was opened in 1970. After both Maxwells died later in the seventies, Kennedy continued to place valuable ceremonial rugs and other art in the museum. "These collections are used in public exhibitions," noted Museum Director J. J. Brody, "but perhaps of greater importance to us, they are used in training graduate and undergraduate students, and also researchers from all over the world. Ed Kennedy's cash contributions to the museum have gone to support these research activities. Space in which to examine objects and to study them generally is difficult to acquire, and it is rare indeed that a private donor will support the research use of collections." To recognize this assistance, the Museum Association later instituted the Ruth E. Kennedy Memorial Lectureship, honoring an outstanding doctoral candidate in anthropology each year.

Although their focus remained on weavings, in the seventies the Kennedys began increasing jewelry purchases as well, until this also became a substantial segment of their Southwest Native American art collection.

Several years later, Edwin Kennedy helped finance a costly long-term project to rebuild the churro herd, which had dwindled to fifty sheep running free on the Navajo reservation. Lyle McNeal, a professor of agriculture at Utah Southern University, headed the effort to round up these remaining churros and carry out a breeding program. In addition to regular annual gifts to the university in support of what officially was called its Navajo Sheep Preservation and Development Project, Kennedy provided emergency funds whenever a crisis seem imminent. This continued for well over a decade, during which time the herd increased twelvefold, providing the wool to restore the beauty and craftsmanship of Navajo weaving to the classic period of the mid-1800s, and help boost the tribe's economy.

Chapter 13   Conflicts of Interests

> *Ed Kennedy had the gift of patience. He always weighed his words to the extent that there was no waste in his conversations. I always felt I had learned something after talking with him.*
> —George H. Heyman, Jr.
> Investment Banker

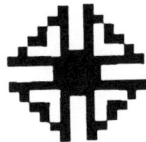

The death of Robert Lehman in 1969 left Lehman Brothers groping for leadership. Joseph A. Thomas, a longtime partner who was on the boards of such important corporations as Litton Industries and Black & Decker, was the overwhelming choice of most colleagues, including Edwin Kennedy, to become chief executive officer, but within a few months he stepped down as chairman, citing health problems. "That left a void for a while," Kennedy said, "but it wasn't reflected much in business transactions because partners still operated rather independently."

Coordination was the missing ingredient, and it was only partially restored with selection of another veteran partner, Frederick L. Ehrman, as the new board chairman. Characteristically, Kennedy never made a negative remark about Ehrman, whom many others regarded as an excellent investment banker, but a gruff, unpopular chairman who lacked the diplomatic finesse of his predecessor. Bickering among partners became increasingly prevalent, although Kennedy insisted it did not reach the "chaotic proportions" reported in the business press. One notable incident involving Occidental Oil, he said, illustrated that the firm's integrity remained intact.

The episode began on the eve of a two-week trip Ed and Ruth took to Europe in September 1970. Having heard rumors that Armand Hammer might be thinking of initiating a large underwriting through Lehman Brothers, Kennedy telephoned Fred Ehrman to assert his opposition to such an arrangement.

"How long will you be gone?" asked Ehrman.

"Two weeks."

"Well, don't worry, nothing is going to happen in that time."

As Kennedy and his wife were preparing to leave Rome at the end of their vacation, however, he received an overseas call from Lehman Partner Robert McCabe, relaying a message from Ehrman that the Executive Committee had agreed tentatively to underwrite a $125 million convertible bond issue for Occidental Oil.

"Tell Fred that the first thing I shall do when I get home will be to consult my personal counsel on what I should do," Kennedy replied.

Such a comment from a conservative partner raised a red flag in the board room. Less than half an hour after returning to the Lehman building, Kennedy was seated at a table with members of the Executive Committee, answering questions about the reasons for his strong opposition to the request of a million-dollar-a-year client. His answers, including some of the things he had told Bobbie Lehman two years earlier, were intentionally and obviously vague, prompting Ehrman to ask, "Ed, do you know something that you are not telling us?"

Hesitating briefly to emphasize his resolve as he looked at the chairman, Kennedy said firmly, "Fred, you have no right to ask me that." Without further discussion, the committee voted to discontinue Lehman's lucrative relationship with Hammer, despite his wealth and influence. "I was never more proud of Lehman Brothers than I was at that moment," Kennedy recalled.

Before the end of the year, Walter Davis resigned from the presidency of Occidental—an act he had been contemplating for several months. Afterwards, when he moved on to highly successful entrepreneurial projects in various fields, he and Kennedy met often, primarily to enjoy the camaraderie, but also to exchange ideas on business and philanthropy. Neither ever disclosed the information Kennedy had withheld from Lehman's Executive Committee.

Some Lehman Brothers problems were unrelated to administrative changes. Competition, reaching a degree of polarization, had developed over the past few years between the traditional banking partners and a more recently organized assemblage of "traders." The latter was headed aggressively by Lewis L. Glucksman, who had been hired in 1962 to form a commercial paper subsidiary, thereby moving the company for the first time into direct purchases and sales of securities. Glucksman's group had expanded rapidly, accounting for a substantial share of total Lehman profits, but the volatile personality of its leader clashed noticeably with the conservative nature of most banking partners. When thrust together on specific projects, Kennedy and Glucksman worked in subdued harmony, revealing no sign of strain, even to each other. Otherwise, however, their relationship was limited to minimum requirements of partnership cordiality.

Factions grew within the company, with partners reported to be less willing to share information with colleagues, an attitude that was painful to Kennedy. A senior partner observed, "Some members were speaking of their own, individual clients, instead of referring to them as the firm's clients, and this didn't fit Ed's strong feeling that the overall institution was of prime importance."

Several partners left the firm, withdrawing their invested funds and thereby depressing Lehman's capital, which was becoming dangerously drained. This occurred at a time when the administration of President Richard M. Nixon was attempting to curtail economic expansion as a means of combating inflation. Industrial output and investment declined accordingly.

To raise additional capital, overcome problems of high tax rates on partnerships, and be able to reinvest earnings, Lehman Brothers was incorporated on October 30, 1970. Except for the transfer of business functions to Lehman Brothers Incorporated, however, the only notable changes were in titles, from "partners" to "managing directors." And despite admitted internal problems, the firm broadened its sphere of influence. In 1971, credit leasing and real estate activities were consolidated in a new subsidiary, Lehman Special Services, headed by William G. Baker, Jr., a managing director. The following year, the company founded Lehman Government Securities, whose chairman, "Lew" Glucksman, also continued as chairman of Lehman Commercial Paper. At the same time, it responded to growth of international business and investment opportunities by creating Lehman Brothers Limited, headed by George W. Ball, former undersecretary of state in the Kennedy and Johnson administrations; Ball had joined Lehman as a partner in 1967. An office established in London exchanged daily information with New York and Lehman Brothers, S.A. in Paris. Domestic offices of the firm and its affiliates outside New York by then were located in Chicago, Dallas, Houston, Los Angeles, San Francisco, Atlanta, and Washington, D.C.

In the spring of 1973, Lehman reported having a staff of 1,261 persons. The firm managed or participated annually in more than one-half of all financings for corporations, governments, and governmental units in the United States. It had managed or co-managed more than $6 billion of registered corporate underwritings and $604 million of municipal underwritings, as well as arranging $915 million of private placements during the previous year. It showed a growth in The Lehman Corporation, its non-leveraged, diversified investment company, and in The One William Street Fund, its no-load mutual fund.

Yet, Lehman's troubles persisted. In addition to the unsteadiness perceived in overall management, the company suffered financially when Commercial Paper, which had generated good profits in previous years, sustained a near-mortal loss. Playing a hunch that interest rates would drop, Glucksman had invested a large segment of the company's own capital in government bonds. Instead, rates went up, collapsing the bond market in July 1973, and cutting deeply into Lehman's reserves. "Lew made a great big roll of the dice and lost," explained a disgruntled managing director. A few years later, Glucksman's commercial paper organization made a comeback, but in 1973, the gamble was devastating. An obviously shaken Lehman auditor had the unpleasant task of reporting to the executive committee that instead of anticipated strong profits, the fiscal year would end with an immense loss.

These varied, but related circumstances of the preceding three years funnelled quickly into a decisive agreement among managing directors that a strong leader, capable of making some tough decisions on cutting costs and tightening controls, was needed to replace Ehrman, who was then sixty-eight and in poor health. Action was initiated so rapidly that the man they chose for the job was taken by surprise. He had been with the firm for only six weeks, and had no prior experience in investment banking.

Peter G. Peterson had grown up in Kearney, Nebraska, where his Greek-immigrant parents owned a restaurant. Educated at Northwestern University and the University of Chicago, he had become president of Bell & Howell at the age of thirty-four. Ten years later, he moved to Washington, serving first as presidential adviser on international economic affairs, then as secretary of commerce in the Nixon cabinet. When political differences uncoupled that alliance, he was lured to New York by Lehman Brothers as vice chairman of the board in June 1973. Peterson had contemplated the opportunity somewhat wistfully. "I didn't know much about investment banking, nor whether I would even like it at that time," he said later, "but I had run a corporation and been in government, and I wanted to be involved in corporate investments in this country and abroad."

Instead of learning the business gradually, as he intended, Peterson was invited to attend a July 19, 1973 meeting of nine senior managing directors, not including Chairman Ehrman, in

George Ball's apartment. Lehman President F. Warren Hellman presided. "I remember that when each person at the table was asked to comment on who could lead the company out of its abyss, I asked to be the last to talk, because everyone there knew more about the company and its problem than I," Peterson said. Nevertheless, the group was unanimous in its selection. Early in August 1973, Peterson succeeded Ehrman as chairman of the board. In doing so, he accepted the task of restructuring the firm.

During what the new chairman described as "a very stressful period," of reducing staffs by 35 percent, honing expenditures, and exchanging Lehman stock for a capital infusion from prestigious Banca Commerciale Italiana, Peterson often sought the counsel of veteran managing directors, who still were referred to as "partners" in general conversations, and even by the press. He retained vivid memories of discussions with Kennedy:

> Ed was very concerned about the firm, and I got the impression he was supportive of my doing these things. He still was uninterested in participating in management, but I knew his feelings. I always thought of him as a positive role model, as contrasted to the transaction-driven type of banker. Ed was more rooted in understanding substance and building long-term relationships with clients, identifying himself with their interests. They knew he was in the trenches with them, not just looking for fees. It always was a pleasure to talk with him, because he was one of a relatively small number not interested in politics and protecting one's turf, and he was unfailingly modest, in a business not noted for a lack of hubris. He didn't want to have anything to do with what you might call centrifugal forces that can vulcanize a firm. In a time of turmoil and difficult decisions, it was nice to have people like that who were part of the solution instead of the problem.

In a successful revival, Lehman Brothers penetrated deeper into foreign territory, bringing international banks together to finance projects in Europe and growth areas of the Middle East. It became banking adviser to Algeria's national oil company following a gradual worldwide adjustment to energy problems wrought by an October 17, 1973 crude-oil embargo imposed by eleven Arab states on the United States and other countries deemed friendly to Israel. Domestically, the company negotiated one of the largest primary industrial equity offerings in history, one million shares of Halliburton Corporation stock at $176. On January 1, 1975, Lehman increased its equity position by purchasing the brokerage firm of Abraham and Company—the first merger for both organizations.

By then, Edwin Kennedy, having passed the age of seventy, was gradually reducing his work load. Many of the seasoned partners with whom he had worked for three decades had retired, as had Gen. Lucius D. Clay, hero of the 1948–49 Berlin Air Lift, who was a Lehman partner for nine years after serving twelve years as chairman of Continental Can Corporation. Others, including Fred Ehrman, Monroe Gutman, and Paul Mazur, had died. James Glanville developed many of the new oil company accounts, and William C. Morris, a managing director who had joined Lehman in 1967, was becoming increasingly involved by handling public offers for the Oil Department, along with his other duties. Although Kennedy declared quite sincerely that he was "winding down" his schedule, those men and others found it difficult to detect the professed change of pace.

George H. Heyman, Jr., who came to Lehman Brothers from Abraham and Company in the merger and became chairman of the investment committee, had known Kennedy "by his legendary accomplishments and through investing in several companies he had been instrumental in financing," but the two had never met before 1975. They subsequently became good friends. "I got to know Ed well when I went with him on a few trips to the West Coast," Heyman said later. "He was older than I, but he would get up at 5:30 each morning, to tramp around the oil fields, all the while quietly asking questions as I was told he had done for many many years. If that was slowing down, I can only imagine what he was like in his forties and fifties."

Heyman also noted that Kennedy seemingly had no touch of vanity, explaining, "He had plenty of money, and he wasn't afraid to spend it, but the notion of having a limousine never entered his mind. He took the train into the city and taxis or subways around Manhattan. That was a little unusual in the financial district, where people in his position come to the conclusion they have to travel ten blocks in a limousine that is two blocks long."

Like others, Heyman marveled at Kennedy's ability to control emotions in a storm of controversy. "He would not abide being cheated, but he could work calmly toward solving a problem of severe magnitude if he believed there was no bad intention," Heyman said. "On one memorable occasion I was asked to complete formalities on a deal Ed had set up to finance a West Coast developer of oil properties. In the end, it became apparent the man had made representations that were not true. I was fuming, but Ed patiently asked him questions, set him straight on what he had done wrong, and politely cancelled the deal, although it meant some financial loss to Lehman Brothers. He concluded that the man had meant well, but promised more than he could deliver." As to the loss, Heyman said candidly, "No one associated with investments bats a thousand. Most are under three hundred and Ed was among the tops in average. If you are a bad loser in this business, you had better get into something else."

William Morris explained Kennedy's demeanor another way: "When something was done that he didn't like, or when he thought something within the firm was being left untended, he pointed it out. But he didn't throw his shoe at you first. He pointed it out in a civilized, but forceful way."

Self-control was, in fact, so ingrained in Kennedy's personality that his only display of anger in a business situation gnawed at him for the rest of his career, and on into retirement, even though the story had a happy ending.

The incident involved Tosco, with which Kennedy remained vitally involved as a shareholder, director, and financial adviser. The company was clinging tenaciously to hopes for shale oil production while protecting its equity through acquisitions of conventional refineries. The first such investment was in a refinery near Bakersfield, California, purchased from Signal Oil and Gas Corporation in 1970. Two years later, it added a second facility, purchased from Monsanto in El Dorado, Arkansas. Monsanto had acquired the former independent refiner-marketer known as Lion Oil Company in order to control crude oil for its chemical production, but interest had waned and it was put on the market. Kennedy arranged financing for the two refinery purchases through long-term funding by Equitable Life Assurance, Prudential Insurance, and First National Bank of St. Paul, primarily on the strength of his record in oil.

By 1974, Tosco's annual gross and net figures from the refineries assured a sufficient cash flow to plan the nation's first commercial shale oil production plant. An oil crisis dating to the 1973 Arab embargo had awakened the United States from its nonchalance toward domestic production. With prices rising accordingly, Tosco had anxious customers urgently encouraging development of shale oil. When the federal government, motivated by the influence of President Jimmy Carter, opened up more of its land in the shale regions of Colorado, Wyoming, and Utah for competitive bidding, major oil companies leaped at the opportunity to lease properties and develop economical and environmentally acceptable processes to extract high-priced crude. In assessing Tosco's position, *Forbes* magazine reported on April 1, 1974 that prospects for its investors "have never looked better." A year later, optimism continued to dominate predictions by producers and analysts, but no commercial operation had surfaced, and Colony Development Corporation activities again were slipping into limbo.

Meanwhile, Tosco's largest and most complex acquisition, and the one that catapulted it into the status of a major oil company, resulted from a seeming impasse between non-related federal regulations and Phillips Petroleum. To comply with terms of a divestiture decree from a federal judge in California, Phillips was ordered to sell its huge Avon Refinery on San Francisco Bay, near the city of Duncan, California. None of the other oil giants was permitted to purchase Avon, however, and no small company had adequate resources for such an acquisition, which included not only the refinery, but also port facilities, terminals, and hundreds of service stations. Phillips faced the dilemma of being ordered to sell an extremely valuable network of properties for which there was no buyer.

Enter Edwin Kennedy. Recognizing an opportunity to move Tosco into the major leagues of oil refining, Kennedy developed a plan to purchase Avon. "Officially, the enormous undertaking was the work of the Lehman Energy Department," observed Morton Winston, Tosco's key figure in coordinating the transaction, "but it was Ed's brainchild, and it was his reputation that made the strategy possible." Winston's reference was to a three-pronged projection: giving Phillips an issue of preferred stock in Tosco; on the basis of that expanded equity, raising a private placement of senior debt from a consortium of banks capable of putting up money on such a large scale; and devising a system of selling off service stations and other auxiliary properties for additional financing as the plan unfolded. William Morris, who worked with Kennedy on the project and became a member of the Tosco board, referred to the purchase as "a mouse swallowing an elephant." The Avon Refinery and its associated properties were many times the size of Tosco.

Execution consumed two years of overcoming such obstacles as California usury laws coming into conflict with the Federal Reserve Board, driving interest rates into double-digit figures to stop inflation. But in 1976, Tosco became sole owner of Avon Refinery. "The procedure worked just as Ed intended," Winston said, "and many industrial leaders have hailed it as America's first real leveraged buyout."

Kennedy himself opposed categorizing business dealings, considering each to be custom-designed for its own specific needs, and vehemently differentiated between his arrangements for the Avon purchase and the ensuing LBO craze that brought on junk-bond atrocities of the 1980s. "Never in my career did I buy or sell a junk bond," he said with conviction.

While negotiations with Phillips were under way, Winston succeeded Hein Koolsbergen as president and chief executive officer of Tosco. Three years later, when the 1979 Iranian Revolution ignited another surge in OPEC crude oil prices, Tosco attempted to revive dormant shale oil activities by again planning construction of the long-sought commercial plant.

To facilitate that effort, Arco in 1980 sold its 60 percent interest to Exxon, which then joined Tosco in obtaining a government loan guarantee of $1.1 billion. This arrangement included a clause, orchestrated by Winston, in which Exxon agreed to purchase Tosco's interest if it should decide to withdraw from the project. Such a reckoning seemed remote indeed, with wellhead prices doubling from 1979 levels to forty dollars a barrel by the end of 1980. Analysts projected a continuing rise to fifty or even sixty dollars by 1986, the target date for completion of Colony Development's 47,000-barrel-a-day plant. In addition, Exxon's own domestic petroleum reserves had dropped by 24 percent in the previous three years.

Several factors, however, were missing from the formula for success. Instead of following the predicted pattern, oil demand sputtered under nationwide efforts to conserve energy, and OPEC nations reopened petroleum flood gates to discourage the development of synfuels. Exxon, also citing skyrocketing construction overrides, abruptly exercised its withdrawal option in May 1982, paying Tosco a premium price of $380 million. Unable to complete construction alone, Tosco abandoned the Colony project—again shelving its aspirations for oil shale—but realized a profit of $220 million after paying off government-guaranteed loans and taxes of $160 million.

Bolstered by this large infusion of cash from Exxon, the company continued to grow, moving into production, particularly in heavy California crude oil, and purchasing a fourth refinery, in Duncan, Oklahoma, from Sun Oil Company.

Meanwhile, a new federal regulation outlawing "cross-directorships" dictated that Kennedy could no longer be a member of two oil company boards. Because of his long-standing dedication to the workings of Kerr-McGee, he resigned as a director of Tosco, but remained active as its investment adviser. In this capacity, he opposed, but could not vote against the Duncan Refinery purchase, which he warned would dangerously increase the company's debt service.

Later, Kennedy voiced even stronger objection to Tosco's intended acquisition of AZL Resources Corporation, a Phoenix agricultural equipment company with heavy investment in oil production. AZL was in the process of converting to an energy company, and Winston hoped to continue that move by liquidating the agricultural operations. Contending that the timing was wrong because oil prices were destined to go down and Tosco could not afford exploration without active field partners, Kennedy firmly advised against any such purchase. When the debate between president and adviser persisted, Kennedy became increasingly angry, speaking in a manner that openly reflected his feelings. He became even more disturbed when the board, upon Winston's recommendation, voted unanimously to purchase AZL, but he vowed to "never again speak in anger."

The acquisition proved to be a bad mistake. Oil prices continued to fall, and field partners became either unable or unwilling to assist in exploration. "It might have been fate," said a colleague, "but Ed's intuition about fate is amazing."

Bankers who financed the AZL purchase became involved, forcing liquidation of assets at a low point in the marketplace and insisting that Winston resign, but during a heated meeting with bank representatives, Tosco directors chose to back their president. Kennedy, who had attended the meeting as company adviser, left while the discussion continued, and headed for the elevator. Before he reached it, however, he was stopped by Winston, who had followed him out of the meeting.

"What do you suggest that I do?" the Tosco president asked.

"You should resign," Kennedy answered. "As tough as that might be, and right or wrong, things will be worse if you don't do that." Winston turned, walked back into the board room, and resigned as CEO, although he remained on the board for more than a year.

Kennedy nursed no personal animosity toward Winston. They remained friends, with a mutual respect that would draw them together again, less than a decade later, in two exciting new business ventures. "Despite any disagreements we had, and in bad times following my resignation as president of

Tosco, I had the unfailing human support of Ed Kennedy," Winston recalled with obvious deep feeling. "You make mistakes and you don't make mistakes, and Ed opposed me in some of my oil company endeavors, but I always had his support as a human being; and that is one of the most important things I've ever possessed."

In the years ahead, Tosco sold three of its refineries, paring operations to Avon, estimated in the nineties to be worth one billion dollars, and marketing gasoline, diesel fuel, and petroleum coke in the United States and abroad.

In December 1977, with its business again thriving at a pace that resurrected its prestige on Wall Street, Lehman Brothers announced a merger with another illustrious investment banking firm, Kuhn, Loeb, best known for having helped finance the expansion of America's railroads and steel mills early in the century. The merger brought an addition of more blue-chip clients, along with an increase in total capital that had been missing since the days when Bobbie Lehman could reach into his own immense private reserves for instant financial transfusions whenever necessary. Peter Peterson emerged as the chief executive officer of Lehman Brothers Kuhn Loeb Incorporated, with Harvey M. Krueger, former Kuhn, Loeb CEO, heading the combined investment-banking operation.

"The merger didn't change much, except that it brought in more people," Kennedy observed. The firm remained a private corporation.

In moving closer to retirement, Kennedy devoted less time to developing new business, but continued to help build companies with whom he held close affiliations. Foremost among these was Kerr-McGee Oil, where he remained a director, a major shareholder, and, since 1966, a member of the executive committee. Kennedy also was instrumental in the addition of his Lehman Brothers colleague, William Morris, to the Kerr-McGee board. No stranger to the company, Morris had worked on several Kerr-McGee financial projects in recent years. Headquartered in the modern Kerr-McGee Center in

Oklahoma City, the company in 1977 had grown, principally through acquisitions, from the small producer Kennedy assisted nearly thirty years earlier to a diversified energy corporation with twelve subsidiaries active in worldwide onshore and offshore drilling, refining, gasoline merchandising through two thousand retail stations, uranium and coal mining, natural gas processing, and production of various chemicals. Based on such expansive resources, some media observers suggested that the company might become a takeover target, but Dean McGee shrugged off such rumors. At seventy-three, he was more intent on making plans for a succession of leadership, something Edwin Kennedy, who was the same age, urged him to do. Asked by a *Wall Street Journal* reporter how he knew it was time to step down, the laconic McGee replied, "That's easy; my age." Deteriorating health following knee surgery, however, was more germane to his decision.

During what McGee called his "phasing out" process, he sought and received advice frequently from Kennedy. Ironically, similar groundwork Kennedy had prepared for himself over a period of years was soon to be impaired.

Chairman Peterson was greatly impressed by "Ed Kennedy's long-range view of Lehman Brothers in perpetuity, based on a belief that the firm was more important than any single member." It was for that reason Peterson and others correctly surmised that one of the saddest moments in Kennedy's business life occurred in 1978, when he discovered abruptly that plans for his succession were shattered.

While he was on a vacation with his family at the Canadian lodge on Calabogie Lake, Kennedy learned that James Glanville, whom he had groomed as his successor in oil affairs and who had already assumed a large share of that responsibility, had left Lehman Brothers to join a competing banking house, Lazard Freres & Company. Shaken by the news, Kennedy reacted as might have been expected, in silence. But the hurt was deep and long lasting. "Ed's grave personal disappointment was intensified by his loyalty to the company," said a sympathetic partner, Walter Lubanko, who had worked with Kennedy on many occasions.

Glanville, feeling that attempts at providing an explanation would be futile, especially over the crackling telephone lines to Calabogie, said only that he owed his success to Kennedy, and therefore was sorry to disappoint him. "I never had a chance to talk it out with Ed," Glanville would say more than a decade later. "Also, I didn't really think it would be fruitful to explain that I was so disappointed in some problems I envisioned at Lehman Brothers that I didn't think it would be a place where I wanted to spend the next ten years of my life."

The two men never became business or personal enemies, but their friendship didn't resume until well after Kennedy's retirement several years later. "We didn't nurture animosity," Glanville said. "We just were in different worlds, doing things in different places."

After Glanville's departure, William Morris became administrative head of the Energy Department. "Ed still outranked me in terms of longevity and experience, and even though he was in semi-retirement, we continued to work together," Morris said. "There wasn't any formal structure to the relationship, but it worked fine, as far as I could tell. We had individual client dealings, and cooperated on others. As always, Ed loved the external aspects of investment banking, but had no interest in the internal, day-to-day administrative details of the firm. I don't remember exchanging one cross word during the years we were together."

William D. Forster, a young managing director, also began channeling efforts into business of the Oil Department, and Jack Lentz gave the group a steady presence in the oil- and gas-rich Southwest, operating out of Lehman's Houston office. Kennedy quickly became confident once again that the department he had organized nearly four decades earlier remained "in good hands" for the future.

Changes in the investment world were occurring so rapidly, however, that the future was destined to embrace a shift in emphasis that sidestepped the values on which Edwin Kennedy had built his reputation. Many observers traced the transformation to 1975, when deregulation that had been creeping in since the late sixties brought on what Wall Street termed "May Day" in the brokerage business. In a dramatic display of power, the Securities and Exchange Commission on May 1, 1975, had replaced the fixed-rate regulation—which had been in effect for more than forty years—with a system of negotiated rates. Although previous fixed brokerage commissions and underwriting spreads had in effect made investment banking a regulated business, they had assured a stability that enabled men like Kennedy to concentrate on helping build the security and productivity of client companies. Deregulation ushered in fierce competition from the discount brokerage sector, as well as blood-letting price wars among banking houses, seemingly desirable from the vantage of investors, but counterproductive to the development of close client relationships. By the end of the seventies, it was evident that underwriting would be going to those who could raise money cheapest. Personal trust and even integrity were losing ground to bottom-line financial figures as primary considerations. In a growing number of transactions, industrial productivity had little to do with conglomerate manipulations.

The volatility brought about by the growing scramble for hostile takeovers, often with little regard for products or employees, sometimes created what Peter Peterson had described as "centrifugal forces" within investment banking firms. Indeed, during the latter half of the seventies, Lehman traders were located at 55 Water Street, with bankers remaining at One William Street. When Peterson announced plans to consolidate operations at 55 Water Street—based on inadequate space at One William Street following the merger with Kuhn, Loeb—some investment bankers objected to being in such close proximity to their own firm's trading operations. Nevertheless, the move took place in 1980.

Kennedy had an office in the Water Street building, but he used it only as a home base from which he tended business accounts unrelated to the new trend toward cut-throat competition. He was wary of possible repercussions on the horizon. Yet, his career had spanned other socioeconomic metamorphoses, and a new drift from the bearing he advocated was not strong enough to diminish his enthusiasm for the oil investment business, nor his loyalty to Lehman Brothers.

Reflecting on the late seventies, Kennedy realized his concern for the health of his wife had overshadowed all other interests, although Ruth herself refused to let it alter the pattern of their lives. In respecting that wish, Edwin managed to disguise his anxiety, as the couple continued their varied activities together. No one outside the family and circle of close friends detected a change in Ruth's vigor, and indeed, her enthusiasm never dwindled.

Chapter 14   **Continuing Commitments**

> *In the United States, universities and colleges are governed as trusts by volunteer trustees. When you add to this the strong American tradition of private philanthropy, you have a distinctive American heritage in education.*
>
> —Dr. Charles J. Ping
> President, Ohio University

In a halftime ceremony at Ohio University's Homecoming football game on October 30, 1971, Edwin Kennedy was presented an award as "Alumnus of the Year." The honor—a particular source of pride because undergraduates had made the selection—was bestowed by Jeffrey Brickman, president of the Undergraduate Alumni Council, on behalf of the university's 18,673 students. At the same program, Laurel Lee Schaefer, a June graduate, received special recognition as having recently been crowned the 1972 Miss America. The two recipients then were driven around the stadium track while the Ohio University band played a medley of songs in their honor. That evening, the annual Alumni Awards Banquet was the scene of a more formal announcement of Kennedy's honor. Although Kennedy greatly appreciated the distinction afforded by students of his alma mater, he expressed regret that illness prevented his wife from being with him.

A birthmark had developed into a melanoma on one of Ruth Kennedy's feet, requiring an immediate operation, and a lengthy period of recovery. Fortunately, the surgery removed all traces of malignancy, enabling Ruth to resume her active life, and, in fact, accept grandson Danny into the household after Eddie and Margaret were divorced in Canada. Margaret moved with the couple's daughter, Patty, to Florida. Later, when lightning struck Eddie's lumber mill, precipitating the close of his business, he returned to New Jersey also, and in 1973, Patty joined the family at New Vernon when her mother, who died three months later, no longer was able to care for her.

Consequently, Christa and Jeff Cook, who had contemplated moving into a home they had purchased in nearby Lincoln Park, agreed to stay with the Kennedys, and Danny, Susanne, and Patty grew up as brother and sisters. Jeff Cook became disenchanted with corporate life, and, convinced he preferred retailing, explored a variety of possibilities, eventually accepting a position as manager of the Mendham Hardware and Paint Company, ten miles from New Vernon. The new career proved to be so satisfying that Cook purchased the Mendham store a decade later, building the business substantially through the years, with the assistance of Christa, who worked with him regularly.

Edwin Kennedy had honored financial commitments to higher education and carried out his duties as a trustee of Ohio University, Hiram, and Juniata as the fires of student discontent—fanned by killings of demonstrators at Kent State and Jackson State universities in 1970 and the United States movement into Cambodia in 1971—dragged on into the seventies. Yet, he hesitated to launch new projects amidst the uncertainty of campus fortunes.

Following lengthy studies and discussions, a President's Commission on Campus Unrest, appointed by Richard Nixon, did nothing more than condemn student participants, police, and college administrators, offering nothing in terms of a solution. Tensions began to ease only with the end of American involvement in Cambodia and Vietnam and official dissolution of the military draft on June 30, 1973.

In May 1974, Kennedy began his second term as chairman of the Ohio University Board of Trustees, just prior to the resignation of President Sowle. Dr. Harry B. Crewson, who had been a member of the economics faculty since 1949, was named interim president while a search committee headed by

Dr. Alan R. Booth, professor of history, interviewed candidates for the position. Kennedy was a member of that committee.

In the dying embers of confrontation, order gradually was restored, but there were wounds to be healed on campuses across the country. At Ohio University, this task was faced by Dr. Charles J. Ping, who succeeded Dr. Crewson as president on September 1, 1975. A graduate of Southwestern at Memphis and the Louisville Presbyterian Theological Seminary, with a Ph.D. from Duke University, Ping came to Ohio from Central Michigan University, where he had been a professor of philosophy, and since 1969, provost. He also had served during the past six summers as a lecturer at the Harvard University Institute for Educational Management.

"Charlie Ping told me he was well aware of Ohio University's problems, which were great at that time," Kennedy recalled, "but he was impressed with the people there, and especially the deep interest they had in the school, something he considered unusually strong for a large public institution." Indeed, Ping described the university as "troubled, but rich in people, place, and history." With that background, he initiated steps to recover lost confidence among faculty and students and to revitalize programs that had been eroded by the atmosphere of campus turmoil. The Kennedys pledged their full support.

Although Edwin had been among those instrumental in selecting the new president, he no longer was a member of the board at the beginning of the Ping administration. His sixteenth and final year as a trustee had ended in May 1975, and by law, he was not eligible for reappointment. He did, however, remain a member of the University Fund Board, and was encouraged by President Ping to proffer a voice of experience to other programs in which he was interested.

"I quickly became aware of how important the Kennedy gifts and presence were to Ohio University," President Ping said. "The Kennedy Lecture Series bring a steady stream of remarkable people to the campus, and I feel certain the Distinguished Professors awards have helped make it attractive for outstanding scholars, who also are effective teachers, to remain here for long tenures. Research support, also through the Baker Fund, offers similar inducements. Furthermore, I think this first endowment established by Ed and Ruth inspired a level of private support making a margin of difference in the life of the university."

In recognition of these and other contributions, the Kennedys were honored at a formal dinner on March 6, 1976, held in conjunction with the inauguration of Dr. Ping as eighteenth president of Ohio University. The evening's program spotlighted presentation of the Founders Citation, the university's highest honor, to Edwin, something he thereafter considered to be a highlight of his life. He was pleased that former President John Baker was selected to be the major speaker, following the presentation by President Ping. "Ed and Ruth Kennedy have shown a faith in education comparable with that of the founders," Baker told an audience of several hundred educators and friends, "in considering education as vital to the development of the individual and the nation, in recognizing the worth and dignity of every man and woman, and in emphasizing the need to provide equal opportunities for all."

Kennedy used his brief acceptance talk to pay tribute to his wife and reaffirm a strong belief in the future of their alma mater. He also used the occasion as a forum for expressing his concern over the nation's attitude toward energy:

> I long have felt that the worst thing that can happen to a people, excepting only invasion and occupation, is inflation. Now I'm not so sure. The horrendous problem of our future energy supply and its cost may approach such a standard of seriousness. If we continue to permit politics to transcend rationality in seeking solutions to both of these problems then the structure of our society, including our individual freedom, our national strength, and our economic well-being are in grave jeopardy.
>
> . . . . Our legislators provide no leadership, but rather compete with each other to attract political support by restrictive or even punitive legislation on our energy industries. Each time you buy a gallon of gasoline, five cents of the total, or in the aggregate $6 billion per year on gasoline alone, is due to the cost of regulation by

the Washington bureaucrats, eleven cents comprises gasoline taxes, and one cent is profit to the venture capital system that made it all possible. Long ago I learned that when politics and economics meet, truth is the first casualty, logic the second.

Kennedy could have, but did not reveal that his admonition was backed by intimate familiarity with such a collision, not in the United States, but in one of several officially allied nations where both truth and logic seemed to be endangered species.

That nation was Panama. Although summer excursions to the private lake-front lodge in Canada still ranked at the top of the Kennedy family vacation plans, Christa and the children occasionally accompanied "Oma" and "Opa" on winter flights to the commercial Tropic Star Lodge complex, where deep sea fishing was a thrilling attraction. Even grammar-school students Susanne and Patty caught sizable sailfish. Side trips in small aircraft provided additional adventures to the San Blas Islands and other exotic locales.

Having owned Tropic Star since 1968, Kennedy followed both economic and political trends in Panama, which had since been transformed from a democracy to a dictatorship after the Guardia Nacional, headed by Gen. Omar Torrijos, had overthrown the government. One of the powerful figures whom Kennedy had come to know, albeit reluctantly, was Lt. Col. Manuel Noriega, information officer of "The Guard." Introduced to a gracious Noriega at guard headquarters by the chief justice of the Panamanian Supreme Court, Kennedy had felt uneasy in the relationship that followed.

Noriega remained amiable in subsequent encounters. His exceptional hospitality, in fact, included meeting Kennedy several times when he arrived at Tocumen International Airport in Panama City. Nevertheless, Edwin confessed to Ruth and intimate friends that he had formed a negative opinion of Noriega which "could not be altered by a smile and a handshake." The most disturbing disclosure, he said, was that Noriega "learned of my arrival through complete monitoring of all incoming and outgoing telephone calls." Beyond that, Kennedy based his mistrust of the man who was among competitors mounting behind-the-scenes campaigns to succeed Torrijos as dictator simply on a feeling of antipathy, honed by analytical experience. Noriega's insistence on meeting Edwin at the airport, although somewhat baffling, could be attributed to his desire to foster friendship with a partner in an important investment banking house—one of many contacts that might be important some day as the aspiring dictator nurtured political ties to the United States (which later proved to include an undercover connection with the CIA).

Reasonably confident that Noriega would become the protagonist in any open fight for leadership of the country, and anticipating dire consequences for foreign investors, Kennedy began looking for an opportunity to sell the Tropic Star complex. He felt no sense of urgency, but when a buyer emerged in 1976, he sold out. In the language of investment banking, that sale proved to be prudent. Noriega eventually took command of the guard, which he renamed the Panama Defense Forces, thereby becoming dictator of Panama in 1983. He remained in that position until he was ousted and arrested by United States Armed Forces on January 3, 1990, following what a biographer alleged to be "a career of drug running, torturing political enemies, and extorting a billion dollars from the people of Panama."

During the last three years of the seventies, Kennedy served as honorary chairman of Ohio University's first capital campaign, the 1804 Fund, so named because the university was founded in 1804. The drive proved highly successful, exceeding its $14 million goal by $9 million. At Juniata College, where he was commencement speaker in 1977, Kennedy had been honorary chairman of a fund-raising campaign, the Margin of Difference, which topped its $10-million goal in time for the college's centennial in 1976. Following that successful drive, he was appointed honorary chairman of Juniata's Century II campaign. "His gift, the largest of the campaign, moved the drive ahead quickly, and motivated others to raise their sights in making commitments," said Juniata President Frederick M. Binder. The gift Binder referred to was a challenge grant to complete the financing of a $4.5 million sports and recreation complex that had held high priority for several years. When it later appeared that the challenge would not be met, Kennedy made an impassioned appeal to the board—reminiscent of his entreaties to Hiram trustees on two occasions in the sixties—and added $400,000 to his original pledge. Again, the prod was effective. When the goal was reached, figures showed that trustees had committed 43 percent of the total.

The Kennedys' support of education was unflagging, despite the dark clouds that illness had placed on their personal horizon. Although Ruth's recovery from the melanoma on her foot was complete, an early stage of breast cancer had been discovered shortly after a family trip to Canada in the mid-seventies. The progressive seriousness of Ruth's condition as the cancer spread during the next few years, however, was difficult for others to detect. "She was unbelievable," said Christa. "I would take her for therapy, and when we came home, she would rest for a couple of days and then be ready to do things again. She never complained. Occasionally she would get pneumonia and go to the hospital, but she always would say, 'Don't worry, I'll be back soon,' and sure enough, when she returned a week or so later, she would say, 'I'm fine; no problem.' Even when she became dangerously ill, you wouldn't have known it by her attitude. She tired easily, of course, but she still loved to shop. And she never lost her sense of humor."

Despite her failing health, Ruth remained sympathetic with the plight of other people, helping them in ways that seemed unique to the few who knew of her actions. Each month, she paid electric bills for area families in arrears because of genuine financial difficulties. Only a representative of the power company knew their identities, and the families were not told the source of the payments. She readily accepted her Social Security checks, explaining that the money was justly due her, but she used it all to help people in need, always anonymously.

In September 1980, Ruth made reservations for the family to go to Hawaii the following February. But in November it became necessary for her to enter the hospital again. Before she left, Christa recalled, Ruth walked slowly through every room in the house, and calmly told her, "Christine, I don't think I'm coming back this time." Twenty days later, on December 12, 1980, Ruth Kennedy died.

On June 5, 1982, Hiram College dedicated its newly completed Ruth E. Kennedy Memorial Nature Trail, winding two miles through its forested biological field station. Conceived and built by students and financed by Edwin Kennedy, the trail leads hikers past ponds, streams, bogs, and rare stands of trees, also providing ready access to specified research areas for the study of plants and wildlife. Continuing plantings and development, carried out entirely by students and faculty members, helped make it an increasingly popular and highly publicized attraction for visitors, as well as students and other researchers. An introduction to the Trail Map, written by Dr. Martin Huehner, paid tribute to "a wonderful lady who had much love for the Hiram College Field Station." From the time it was opened, Edwin Kennedy never failed to walk the trail when he visited the college.

Less than a year after completion of Hiram's nature trail, Juniata College acknowledged financial and inspirational support for its newest building by naming the modern facility The Ruth E. and Edwin L. Kennedy Sports-Recreation Center. Speaking at the dedication ceremony on April 17, 1983, President Binder described the center as "a colossus which will serve the varsity sports and recreational needs of Juniata students for generations to come."

Seated on the platform with representative administrators, faculty, students, and special guests, Edwin Kennedy was filled with emotion. It was the first time his wife was not with him to share such a moment. And when he glanced toward the audience at the mention of Ruth's name, he noticed that Christa and Susanne were crying.

Most of Kennedy's friends believed Edwin would sell the large house in New Vernon, filled as it was with reminders of Ruth. But they underestimated his determination to value such memories without letting them become diluted by the deep sadness he felt, and in truth, did not try to avoid. Lively family discussions at the dinner table continued, and young friends were welcomed, as always, into the Kennedy home. "All my friends have adopted Opa as their grandfather too," said an admiring Susanne ten years later. "None of them calls him Mr. Kennedy; they all call him Opa. They don't remember Oma very well, because I was only in the seventh grade when she passed away, but we all notice that when someone talks about her, Opa really gets this glow about him, and they can tell the way he speaks how much he was in love with her."

On Edwin's eightieth birthday in 1984, Christa organized a party that attracted members of his family and many close friends from throughout the United States. Ruth's niece, Nancy Bletzer remembered, "Uncle Ed and everyone else had a marvelous time, and I think one of the highlights for him was when all of Susanne's teenage girl friends surrounded him on the stairway for a photograph."

The lodge in Canada remained a happy summer retreat for the immediate family, relatives, and friends. "Opa still loved to water ski, and he was well known around the lake," Susanne said. "When people saw him skimming along behind the boat, they would rush to the shore with cameras. They wanted pictures of this octogenarian skiing. We all thought that was the neatest thing." Fred Linville was convinced his uncle continued to water ski well into his eighties "not to prove anything, but because he still liked to be part of what was going on."

At Thanksgiving in 1983, Kennedy organized a family reunion at the Worthington Inn near Columbus, Ohio. As part of the holiday festivities, the entire group visited the homestead farm at Kirkpatrick and other sites that were prominent in the memories of Edwin and his brothers and sisters. Deeply touched by the experience, Kennedy assumed the leadership in making it an annual tradition.

When Ohio University sponsored an alumni tour of Russia, Kennedy and his sister, Gladys Linville, made the trip together. "That was the best vacation I ever had, because it was so interesting," Gladys recalled. "Edwin is not a typical tourist. He had to stop at every bookstore to look through all the volumes he could find that were written by Russians, but in English. On the return trip, he had his suitcases so heavy with books that he could barely lift them. And after he got home, he read them all." A year later, Edwin and Gladys, this time accompanied by Christa, Susanne, and Patty, attended a special Jubilee performance of the famed Passion Play in Oberammergau, Germany, then toured France and Italy.

Determined to carry on the interests shared so closely with his wife, Kennedy remained vitally involved in education. When a neighbor who was chairman of the board of Hampden-Sydney College in Virginia asked him to accept appointment to fill an unexpired term as a trustee, Kennedy accepted. Studying everything he could find on the history and workings of the college, one of only two remaining non-military all-male schools in the country (the other being Wabash College in Indiana), he was impressed with its high academic standing and its record of having the nation's largest percentage of graduates listed in "Who's Who." Soon elected to a full term, he introduced one of his favorite topics, deferred maintenance and obsolescence, requesting that a study be made by administrators for an early report.

"Ed was the fiscal conscience of the board," said Josiah Bunting III, then president of the college. "Two things in particular impressed me about his work for Hampden-Sydney. First, his extraordinary grasp of the details of every aspect of our business operation and the management of our endowment; and, second, his unhesitating willingness to speak up—usually at the end of our plenary sessions, when an excess of zeal had swept us to conclusions he thought too expensive or otherwise unwarranted. In measured and solemn and unadorned language, he lectured us on our primary fiscal responsibilities. Invariably he was right on the money. He believes with a steely

Continuing Commitments

quiet passion that education is our last hope, and that his service on the boards of educational institutions is the best means of helping make that hope live, making it, perhaps, reality."

Veteran Trustee Henry Spaulding agreed. "Hampden-Sydney is a very old school with some very old buildings, and we truthfully had not addressed the problem of maintenance as carefully as we should have done," admitted Spaulding, a Richmond, Virginia investment counselor. "Ed pointed out the dangers of the situation, and we have since spent a lot of money in catching up on neglected maintenance."

Spaulding also remembered an incident that contradicted Kennedy's self-criticism of what he considered a deficiency in the ability to speak spontaneously: "When Mr. Bunting announced his plan to resign as president, Ed made the most eloquent and endearing tribute I have ever heard. And it was entirely off the cuff. It was an extraordinary expression of gratitude to a deserving man. I have never forgotten it." Bunting, who believed that no person should remain in a college presidency for more than ten years, left Hampden-Sydney to become headmaster of Lawrenceville School in New Jersey.

An honorary member of the Hiram Board of Trustees since reaching the maximum age for regular membership in 1974, Kennedy underwrote the replacement of worn and obsolete equipment in a language laboratory he and Ruth had funded in the sixties. The new contribution provided for thirty-five stations containing up-dated audio-tape features for instruction and study, and a reserve account for future steps to match the accelerating pace of technology.

Still a member of the Juniata board, he contributed time and money regularly to that school. He provided financial support to Ohio Northern University and Findlay College, and made contributions to Cottey College in Ruth's memory. He continued to support the Maxwell Museum at the University of New Mexico and to attend Ruth Kennedy Memorial Lectures there. Support of the churro sheep development program was a continuing commitment to Utah Southern University.

The extent of this progressive involvement culminated in Kennedy's selection by the Council for Advancement and Support of Education as 1985 Volunteer of the Year. CASE described the honor as focusing "primarily on achievement for the past five years." Kennedy's nomination for the national award had been the brainchild of Jack G. Ellis, Ohio University vice president for development. Having served as executive director of the Ohio University Foundation since 1973, including the one year since becoming a vice president, Ellis had first-hand knowledge of Kennedy's behind-the-scenes educational endeavors, as well as those that received media attention. Documenting these, he had taken the initiative of obtaining endorsements from the other eight institutions and structuring the successful proposal.

In an introduction to the nomination, Ohio University President Ping noted, "Still steadfast in his loyal enthusiasm as he approaches his eighty-first birthday, Ed Kennedy remains active in the affairs of the university. He has been a valued friend and counselor of five presidents of the university. Such involvement at a single institution is exemplary. Such involvement at nine institutions is extraordinary. Few individuals contribute so much of themselves—time, talent, possessions. Few individuals have so broad and varied an impact on educational institutions."

Three days after the awards program in Washington, Kennedy was back at work in his New York City office, but he was troubled by what had been happening to the company he had served for four decades.

Chapter 15   Riding the Cycles

We are only as good as the times we are in.
—Michael David-Weill
Lazard Freres

With $250 million in capital, and profits exceeding $15 million a month over the previous year, Lehman Brothers in the spring of 1983 had rebounded to an earnings level unmatched in its long history. Yet conflicts within the board of directors were beginning to surface. They became intense in mid-May, when Chairman Peterson made an unusual move, one that Kennedy opposed: he named Lewis Glucksman co-chief executive officer.

Within weeks a brusque power struggle confirmed suspicions that Glucksman would use that position as a launching pad to oust the man who put him there. Following futile attempts to fashion a gradual transition of authority, with George Ball serving as an intermediary, Peterson announced his resignation on July 25, leaving Glucksman alone at the top of Lehman Brothers Kuhn Loeb.

Edwin Kennedy, on the eve of retirement, was in a minority group that feared for the life of the firm. Most managing directors, including a vast majority of the board, believed that Glucksman's abrasiveness was offset by his proven expertise, and remained as optimistic as a trader in a bull market. On October 1, 1983, the first day of the new fiscal year, Edwin Kennedy officially retired from Lehman Brothers Kuhn Loeb. As a managing director emeritus, he continued to have an office, and used it frequently, although he was privately disturbed by what was happening at 55 Water Street.

Peter Peterson remained chairman to assist with the changing of the guard until the end of the year. Then he left to form a venture capital firm with a friend, Eli Jacobs. After little more than a year, Peterson and another former Lehman partner, Stephen Schwarzman, founded what soon became a thriving Park Avenue investment banking and venture capital partnership, The Blackstone Group.

No one questioned Lew Glucksman's dedication to the job. His normal work day began before six a.m., and his competitive spirit permeated the company. As a trader, however, he remained combative with the investment bankers, a sentiment reflected in shuffled positions, promotions, and bonuses. Feeling the squeeze, discouraged managing directors (still known as partners in Wall Street parlance) fled to other firms, just as trading profits began to fall in a shrinking market. Many of those who remained became deeply concerned about the personal capital they had invested in the company.

Worries about capital, in fact, became the major topics at directors' meetings in the early months of 1984, and word soon circulated along Wall Street that Lehman would either have to go public or find a friendly buyer. Some reports intimated that top Lehman officers were no longer able to manage the firm. Such news soon reached the attention of Shearson/American Express, which was interested in fitting another blue-chip company into its financial package. Lehman Brothers offered strength in banking and securities trading, areas where Shearson, principally a brokerage firm, had admitted weaknesses. American Express, a diversified business superpower, had purchased Shearson Loeb Rhoades in 1981 for conversion to an investment banking subsidiary of the parent company.

With ledgers revealing a precipitous slide in profits from the previous year, Glucksman and the Lehman Brothers board decided to investigate the possibility of a merger. Negotiations subsequently began on April 3, 1984, and a month later, Lehman Brothers became the eighteenth firm to merge into the giant Shearson/American Express conglomerate. Nine months after changing leadership and 134 years after its founding, Lehman Brothers relinquished its position as an independent investment banking house. "That was the end of Lehman Brothers as I had known it," said a disheartened Edwin Kennedy, "but I will always remember the many years that we were among the leaders of our industry."

Lehman managing directors (partners) received $325 million of the $360 million purchase price. Fifty-seven of the seventy-two remaining at the time of sale were asked to stay, and to certify that if they should leave, they would not join a competing firm within a ninety-mile radius for at least three years. Peter A. Cohen, who had headed Shearson/American Express for the past two years, continued as chairman and chief executive officer of the expanded organization.

The subsidiary's name was changed to Shearson Lehman/American Express immediately following the merger. This, however, soon was revised to Shearson/Lehman Brothers. "The idea was to capture the mystique of the Lehman Brothers tradition in banking, but the firm had neither the people nor the method of operation to do it," Kennedy noted candidly, with no indication of resentment. "It is remotely possible that such a standing in the financial community can be restored many years from now, but the most critical objective after the merger became keeping Shearson/Lehman from fading out of existence."

The balance of Edwin Kennedy's business interests tilted toward personal investments in support of his philanthropies and the long-range welfare of his family. He maintained regular contact with several former associates, however, and never missed a meeting of the Kerr-McGee board of directors. "Ed's knowledge of the energy and minerals businesses was extremely valuable at a time of transition for our company," observed Frank A. McPherson, who had succeeded Dean McGee as chairman and chief executive officer in April 1983. The transition McPherson referred to was not the change in leadership, but the resharpening of Kerr-McGee's focus, which had broadened during the preceding twenty-five years. The change in strategy was prompted by a slowing economy in which the business environment was becoming increasingly unforgiving for a company with a widely diversified portfolio of assets.

Like others in the fickle energy industry, Kerr-McGee sought a more stable position by concentrating on strengths in its three major segments—oil exploration/production, chemicals, and coal—while divesting what had become negative elements from the expanded asset base that served well during a period of worldwide expansion, but perhaps had been boosted artificially by periodic spurts of inflation. What had been a gentle curve of the business cycle—reliable for long-term planning—now was a bouncing wave of highs and lows. "I spent many hours talking with Ed on the telephone, primarily about refining and marketing, two activities that probably are the most unpredictable parts of the business, but also about establishing good exploration and production operations in the North Sea," McPherson said. "Ed still was among the most knowledgeable persons on the financial aspects of those things."

America's energy programs indeed stimulated Kennedy's thinking nearly as much as in the days when he was in the thick of the action, and if asked, he did not gild opinions of past mistakes that he believed should earn more respect as barometers of the future. Neither did his conservatism offer political asylum to those he held responsible for the nation's energy policies. "Jimmy Carter tried to do something about an intelligent policy that would significantly help develop alternative sources of fuel," he maintained, "but Congress wasn't ready for it." Addressing the subject of shale oil, with which he was intimately familiar, he regretted that legislators in the seventies made decisions based on assumptions of oil being abundant and gasoline forever cheap. "No one paid attention to well-documented forecasts that the time would come in which we would impinge on our natural reserve of oil," he said. "The American people get the impression that what's here today remains forever, so the only thoughtful response we see is when a crisis becomes headline news. Then when oil seems abundant again, the government and the people forget it once more."

That cycle happened again in the eighties, he observed with obvious regret: "Consequently, I consider the Reagan administration's lack of interest in a long-range energy policy to be a catastrophe." Eventually, he insisted, the United States will have to develop alternate sources of energy, "which can't come about overnight, so it seems quite obvious that these programs need encouragement ahead of time, and we just aren't providing it now."

Predicting that OPEC nations would have 75 percent of the world's oil in 1995, Kennedy asked, "How do you conduct foreign affairs where that much of the world's oil is owned, produced, and controlled by people who hate you?" He feigned agreement with protestors and some political candidates who insisted that conservation can make the nation nearly self-sufficient in oil, but added the disclaimer, "if we are willing to drive small cars and pay four or five dollars a gallon for gasoline." Because Kennedy foresaw no hope for such an alternative, he advocated a government policy of encouraging the search for such synthetics as a solvent extraction of bituman from tar sands and eventually oil shale, as well as research on solar energy, clean coal conversion, and various exotic methods that he envisioned as becoming auxiliary, rather than major sources.

"We must try these ideas and see which work best," he said assertively. "Then the American genius will bring the cost down, and we can tell Arab nations we won't pay their asking prices for oil; we can use our own." He expected nuclear power to regain sufficient public acceptance for further expansion, "but apparently not in the near future."

Those observations echoed the contentions he alone had expressed along Wall Street in the sixties with an intensity that in some quarters had earned him the nickname "Oil Shale Kennedy."

Shearson Lehman remained at its Water Street quarters for two years after the 1984 merger, then joined its parent company

Brothers and sisters at an eighties reunion: Gladys (left), Helen, Edwin, Robert, and Richard.

Christa's wedding day, December 19, 1964.

Skiing on the Calabogie.

One of several world record catches by son, Eddie.

Relaxing in Panama.

With Charles Ping and John Baker in 1986.

Collector Kennedy at Ohio University showing, June 1992.

Hiram's Kennedy Center.

The Kennedy home in New Vernon.

Hiram students ready to walk the Memorial Trail, 1991.

Salmon fishing in Alaska.

Surrounded by granddaughter Susanne (second from left) and high school friends at eightieth birthday party.

Ruth and grandson Danny at New Vernon.

Granddaughter Patty Kennedy.

Son Eddie, at home in Santa Fe, 1992.

in the American Express Tower of the World Financial Center. The firm provided Kennedy a "retirement office" on the 101st floor of the adjacent World Trade Center, from which he could look out over Lower Manhattan and the Hudson River. Peering down on the striking modern complex of waterfront buildings and terraces comprising the World Financial Center drew forth memories of the time it had been the site of a wharf where he arrived for many years by ferry from Hoboken on the second leg of his daily commute—the first being a train from Madison, near his home in New Vernon.

"Going to the office about twice a week was important to me," he said. "The atmosphere was strange to me, because, realistically, no one really cares whether or not a retired partner is there, but it was helpful to use the Lehman library and to decelerate, rather than just cut off my business affairs, even if nearly all were personal and carried out by telephone, which I could have done at home." He did, however, continue to represent the firm in dealings with Kerr-McGee, where he remained a member of the board until May 8, 1990, eight months after Dean McGee died.

If Kennedy felt unnoticed at his new office, he certainly was not forgotten. When a team of entrepreneurs contemplated launching an expensive tertiary oil recovery project in late 1984, they asked Kennedy to attend their first organizational meeting as an adviser. There he met a young Kidder Peabody investment banker, Griffith R. Morris, who was invited to take over the financing. Seeing that Kennedy would have great influence with the group, and considering him "the only really knowledgeable person in what otherwise was a collection of young high-rollers," Morris decided to "get a read on the man, as we often did in that business," by contacting several Shearson-Lehman bankers who had known Kennedy during the past fifteen or twenty years. He was greatly impressed with their reports:

> In one conference call, two of these men provided what proved to be a consensus among all with whom I spoke. In essence, they

Riding the Cycles

told me, "Griff, whatever word you ascribe to gentlemen of the old school, to integrity, to financial knowledge, skill, background, experience, and success in our business, Ed Kennedy is the best example either of us has ever known. There are few people on Wall Street even close to his standard. We don't care what kind of project you are talking about, if you choose to involve yourself, it will not be to your detriment. Kennedy will never let anyone with whom he is associated make a professional, personal, intellectual, legal, moral, or financial compromise." Well, I had never heard endorsements like that in our industry. But in time, I discovered they all were true.

At one of the meetings, after Kennedy had condensed a lengthy conversation into a succinct statement, as was his custom, a young attorney stared at him and asked, "Tell me, Mr. Kennedy, just how old are you?" Morris recalled that everyone except Kennedy appeared embarrassed by such a question that had nothing to do with the subject at hand, but Kennedy's reply relieved the tension immediately. "Let me answer that with a quote from Mr. Bob Hope," said Kennedy. "When I drop something on the floor, or when I bend over to tie my shoelaces, I try to think of other things I should do while I'm down there."

When Kidder Peabody was purchased by General Electric a year later, Morris resigned to form his own financial and management consulting firm, focusing on utilities and other energy-related industries. Kennedy continued as a friend, confidant, and informal adviser, as well as a partner on some ventures. When one project soured and Morris confided his discouragement, his mentor replied, "Griff, if I made a list of all the things I tried that did not work, it would be miles long. And when I make a list of things I did right, it is very short. But the results of the latter have been big enough to overcome those on the long list. That is the way you do it."

Morris followed that formula to carve a successful career as the friendship with Kennedy deepened. "I never even think of an age difference," Morris once observed, "I just know he is the most trusted friend a person can have. You would buy a used car from him. If he says it is raining, you don't bother to look out the window."

Spectacular gains in all phases of its business made Shearson Lehman the envy of Wall Street during 1986 and most of 1987. Its record earnings, indeed, proved a boon to the overall profits of American Express, and optimism approached euphoria in the board room. Having transformed operations from domestic retail brokerage into full-service global banking with the acquisition of Lehman Brothers, the company had sold its stock publicly and added Japan's largest insurance firm, Nippon Life, as a 13-percent equity investor that spring, reducing American Express interest in the subsidiary to 61 percent. Now it aspired to challenge the undisputed brokerage leadership of Merrill Lynch, Pierce, Fenner & Smith. Peter Cohen believed that opportunity appeared when E. F. Hutton & Company, crippled from recent scandals, decided in late 1987 to seek a buyer.

The securities industry had experienced a paralyzing market crash on October 19, but Cohen viewed that as a boost to his bargaining position, rather than a signal to retrench. On December 2, after less than two weeks of negotiations, Shearson Lehman bought the eighty-three-year-old Hutton firm for $960 million, representing $29.25 a share—only slightly more than half of the asking price.

Hutton had pleaded guilty to a check-overdrafting scheme in 1985 and had been accused by federal prosecutors of money-laundering in 1987. The New York Stock Exchange was moving to censure two former senior officers. A disillusioned Edwin Kennedy, happy to be an outside observer with only the physical location of his complimentary office still connecting him to the successor firm of his former employer, had his own view of the purchase: "Buying Hutton was a disaster."

Euromoney magazine, however, named Peter Cohen 1987 Banker of the Year, and *Institutional Investor* published a glowing cover story about what had taken place. But problems hounding Shearson Lehman Hutton would soon draw different comments from the press. *Newsweek* in December 1989 referred to

"The slide of Shearson Lehman," reporting, "Weak earnings and a string of embarrassing and costly management fiascos have taken a hefty toll." One of the most publicized examples was representing RJR Nabisco CEO F. Ross Johnson, an American Express director, in a losing bid to take that company private in 1988. Outmaneuvered by leveraged buyout specialist Kohlberg Kravis Roberts & Company, Shearson lost well over $200 million in fees and a great deal of prestige as an adviser for takeovers in what proved to be the largest LBO up to that time.

Blamed for a variety of blunders and undue extravagance—Shearson had bought three Gulfstream jets and built a $25-million conference center at a Colorado ski resort, for example—Peter Cohen was fired by American Express CEO James D. Robinson on January 29, 1990. Heading the list of accusations was the lamentable purchase of E. F. Hutton, although Cohen had defenders who insisted he was a scapegoat. Six months later, the subsidiary was divided into two divisions, Lehman Brothers for investment banking and capital markets, and Shearson Lehman Brothers for brokerage and asset management, thereby erasing the reference to Hutton. Howard L. Clark Jr., former American Express chief financial officer, was selected to replace Cohen as CEO.

In March 1990, American Express bought all Shearson Lehman public stock except a relatively small number of preferred shares owned by Nippon Life Insurance Company, in an effort to overcome a 77-percent drop in earnings over the preceding three years. It also provided a direct infusion of cash and financed an extensive reorganization plan that included laying off 6 percent of its 35,000 employees. The combined price tag for these revitalizing efforts was reported to be more than $2 billion. Lehman Corporation, the sixty-one-year-old internal investment company that had weathered depressions and stock-market crashes, was sold to Salomon Brothers, whose long-standing reputation as a powerful Wall Street firm soon was marred by billion-dollar United States bond trading violations.

Shearson Lehman, of course, was not alone in the series of incidents striking fear and anger into professional and lay investors through what had become known as the excesses of the eighties. The firm's problems were, in fact, eclipsed by a core of white collar felons whose disquieting violations of the law echoed through the Wall Street canyon.

The first discordant note had been trumpeted from the investment house of Drexel Burnham Lambert, where a young deal-making managing director named Dennis Levine was trading on and selling insider information. Arrested in 1986 for breaking regulations of the Securities and Exchange Commission, Levine quickly led federal investigators to 49-year-old Ivan Boesky, known as the "arbitrage king of Wall Street," triggering what proved to be the biggest insider trading scam in history.

For years, Boesky had convinced investors that he possessed a remarkable prescience regarding possible takeovers. Buying stocks through a heavily financed partnership before such mergers were announced had made the duplicitous manipulator one of the wealthiest men in the world. When he faced irrefutable evidence that his genius was in truth linked to advance knowledge, Boesky sought leniency in his virtually assured prosecution by informing on other insider rings. The resulting chain reaction careened across the country, striking a host of financial charlatans, the most notorious of whom was Drexel Burnham's Michael Milken.

At the age of thirty-nine, Milken already had acquired an estimated $1.3 billion net worth as a junk-bond specialist who accounted for a quarter of Drexel's considerable revenues. Although he denied charges of selling insider information to Boesky and others, even after being found guilty of securities fraud and sentenced to a ten-year prison term in 1990, Milken was ousted from the firm as part of a deal with the government, in which Drexel pleaded guilty to six counts of mail and securities fraud.

In setting an early pace for the creation of a junk-bond market to finance hostile leveraged buyouts, Milken had placed the bonds with cooperating owners of savings and loan or insurance companies. This, in effect, provided what one Wall

Street analyst labeled "a self-sufficient LBO takeover machine," tying Milken and others to a related problem smoldering beneath the surface of public disclosure.

Fueled by another deregulation binge started in the early eighties, new savings and loan companies had been sprouting at a mind-boggling rate. Junk bonds made it possible to organize a thrift institution in a period of three months by borrowing as much as 80 percent of the necessary capital from eager banks, which also benefited from deregulation. No longer saddled with low-interest, fixed-rate loans, financial organizations paid high dividends to eager depositors and charged uncomplaining borrowers slightly higher rates of interest. Everyone was protected by a government shield guaranteeing individual deposits up to $100,000. It was not unusual for an S&L to appreciate 50 percent in one year, making it profitable to operate for a short time, then sell out to a larger firm. Investors in one Florida thrift made a large profit by selling out before their company opened its doors for business.

Many organizing groups had little or no experience in banking. But when thrifts became troubled, the Federal Savings and Loan Insurance Corporation (FSLIC) arranged mergers with healthier competitors. To help facilitate this band-aid repair, the FSLIC subsidized takeover companies by reimbursing them for ongoing losses from the acquired thrifts.

Deregulation brought a similar revolution in operations of banks, insurance companies, and securities firms, all of whom were invading each others' financial territories, which previously had been protected by legislation. Even department stores and manufacturing companies were joining what *U. S. News & World Report* labeled a "financial free-for-all" and William Isaac, chairman of the Federal Deposit Insurance Corporation, described as "a prescription for disaster." Explanations of how America reached such a point of financial decadence were numerous and varied: greed, crumbling of regulations that had directed banking since the Great Depression, emergence of young manipulators who learned questionable uses of financial instruments in business schools, and many others.

Many financial groups, including those formed by independent promoters and investment banking houses, while generally operating within the law, began using their own capital or finding other investors to underwrite hostile leveraged acquisitions. Overwhelmed by the fast profits that could be made, they abandoned old philosophies of helping client companies determine methods of expanding or in other ways increasing equity, to a new "transaction" orientation.

The typical transactor convinced a company that it should make a specific acquisition through a leveraged buyout. Preplanned procedures and cost figures were elucidated flamboyantly to chief executive officers, along with the strategic reason to buy. It was further explained that the transaction could be accomplished whether or not directors of a target company chose to be acquired. Backed by the acquiring company's balance sheet and the investment banker's ability to raise money, it was possible to circumvent the other board and deal directly with stockholders. With the plan approved, the transactor then confronted officers of the target company with what came to be known on the Street as a "bear-hug" proposal: Advantages of selling out were outlined politely, but if rebuffed, the transactor pronounced that the deal would be made, whether it was friendly or hostile. In the latter instance, enough stock would be purchased directly from shareholders to take over the company.

Many companies succumbed. Others quickly initiated fundraising efforts, through other investment banking houses, to fend off the attack. Thus, investment bankers were involved on both sides—the offense and the defense. In both instances, they derived large fees from the transactions. Relatively low values, in terms of the stock market, added greatly to the enticement for such practices, and all Wall Street investment houses became involved in one way or another.

Not all takeovers were selfishly motivated. Some companies honestly believed the LBO system was necessary for their growth, and also would benefit the acquired firms. A few hostile transactions even became friendly by the time they were concluded. But the prevailing impetus came from the prospect of profitable transactions.

Not surprisingly, this sophistry was far-removed from the kind of relationship Edwin Kennedy had maintained with client companies during his entire career. One approach was that of the salesman with a preconceived point of view, and the other an adviser with a long-term commitment to his client-company's welfare—a stranger wanting to knock off a fee versus a trusted friend helping with a firm's corporate finances. "The motivation in my day was an acquisition for an operating use, not a financial one where people outside the companies could make a lot of money," Kennedy explained.

Kennedy never was openly critical of the new wave in investment banking. He described methods of the eighties only as being "different." Nevertheless, he was distressed to see Phillips Petroleum, Union Oil, and others become saddled with heavy interest payments on debts accrued in fighting off hostile takeovers. It bothered him to read *Financial News* reports of companies writing off hundreds of millions of dollars and going into bankruptcy because benefits expected from highly leveraged acquisitions failed to materialize. He suffered to see Bloomingdale's try unsuccessfully to protect its operations from a hostile takeover by real estate-oriented Campeau Corporation of Canada, which subsequently put the New York-based department store dynasty into bankruptcy. "Bloomingdale's was one of the great stores of the world," he murmured almost musingly. "It was alive. It is in Chapter Eleven. Campeau borrowed so much money to take it over that he couldn't carry it." By contrast, he remembered such acquisitions as the one he negotiated in the sixties between Kerr-McGee and American Potash, with no loss of employment and increased revenues for both groups.

Illegal insider trading, which had reached a zenith just prior to Boesky's confession in 1986 (and subsequent three-year prison sentence), was another corruption that Kennedy considered most damaging to America and the reputation of investment banking. He recalled having rejected as immoral many opportunities to purchase stock of oil companies ahead of announcements that they were going to sell out, even though it would have been legal to do so at that time. "That is the way people in our business operated then," he said. "I'm not certain what changed. It's like crime on the streets. There is no shortage of theories on what happened, but it is difficult to find cures." Walter Lubanko, who had left Lehman Brothers in 1978 to become an independent investment adviser, was equally perplexed. "Somehow, Wall Street firms underwent such a metamorphosis that you can't even compare what they are now with what they were in the past," he said. "It's a completely different ball game."

Colleagues considered Kennedy a builder, attuned to increasing productivity, sometimes to a fault from the viewpoint of personal gain. He never sold a stock short, even though he frequently recognized good opportunities to increase his income by doing so, because he did not enjoy gearing investments to negative cycles of the economy. Such an outlook simply was not in keeping with his optimistic temperament. "If Ed had still been full-time on the Street during the last half of the eighties, he would not have been caught up in what was going on," observed George Heyman. "He would have done his own thing, and he would not have been affected by what others did." John Baker described his friend as "a builder of solid companies, not a speculator, manipulator, or destroyer, nor simply a shuffler of corporate securities." Kennedy never compromised that reputation, Baker said, during a career in which he "probably had as many successful mergers to his credit as any investment banker in New York."

Kennedy considered the "purchase of sympathetic legislation through campaign fund contributions" by Charles Keating, Jr., a real estate and banking tycoon, "a textbook example of businessmen and elected officials touching bottom." Keating, who had sold uninsured corporate bonds to investors who thought they were purchasing FSLIC-backed certificates of deposit, was convicted of fraud in 1991 and subsequently sentenced to ten years in prison. Despite such disturbing examples, Kennedy's evaluation of what happened in the eighties was less a grumble than a hope that lessons had been learned. "The most insidious sin is in not recognizing that the world is constantly changing, and therefore failing to seek what is needed for improvement," he said. "We are working at it. Events compel us to. More people recognize that if we don't restore our productivity and reduce the greed factor, we will die. Conducting business is going to become increasingly global, but we certainly have the resources and ability to meet the competition, and we are beginning to wipe out of the system such shortcomings as the pursuit of greed in a manner unjustified by operations."

He took no issue with leveraged equity participation, as long as it was conducted honestly for the growth of productivity, and he was pleased to note that several leaders he still knew at Lehman Brothers, acknowledging the unacceptability of hostile takeovers as procedures for improving business, were putting together imaginative new financial projects. One of these creative thinkers was Jeffrey Hughes, by then head of Lehman Brothers' merchant banking business, who recalled many of Kennedy's attributes as a colleague: his patience ("He always took the time to answer questions in great detail"), his energy ("You could not walk at a leisurely pace with Ed"), and his unstinting willingness to help colleagues and clients alike. "Probably my strongest recollection, however," Hughes said, "is that Ed always looks to the future with uncompromising optimism."

No longer having what he referred to as "regular access to Wall Street investment people and their ideas," Kennedy generated his flow of information alone. On the mailing list of just under two hundred corporations, he examined quarterly and annual reports voraciously, applying a half century of experience to reading between the lines. By following progress through the years, he was able to base decisions on long-range studies, as he had done in business. This required self-discipline, he said, "because when you invest for others, you remain more dispassionate and more careful, and therefore more effective than when you are investing for yourself."

Kennedy prescribed such studied knowledge of a company as essential to recognizing when its stock value is "about to bottom out." When bank failures stunned Wall Street at the beginning of the nineties, driving down stock prices within the entire banking community, he analyzed every element of the business, ruled out the giant money-center firms, and carefully selected three regional leaders he considered certain to rebound vigorously. Then he made purchases near what he anticipated to be the bottom of the downward swing. "Every case is different," he said, remembering the days of directing liquidations during the Great Depression, "so you have to look at individual statements, analyze the long-term performance of management, and maybe even telephone key persons within the organization, most of whom are willing to answer intelligent questions." Six months after he bought the stocks, all three banks recorded record highs.

Like most financial specialists, Kennedy was besieged by friends and acquaintances seeking market tips. Based on his observation that "the typical American wants a single security as safe as a government bond that pays ten percent interest and doubles in one year and one day," and on experience that "if you give wrong advice, you are in trouble," he long ago had devised a standard reply: "What do you want to do, invest, speculate, or gamble?" He insisted that the routine worked. "Within five minutes, I have them so confused they can't wait to drop the subject," he said.

"The real challenge for an investor is to choose risks that fit personal needs, both financially and psychologically," he advised. "Tragedies happen when there is a mismatch. It takes patience. I have a belief that you can expect only a few major buying opportunities in a lifetime, and it takes long-range study to recognize them, along with short-term liquid investments to be ready for them."

Riding the Cycles

Kennedy himself never could resist the clarion call of exciting new investment challenges, even though he momentarily thought it would be possible to reshape his life style into a more leisurely, semi-retirement mode:

> After I retired, I felt free to indulge in working outside the house, something I liked to do many years earlier at Short Hills, before the increasing responsibility of business left me without time to do such things. So I started clearing out the jungle between the driveway and the barn. I took out roots, dug up some things and cut down others, and when I met one objective, I set another one. Christine got after me, but I kept on until I had cleared four acres.

Suggestions that this interest in working the soil had a psychological affinity to childhood memories produced a convincing laugh of denial. Cherished close ties with his family could in no way be identified with farming. He rejected also the oft purported correlation between high-pressure careers and a get-away-from-it-all desire to find tranquility in the land. Both ideas fit the category of "artificial reasoning," which he considered absurd and useless. The most enlightened observation, if one was needed, probably came from Kennedy's sister Gladys, who surmised, "If Edwin thought about removing a vine, he naturally would end up clearing several acres."

Chapter 16 **Renewed Motivations**

> *Ed Kennedy has turned away from opportunities for enormous profit because he mistrusted the people involved; and he has taken what others might consider lunatic long-shots, and come out very well indeed, because he had confidence in the people involved.*
> —*Morton M. Winston*
> *Corporate CEO*
> *1991*

"Old age is difficult," Edwin Kennedy warned a friend in 1991, "because you have no experience on how to handle it." But at age 87, Kennedy's activities prompted William Morris, who had left Shearson Lehman and become CEO of J. & W. Seligman & Company, to note, "I'm not sure Ed has started to wind down yet."

Morris was referring to both business and educational ventures, any of which would have justified the observation. Perhaps the most remarkable common denominator of all these undertakings was Kennedy's long-range view of target dates for fruition. His investment projects offered examples. "When I reached the age of eighty, I told my associates quite honestly that I didn't want to get into any more speculative entrepreneurial ventures," Kennedy explained almost defensively, emphasizing the word *honestly* as though friends familiar with the tolerance level of his restlessness would question the truth of his intentions. "Well, that belief lasted for a few years, but then I couldn't stand it any longer, and when an opportunity arose, I didn't even try to resist temptation."

The initial enticement came from an unexpected source, Morton Winston, whom Kennedy held in high regard despite the differences of opinions that surfaced when both were associated with Tosco. Having returned briefly to the practice of law after resigning as Tosco CEO, Winston organized in late 1985 a small company, NoRad (No Radiation) Corporation, to develop a product that would alleviate sources of both physical discomfort and apparent danger in video display terminals. Working with Winston as co-founder and engineering consultant was a highly respected English inventor, Donald Firth, the former head of Tosco technology development and applications. Firth had joined Tosco following early retirement from a distinguished career as founder and director of the National Engineering Laboratory of Great Britain and deputy chief scientist of the Department of Industry, also in the United Kingdom. Edwin Kennedy and Morton Winston both considered one of Firth's many awards, "British Genius," an apt description of his capabilities.

Winston and Firth began production of their NoRad shield in a room drollishly dubbed "the ODG manufacturing plant," using an acronym of its location—over Donald's garage—in Santa Monica, California. Designed to fit easily over the face of a personal computer, their specially treated micromesh shield, stretched taut and chemically bonded to a rigid frame, prevented glare and reflection, enhanced the optical image, and most importantly, protected the operator from electric and magnetic radiation emanating from the screen. To obtain marketing estimates and direct a sales effort, the co-founders brought in Michael L. Hiles, a former partner in a communications engineering firm specializing in the design and installation of internal communications products for Fortune 500 clients.

"When we were certain we had a market and could expand into widespread sales, I went to see the best man I knew who could set up the necessary financing—Ed Kennedy," Winston said later. Kennedy reacted optimistically, happy for a logical reason to abandon his earlier resolve concerning retirement. "The product was more than just a hope on paper," he explained. "They were making and selling the screens. I was well aware of Donald Firth's creativity, and Mort Winston had one of the best minds I had ever encountered. Moreover, I had decided by then that if a man still has decent health, he shouldn't let age interfere with getting involved in projects that appeal to him."

After attempting unsuccessfully to interest former Lehman associates to join in the new venture, Kennedy found a receptive respondent in Charles Maxwell, who had become vice chairman of C. J. Lawrence Incorporated. Maintaining low profiles, the two longtime friends personally funded NoRad's entry into the international marketplace near the end of the eighties. And although he declined Winston's invitation to join the board, Kennedy took part in some of the decision making, as did Maxwell; still he credited NoRad officers with the success that followed. "In August of 1989, I was told to watch the NBC Sunday Today program, and there was Mort with a six-minute segment devoted to the NoRad Shield," Kennedy said with an expression of awe. "I never understood exactly how he managed to obtain such a long stint on a program seen by millions of viewers, but that actually started us off in great style."

Further impetus came from widespread media coverage relating computer terminals to an assortment of potential health problems. A December 1989 story in the New York, London, Paris, and Frankfort editions of *Financial Times* typified this concern:

> One of the most hotly debated issues about the safety of computers is whether the non-ionising electromagnetic radiation that all types of computer terminals emit constitutes a health risk. Until recently, most scientists believed that these types of very-low frequency (VLF) and extremely low-frequency (ELF) radiations and the electric and magnetic fields that they create had no biological effects. Now they are not so sure.

When an independent laboratory tested how well five commercially available products met United States military specifications, researchers found that the NoRad shield was the most effective protection against computer radiation. Consequently, NoRad increased its models to fit various shapes and sizes of screens, and introduced a custom-made shield for the popular Macintosh Classic in January 1991. By then, Michael Hiles had become president and CEO of NoRad, with Winston serving as chairman of the board, albeit no longer associated with day-to-day operations.

The administrative change paralleled the emergence of another company that required both the full attention of Winston and Firth and substantial financial backing from Maxwell and Kennedy. All four men were convinced that this new effort could lead to a revolutionary advancement in materials handling. Consequently, development and testing had been guarded from premature public disclosure until Firth obtained a patent in January 1991.

Since the early eighties, when Tosco was building an oil shale processing plant, Winston had been intrigued with a machine Firth designed to improve existing methods of materials handling. A full-scale demonstration model worked successfully, so Tosco had it patented, but when the plant construction project was scuttled, the company shelved, then forgot the machine. Years later, Winston revived the concept and negotiated a royalty agreement for further development and possible sales. Backed by that arrangement and development funds from Peabody Coal Company, Winston and Firth launched the Solids Transport and Metering Corporation, soon known as Stamet. Their goal was to introduce a new materials-handling technology that could be applied to a wide range of granular solids.

While suffering several failures with coal, Firth was able to solve each successive problem until the machine worked to everyone's satisfaction. At precisely that moment, however, Peabody and its parent company, Newmont Mining, became entangled in a maze of corporate raiding, leading to purchase by the Hanson Trust Company. Although Peabody considered moving forward with the Stamet project, internal troubles prevented it from doing so. With his instincts providing advance warning, however, Winston already had recruited Maxwell, Kennedy, and a Norwegian investment group to purchase sufficient stock interests to continue the quest. "We realized that if this product could be made to work as we thought it could, and the evidence showed that it would, Stamet could be on the threshold of an industrial breakthrough of great proportions," said an enthusiastic Edwin Kennedy, who again became a company adviser, as well as a major investor.

When refinements were completed, the Firth Solids Pump became U.S. Patent 4,988,239. Kennedy noted that the Patent Office, in its investigation of possible conflicts with existing products, varified the pump's uniqueness "more rapidly than any other with which I had been familiar." Applied to materials as diverse as coal, limestone, lima beans, and flour, the pump was capable of replacing up to three separate materials-handling machines or systems with one efficient, low-cost, easily controlled device. In a single-step continuous operation, particulate solids could be simultaneously moved and accurately measured, delivering a few pounds or hundreds of tons per hour. With only one moving part, the pump was free of the vanes, screws, gears, and other wear-prone components limiting the life and efficiency of existing systems, and it eliminated the need for separate scales or volume measurement equipment.

Winston remembered an example of what he termed "The Ed Kennedy stroke" when Firth received the patent:

> Ed said he always read the regular *New York Times* Saturday section on interesting new patents, and suggested that I should get that newspaper to include our pump. Well, I didn't think getting *Times* coverage would be either possible or important, but I gave it my best effort, just because he wanted it. To my surprise, the paper carried a seven-paragraph story about it on the second of February [1991]. Then I discovered that the head of research for the food machinery division of FMC also read the *Times* on Saturday. He saw the story, got a copy of the patent, assessed it, and invited me to visit him. Soon afterward, we had chances to talk with two other FMC divisions as well.

Executive headquarters for both Stamet and NoRad remained in Santa Monica, but Donald Firth returned to Dartmouth, England, where he continued research and development at a private laboratory. By the spring of 1992, the materials-handling equipment was being installed in Great Britain, the United States, and South Africa.

Overcoming the odds against starting two manufacturing companies almost concurrently in the late 1980s and early 1990s and having both survive was rare indeed. "Ed Kennedy's confidence in me was a major factor," Winston asserted unhesitatingly. "In fact, if he had not believed in what we wanted to do, I probably would not have moved ahead. That is how much weight I place on his judgment, and many other persons feel the same way."

On June 29, 1991, Ohio University announced approval by its Board of Trustees to convert an imposing historic Athens building into an art museum housing collections "reflecting the American tradition." Primary among these would be the Southwest Native American textile and jewelry collections of Edwin and Ruth Kennedy. The decision climaxed a cooperative effort that had been foremost among Kennedy's philanthropic interests in recent years.

Having continued, and in several aspects intensified his zealous pursuit of Navajo art since the death of his wife, Kennedy had come to regard it as a means of helping focus interest on an important American culture. The best way to accomplish that goal, he reasoned, was to offer the collection as a centerpiece for research and study, as well as public display. He had rejected proposals from several art organizations because they did not meet that qualification.

Thinking initially that the collection should "return to the Southwest, from which it had come," Kennedy had gradually concluded that placement at an eastern site would better serve the national interest. "It had become clear to me that an appreciation of Southwestern Native Americans and their craftsmanship was spreading," he observed, "but it garnered less attention in its own back yard, where it understandably was somewhat commonplace." He reasoned that a significant number of valuable pieces could remain at the Maxwell Museum, but the largest segment of his collection should be placed where it could best help extend awareness of the Navajo culture. It was a decision Kennedy reached reluctantly, because of personal friendship with Gil Maxwell, as well as appreciation for the valued support he received from the University of New Mexico and its Maxwell Museum.

In contemplating possible eastern locations, Kennedy's thoughts came to rest on his alma mater. This possibility was enhanced when Ohio University Vice President for Development Jack Ellis suggested privately, "The oldest university in the Northwest Territory, established by the Ordinance of 1787 as a frontier school in what then was Indian territory, might be an appropriate repository for a collection of Native American art."

Ellis and Ohio University President Charles Ping were among the few persons who had seen the extremely valuable textiles and jewelry Kennedy had quietly assembled in a home vault. Although some had been removed for museum shows at Washington, D.C. and Montclair, New Jersey, the danger of theft had made it imperative that the home-base location not be widely disclosed.

"When Ed told me he would consider giving his collection to Ohio University, I was delighted," President Ping said. "My conscience had been cleared by his saying he was not going to place it in the Southwest, so I agreed to pursue the idea without hesitation." In addition to appreciating the intrinsic value of the Kennedy collection, the Ohio University president recognized its potential in helping gain state support he had been seeking to renovate a campus building, Haning Hall (the former Athens Post Office that had been converted to a computer center) as an art museum.

Ping immediately appointed an eleven-member advisory committee to work with the university architect in developing a mission statement for the Board of Trustees. The university hired Bell Exhibit Services of Louisville, Kentucky, headed by Rick and Sue Bell, to analyze the Kennedy collection and submit a comprehensive plan for exhibiting and storing it, and for integrating it into research and academic programs. The Bells, who had studied Navajo history and culture extensively for many years, and who had spent a great deal of time visiting weavers and dealers on the reservations, also were able to formulate detailed methods for preserving and utilizing the collection, and possible procedures for developing the museum into a national center for scholarship.

Meanwhile, Kennedy continued his regular trips to the Southwest, usually accompanied by Christa Cook, as he had done for years. He spent many hours assisting the university in making preparations to transport, store, and catalog the weavings and jewelry. In September 1989, just a few months after the project was initiated, a portion of the collection was put on display at the main gallery of Siegfred Hall, center for the College of Fine Arts. The showing coincided with the first meeting of a National Campaign Council, composed of alumni from across the country. Under the direction of Vice President Ellis, who continued also as executive director of the Ohio University Foundation, this group would become volunteer leaders in an upcoming "Third Century Campaign," whose goal of $100 million made it the largest fundraising effort in the university's history. Kennedy, an honorary co-chair of the campaign and still a member of the Foundation Board, attended the black-tie opening program with his granddaughter, Susanne Cook.

Two months later, John H. Gerber, director of collections and exhibitions, was asked by President Ping to arrange a repeat performance. Puzzled at the request coming so soon after the original show, Gerber became enlightened when he saw the president ushering several state legislators past the examples of chant weaves, silversmithing, turquoise, and coral inlay jewelry. Asked by one congressman to estimate how much of the collection was represented in the show, Gerber answered, "I have calculated that about one-eighteenth of it is here in the gallery."

Soon afterward, the Ohio General Assembly appropriated four million dollars of renovation funding toward establishment of an Ohio University art museum. "I am convinced that the Kennedy gift became the lever that enabled us to persuade the governor and a majority of legislators to support our museum idea," said President Ping. "As far as I know, it was the first time the state provided funding for such a building."

In October 1990, a public exhibit of selected items from the collection, featuring nine large weavings of the premier bead chant, opened at Siegfred Gallery, as part of a program formally kicking off the "Third Century Campaign." The following summer, John Gerber and Vice President for University Relations Martha A. Turnage, who, along with Presidential Assistant Alan H. Geiger assumed leading roles in overall planning for the museum, joined Kennedy and Christa Cook on a tour through the Southwest. Gerber quickly recognized the extent of the reputation Kennedy had gained as a collector through the years:

> I became aware that some of the dealers like Tobe Turpen had kept very high quality pieces in their back rooms, awaiting Ed's arrival. That basically is the reason his collection is unmatched anywhere in the world. Many of the things are direct results of his good relationships with dealers and traders. So when he arrives, they have these items ready for him to see. I call it "in the back room." Also, there is a network out there that amazingly lets all of these people know where Ed is and where his next stop will be. You think of the Southwest as being huge, but in this sense you find it a small community of people. Somehow, they all know Ed Kennedy is in the neighborhood. So Tobe Turpen, who deals with Hollywood stars and others with large amounts of money, still holds back top quality items for Ed. We went into Tobe's home in Gallup, and it was obvious their friendship goes back a long way. We also were welcomed into individual homes of the Navajo, Zuni, and Hopi people.

Kennedy always included a visit with Alberta Thomas on his Southwest itinerary. He considered Alberta, her sister Anna Mae Tanner, and their mother Despah Nez the three best weavers in the Navajo nation. At times he "grub staked" them with advance payments for complex, time-consuming projects. His affinity for Navajo culture stemmed partially from his concentration on ceremonial weavings, rather than those unrelated to specific purposes, but that kindred spirit could be traced also to a mutual love of the outdoors. "I think the Navajo culture is particularly interesting, because the basic element is a close relationship with our environment," he often told friends. "We could learn a lot from it."

Even Kennedy's attire reflected the extent of his absorbing interest in the people he often referred to as "our Southwestern predecessors." Whether at home or on business and pleasure trips, he wore ornamental rings, belt buckles, watch bands and bolo ties from his private assemblage. "When I began wearing silver and turquoise jewelry in the eighties, I was considered peculiar," he admitted, "but now everyone asks where these items can be obtained. Maybe people just indulge me now, but I like to think their curiosity helps spread the message of preserving an important culture."

After studying both the architect's preliminary work and the Bells' recommendations for displaying the collection, the university's Museum Advisory Committee recommended abandoning previous plans to renovate Haning Hall in favor of the hill-top administrative center of a former state mental health complex, which had become available through a chain of legislative events stretching through the previous nineteen years. For decades, the center had been applauded for a program of treatment that included helping mentally ill patients improve self-esteem through productive work in the gardens, fields, and massive dairy barn of its spacious farm. These activities also helped provide food and milk to offset some expenses of maintaining the facility. The institution had been forced to abandon this practice, however, when a federal court in 1973 ruled that patients in mental health facilities could no longer work without pay. The ensuing adjustment left in its wake an expanse of untended agricultural property, from which the City of Athens received thirteen acres for recreational purposes, a local mental health group six acres, and the Southeastern Ohio Cultural Arts Association thirty-five acres. The latter included the historic dairy barn, which the association converted into an imposing art center. After considering other recommendations, the Ohio General Assembly in May 1988 deeded several buildings and 670 acres of the institutional grounds to the university. Thirty of those acres, which contained the main administration building, actually were not physically transferred to the university until 1991, when the state decided to construct a new mental health facility near the city's O'Bleness Memorial Hospital. Of the total tract then under the university's jurisdiction, fifty-seven acres that seemed suitable for development became known as "The Ridges."

A July 2, 1991 editorial written by G. Kenner Bush, publisher of the *Athens Messenger* and a former member of the Ohio University Board of Trustees, analyzed the reasoning behind the museum committee recommendation and its adoption by the board:

> The administration building is the centerpiece for any development of The Ridges. This is the most attractive, architecturally important, and historic structure in the mental health center complex. It is an ideal home for the museum, originally planned for Haning Hall on West Union Street. Haning Hall was never a good site for the museum. It is too small, provides no parking, cannot be expanded, and is practically inaccessible to the general public.
>
> The center's administration building, by contrast, is almost a museum in itself, provides an unchallenged presence relating to both the university and the community, offers almost unlimited opportunities for future expansion, and is easily accessible to all.
>
> The museum of American art will set the stage for everything else that can happen on The Ridges in the years ahead.

Foremost among the weavings and jewelry assembled over a period of thirty-eight years were six complete sets of chant rugs; the only other sets in existence were two Kennedy previously had given to the Maxwell Museum. Interestingly, the rug that completed the last of the ceremonial chant series was created by Vera Begay, who had woven the Yei blanket that motivated Kennedy to begin his collection in 1954. Another of particular historical significance to Kennedy was the last tapestry started by Hosteen Klah, the noted medicine man who had made it possible to copy sacred sand paintings. Still on the loom when Klah died in 1937, it had been completed by his two nieces, who gave it to the wife of a trading post proprietor, who passed it on to her daughter, who sold it to Ed and Ruth Kennedy in 1980.

Although the preponderance of textiles in the Kennedy collection represents the contemporary period of Navajo weavings, which began in 1895, several are from the so-called classic and transitional periods dating to the mid-nineteenth century. Anthropologist Joe Ben Wheat, a noted textile scholar, described the collection as "an extremely valuable resource because of its depth, range, and balance," and several of the weavings were featured in a highly regarded book, *The Song of the Loom,* published in 1987. The wide assortment of jewelry and silverware documented both the history and the artistry of Southwest American Indian tribes during the twentieth century.

A valuable collection of contemporary art, assembled several years earlier by Emeritus Professor of Art Donald Roberts and the late Henry Lin, former dean of the College of Fine Arts, also was slated for placement in the new museum. Roberts was a member of the Museum Advisory Committee, as was Lin's daughter, Maya, whose winning design of Washington's Vietnam Veteran's memorial had led to a highly successful career as an independent architect in New York City.

In responding to media questions, President Ping said the proposed museum would focus on "distinctly American" works of art. "Too many university museums are not focused," he said. "We want this to be a center of instruction and research as part of our public service. There is every reason to believe that the collections will grow."

Kennedy echoed that feeling, but admitted that a new phase in Navajo weaving should be expected to begin within a few years. The era of close affiliations between artisans and trading posts was giving way to the "pick-up-truck age, in which weavers transport their wares from dealer to dealer, seeking the best bids," he said. Kennedy saw no dealer as "a worthy successor to the likes of Tobe Turpen and the late Troy Kennedy," and young weavers were not developing the specialized skills of Despah Nez—who was in her eighties—and her daughters, one of whom was seriously ill. The trend was from quality to what Kennedy termed "tourist orientation." This, of course, would increase the value of existing ceremonial blankets like those in the Kennedy collection, which Turpen called "the finest in the world." Other people have purchased fine rugs, he said, "but there is nothing anywhere that even remotely resembles the collection Ed Kennedy is giving to Ohio University."

Kennedy envisioned the spread of the university's recognition as an important center for research and studies on the Navajo culture, and talked excitedly about it to Charles Ping, John Gerber, and others. He believed it would take many years to develop that potential properly, along with other projects on The Ridges, and cautioned those who seemed anxious to leapfrog into prominence. "Ed gets a little frustrated with some people who don't realize this can't be done in a couple of years, and that it will require a lot of time, energy, and financial commitment," Gerber said. "Here is a man in his late eighties who is looking and working toward a ten-year goal."

Despite his enthusiasm for the museum project and the two new business ventures, Kennedy was involved also with three fundraising programs at Hiram College. As an honorary member of the Board of Trustees, he attended meetings regularly, serving also as an occasional unofficial adviser to Dr. G. Benjamin Oliver, who had become president of the college in 1989.

Hiram had encountered perplexing problems leading to declining enrollments in the late eighties, just as the number of college-age youths reached a downward slope in America's demographic cycle. Admissions officers reported one specific shortcoming: it was difficult to compete with other colleges that possessed what they termed "greater financial flexibility to attract top-ranking high school graduates." With great faith in

President Oliver's ability to overcome this situation, Kennedy had proposed that board members lead the way with personal contributions totalling $100,000 of new money for the 1990–91 operating budget. As an incentive, he pledged the final $20,000 if other members would raise the first 80 percent. When the board quickly attained that goal, Vice President for Development Sylvia Yankey used it as the stimulus for a further three-for-one "Trustee Challenge" to alumni, parents, and friends that in 1992 reached the overall goal of $400,000. A second $20,000 Kennedy pledge at that time enabled her to continue the momentum through another academic year.

During the same period, Kennedy was instrumental in launching an organized program to obtain charitable gifts through deferred giving, which he considered the most feasible long-term method of strengthening a college endowment. Under such a plan, a primary option for alumni and friends is to contribute various types of securities through wills, qualifying for immediate tax deductions, avoiding tax on appreciation, and receiving dividends for the remainder of their lives. In most instances, a college converts such securities to cash, reinvesting in ways that will maximize dividends to donors. Convincing Hiram trustees and officers that this effort would produce "strong and continuing results," Kennedy agreed to organize and chair the Planned Giving Committee. When early success brought an increase in the burden of leadership, he was joined by a newly appointed trustee, Philip L. Warburton, a Hudson, Ohio, attorney and a 1964 graduate of Hiram, as co-chair.

In Kennedy's mind, however, these programs were not sufficient to secure Hiram's stature in the growing competition among liberal arts colleges, forty-eight of which were located in Ohio alone. "Recognizing the need for another major gifts campaign, which would become the largest in Hiram's history, Ed became an early spokesperson for launching such a drive," President Oliver said. "He spoke about it at board meetings, again emphasizing that group's responsibility and involvement, and when the college moved forward with it, he helped me review the plan." By mid-1992, the college had embarked upon a "quiet phase" of the campaign, in which selected alumni and friends were being solicited for large contributions and pledges. The college also established leadership for the official drive, which was scheduled to begin in 1993. Its goal was expected to be $33 million.

"From the time he established his first scholarship and loan funds at Hiram in the fifties, Ed Kennedy has been instrumental in a long series of contributory programs, all of which have been expanded by increased participation through the years," Vice President Yankey observed. "That is his system, and it works. I have come to realize that he appreciates recognition, but unlike many other persons, he doesn't seek it or need it for satisfaction. That is what I consider true philanthropy. With Ed Kennedy, it never is self-serving. The word 'philanthropy' comes from Latin and Greek words meaning 'love for humankind,' which describes very accurately his motivation."

Still an active member of the Juniata College Board of Trustees in 1992, Kennedy played a pivotal role in what President Robert Neff described as "a transitional period in leadership." A former general secretary of the Church of the Brethren in Elgin, Illinois, Neff had been elected president of Juniata in 1986. Soon afterward, he appointed a committee to structure a five-year plan that would bring younger persons onto the thirty-eight-member board. That meant replacing older members who had compiled excellent records of service. "Ed Kennedy and John Baker helped facilitate this delicate shift to a whole new tier of leadership without ill feeling," Neff said. Baker, one of several members who retired during the five-year period, became a trustee emeritus in 1988, and was succeeded on the board by his youngest daughter, Anne, a New York City attorney.

Neff and the new board chair, Harrisburg businessman-investor Klare S. Sunderland, asked Kennedy to continue active membership, however. "We thought it was important for Ed to remain on the board, as a tie to the past, because he still had sound investment judgment, and many fresh ideas," said the college president. "It was a way of stabilizing our shift in leadership, and we convinced him he was greatly needed on the Executive Committee, where he had served since joining the board in 1969."

Thus, at an age when few persons retain the passion or the energy to play active roles in economic and social evolvement, Edwin Kennedy continued to exert his considerable influence as an adviser to business and a friend to education.

Chapter 17   **Reminiscence**

> *Character may be manifested in the great moments, but it is made in the small ones.*
> —*Phillips Brooks*
> *Clergyman, Writer*

With the household reduced to three in 1992, Edwin Kennedy still looked forward to dinner conversations with Christa and Jeff Cook, lingering at the table as before to discuss the hardware business, new ventures, Navajo art, world affairs, and any whimsical events that had taken place. "I doubt that many families laugh as much as we do at the dinner table, partly because of Jeff's humor," Kennedy said, "and I recommend it highly as a buffer against aging."

Events that intrigued him remained vivid in his mind, worth reviving in conversations from time to time. He had been greatly inspired by the Oberammergau Passion Play of 1984, and the history of its performances. At the height of a devastating plague in 1633, survivors in the small Bavarian village had made a promise that if God would lift the affliction, they and their descendents would enact a play depicting the passions of Jesus every ten years. Historians reported that the plague soon ended, without further loss of life in Oberammergau, and in 1664, villagers organized the first performance. Except for a few interruptions necessitated by war—including World War II—the vow was kept. The special series of performances in 1984, marking the three hundred and fiftieth anniversary of the first production, attracted sell-out crowds from around the world. With five hundred performers—all residents or natives of Oberammergau—the eight-hour pageant contained sixteen acts, combining music, drama, and religion. "Everyone who can arrange to go there should see the Passion Play sometime in his or her lifetime," Kennedy advised reflectively.

Although he was a registered Republican during his entire adult life, Kennedy's first vote in a presidential election, when he was a graduate student at Ohio State University, had been for Democrat Alfred E. Smith, America's first Roman Catholic nominee. Opposed to any form of prejudice, he cast that vote in 1928 because many vociferous backers of Herbert Hoover openly opposed Smith on the basis of his religion.

Kennedy continued to develop strong opinions, always through careful study, on events shaping the progress of humankind, whether in the financial world or elsewhere. In trying to determine what the "Desert Storm" conflict of 1991 and its aftermath in the succeeding year would mean to stabilization in the Middle East, he listened to the words of political and industrial leaders and read reports from various writers and analysts, added what he recalled from the past, then formed his own conclusions from the weight of evidence. "That is precisely the way he made decisions in the oil business—weighing and analyzing all available factors and coming up with his own, unique decision—and it certainly worked well for him then," observed a friend.

When John L. Gaddis, Ohio University distinguished professor of history, spoke to a New York alumni group about the end of the Cold War, Kennedy was so fascinated he insisted on Gaddis discussing the topic further at breakfast the next day. Gaddis was happy to accept the invitation, and recalled that "when the conversation moved from the Cold War to technical innovation, I became the questioner, with Ed waxing eloquent on the new concept in materials handling." Several months later, Gaddis, who was director of Ohio University's Contemporary History Institute, was named to an international group sponsored by the Council on Foreign Relations in New York to study the reshaping of America's world role beyond the Cold War. Kennedy followed his progress with intense interest.

During visits to the Ohio University campus, Kennedy enjoyed talking with several faculty members of both long and recent acquaintance. Richard K. Vedder, distinguished professor of economics who had served for several years as chairman of the Kennedy Lecture Series, kept him current on activities, especially those supported by Kennedy endowments. "I always admired Ed for having the insight to focus contributions right at the heart of the intellectual life of the university," Vedder noted. "The money from Ed and Ruth rewards students for excellence, and faculty for expanding the frontier of knowledge. Furthermore, it touches every discipline." Vedder considered Kennedy "unusually bright, with a penchant for asking penetrating, often unpopular questions, in challenging conventional wisdom, while always remaining polite and respectful." He related an incident in 1987 that he considered emblematic of Kennedy's sensitivity to the feelings of others:

> After visiting the campus, Ed was on a tight schedule to make another appointment, so someone had offered to pick him up at the Ohio University Inn, where he had been staying, and drive him to the airport. Unfortunately, the driver did not arrive on time, and I could tell Ed was very concerned, even though he did not say anything. So I offered to get my car, which was at the end of a large parking lot, and pick him up at the Inn. "Oh, no," he said, "I'll go with you to the car." He also insisted on carrying his own bag, which was quite heavy. Well, when we arrived at my car, it had a flat tire. I was never more embarrassed in my life. We hurried back to the Inn, again with him refusing to let me carry the suitcase, and I stormed in as if I owned the place to ask the clerk to get a car immediately. She quickly summoned an assistant who had an old jalopy. We could barely squeeze the suitcase into the back seat, but Ed and the young driver soon were on their way, with Ed unfazed except to apologize to the clerk, the driver, and me, for causing a problem. He had been embarrassed to even hint about needing a ride, and felt he was imposing on us all, even though both the clerk and the driver (a student) were happy to help. And Ed was eighty-three years old.

Encountering unexpected new links to former experiences still excited Kennedy. At the 1990 kickoff of Ohio University's Third Century Campaign, he was approached by New York actor Bill McCutcheon, a 1948 graduate who had received a Tony Award for his performance as the comedy lead in the Broadway revival of Cole Porter's "Anything Goes," as well as four Emmy Awards during several years of playing the role of Uncle Wally on television's "Sesame Street," and an Obie Award for achievements in off-Broadway theater productions. One of two emcees for the gala, McCutcheon told Kennedy, "When I was a struggling young actor in New York back in the early fifties, you invited me to one of the important luncheons at the celebrated Lehman Brothers dining room; that meant a lot to me, and I have never forgotten it." Kennedy quickly recalled that occasion, and was deeply touched by McCutcheon's words. He also enjoyed discovering that the other emcee was Laurel Lea Schaefer, Miss America 1972, with whom he had shared Homecoming honors nineteen years earlier.

While visiting the campus again in the spring of 1992, Kennedy was delighted to meet the son of Albert Ogunsola, whom he had assisted in financing graduate studies leading to a Ph.D. in 1970. Like his father, Femi Ogunsola was studying toward a doctoral degree at the university's College of Education, in preparation for returning to Nigeria as a teacher.

Kennedy savored new associations with young persons in education and business, but also believed strongly in the preservation of old friendships. Keeping in touch by occasional telephone calls and infrequent visits, he noted that "close friendships survive the passage of time." A basic test of "the strength and breadth" of friendship, he philosophized, is "when you finally get together after a long absence, and immediately pick up where you left off, just as if you had been seeing each other regularly."

Relaxing in the large, brown-toned library of his home, surrounded by walls of books, most of which he had read, Kennedy seemed more animated, and certainly more comfortable talking about some of these friends than answering questions concerning his own career. Characteristically preferring the present to the past tense, he emphasized the current accomplishments of persons whose careers extended well into the past. Primary among these men was John Baker, whom Kennedy saw much more often than others because of the short distance between their homes. Still vigorous at age ninety-six, Baker was spending the spring 1992 academic quarter at Ohio University with the title "distinguished visiting trustee professor," participating in courses of varying disciplines, helping prepare an oral history of the 1945–61 era in which he served as president, and taking part in an annual Peace Conference he and his late wife had funded several years earlier.

Walter Davis, while maintaining his entrepreneurial interests, was devoting much of his time to active membership on the North Carolina higher education system Board of Governors. He previously had spent eight years as a trustee of the University of North Carolina, where the library—one of the nation's finest—was named for him in 1985. He had homes and offices in Kitty Hawk, North Carolina, and Midland, Texas, and a suite at Governor's Inn in Research Triangle Park, North Carolina.

Ora Roehl, two years younger than Kennedy, lived in a highrise apartment where he also had an office with a panoramic view of the Charles River and downtown Boston. A financial and management consultant, he served clients throughout the country, as he had done since forming his own company in 1959.

Officially retired at Brooksville, New York, Walter Lubanko spent more time developing business projects than skiing and playing golf. "You don't hang out a shingle for these types of things," he said, "but if someone asks if you are interested, you never say 'no,' because you never know what is going to interest you."

It is more than coincidence that Edwin Kennedy and such long-time consorts represented a breed of leaders who do not view retirement as a distinct phase of life. Classification as workaholics seemed inappropriate, because none nursed a compulsion to carry on financially productive activities, which each described simply as "fun." All had recreational interests, but it would be difficult to imagine any of them highlighting a conversation by describing how he scored a birdie on some long five-par hole or landed a trophy-sized bass. They studied domestic and world events critically, speaking of concerns and hopes for the next century in terms of solutions, rather than worries. In many instances, they took part in helping develop such solutions. Their confederate participants were men and women of widely varying ages, yet they seemed never tempted to choose sides by generations. "I number some elderly forty-year-olds and young octogenarians among my acquaintances," said Kennedy. Like others in his close circle of senior friends, Kennedy found it difficult and "rather boring" to discuss reasons for not settling into armchair retirement, because he rarely thought about such an alternative, except to recall it as an uncomfortable, and therefore very brief experience of the previous decade.

He maintained a vital interest in ongoing activities at the Hiram College Biological Field Station, where his most recent sponsorship was the 1990 planting of several thousand walnut trees. As with his new business ventures, he described this project in terms of its great long-range potential:

> Students planted the trees, and many other students will be involved with taking care of them through the years. Intermediate fast-growing species of hardwoods were planted between the walnut trees to make them grow straight. These can be cut down and used for fence posts within ten or fifteen years, when the walnut trees no longer need their assistance. Meanwhile, it is important to maintain the full stand of walnut trees, so part of my 1992 donation to the bio station and the nature trail is earmarked for replacement of those that didn't survive the first two years. Imagine how beautiful and valuable these walnut trees will be in sixty or seventy years!

Kennedy's reminiscences, admittedly pleasant under proper circumstances, which could be interpreted to mean gentle probing by good friends, invariably sparked recollections of lighthearted episodes he and Ruth had experienced together. For example, questions about the paradox of an investment banker being adverse to using credit in personal transactions summoned forth an incident that led to "surrendering somewhat reluctantly to the pressures of using plastic money." Having attended Ohio University's June 1980 Commencement, then flown on to California to see Ruth's niece, the Kennedys stopped overnight at San Francisco's St. Francis Hotel on their return trip to New Jersey. Kennedy was a part owner of the hotel, by virtue of having invested equity capital for construction of an addition known as The Tower in the early seventies, but such information, understandably, was unknown to the registration clerk. Unable to produce a credit card of any kind, Kennedy was told that he would have to pay cash in advance. "I had no quarrel with that, because we were scheduled for a very early morning flight," Kennedy recalled, "but as the clerk started to do something behind the desk, she overheard Ruth whisper to me that it seemed funny to require advance payment from a part owner." Bothered by the embarrassment of "the very gracious" clerk in the conversation that followed, Kennedy decided it was time to get a credit card.

Influenced by his wife's musicianship, Ed had learned to appreciate and enjoy concerts and operas, which they attended frequently. They watched Metropolitan Opera performances from box seats next to those of Rudolph Bing, and often invited visiting friends to join them for particularly outstanding productions. At home, Ed liked to listen while Ruth played the piano or the organ.

Ruth bequeathed the organ to Hiram College in her will. When members of the music department reluctantly confessed that the organ was too outdated to be used effectively by students, Ed bought the college a new one.

"Ruth and I shared a feeling of gratitude to live in a democratic society with a capitalistic system that gave us an abundant and interesting life together," he said. "We had been extremely poor, and didn't want to be poor again. But we didn't set out to make a lot of money; I only wanted to do my job well, believing that the money then would take care of itself. We soon realized also that we should reinvest in the society that had given us this good life. But how do you do that? We chose the field of education."

Edwin Kennedy believed that life has a pattern. "Events in one's life are not really a series of isolated incidents," he said. "When I look back at the major turning points in my life, every one of them has some connection to education. That has been true from the time Pansy Rauhauser, my high school teacher of ancient history, taught me to think analytically, through all the years, and even today. Education has really formed my life and made it a rich endeavor."

Hesitating briefly to ponder other memorable episodes of the 1900s, he said quietly, almost to himself, "There have been heartaches along with the good things, of course. But I'd like to go through it all again."

As if on cue, a ringing telephone broke the mood, and within a few minutes, Kennedy was agreeing to visit Ohio University shortly after returning from a scheduled California trip to join Ruth's niece at a formal dinner near San Jose and attend a Santa Monica meeting with Morton Winston to discuss new prospects for Stamet Corporation.

Hanging up the phone, Kennedy quickly assured Christa that the expanded travel agenda, which already included a spring excursion to the Navajo reservation, would not interfere with plans to observe his upcoming eighty-eighth birthday at home.

Epilogue

Saundra Theis, a niece of Edwin Kennedy, offered revelatory professional as well as personal observations of her uncle in 1992. Theis, who earned a master's degree in nursing from the University of Colorado and a Ph.D. from Northwestern University, conducted extensive ongoing research in gerontology, the study of aging. "Uncle Edwin is one of the best role models on aging I have ever encountered," she said, noting that much of her research was concentrated on "changes in intelligence" that develop as people grow older. "I have made studies of the mental processes people lose and retain through the years, and I have not met anyone who can match him in maintaining the ability to remember, learn, and analyze. It is fascinating to talk with him about almost anything. And on a personal note, he always is vitally interested in what my family is doing—and all others among his family and friends, for that matter."

Three generations of the Kennedy family had spread to most regions of the United States. Theis, the daughter of Edwin's sister, Gladys Linville, was on the faculty of the University of Illinois at Chicago. Her husband, Lawrence, was with Amoco Oil Company in that city. Their son, Jeff, a recent graduate of Kenyon College in Ohio, was planning to attend graduate school prior to beginning a career as an English teacher. Daughter Jennifer was a senior at Carlton College in Minnesota.

Gladys had moved the previous year from Columbus to Kansas City, where her son, Fred E. Linville, was president of VHA Mid America, Inc., a regional healthcare system of Voluntary Hospitals of America. Fred and his wife, Pat, had two children, Bradley and Cristine.

Both of Kennedy's brothers had retired. Richard and his wife, June, lived in Marion, Ohio, near their older daughter, Peggy Jean, and her young son, Corry. Peggy Jean's daughter, Caroline, was studying to be a nurse in Columbus. The younger daughter of Richard and June, Debra, also lived in Columbus, as did Dorene Baer, the daughter of Kennedy's older sister, Helen, who had died in 1988.

Robert Kennedy and his wife, Patricia, had moved to Hilton Head Island, South Carolina, following retirement. Their son, Michael, an attorney, lived in Phoenix, Arizona, with his wife, Dawn, also an attorney, and three children, Jennifer, Robert, and Kevin. A graduate of Duke University and the University of Virginia Law School, Michael had joined Snell & Wilmer, the largest law firm in Arizona, in 1975. Three years later, he became a founder of Gallagher & Kennedy, which by the early nineties had reached a position of statewide prominence, with seventy lawyers in the firm. Kay Kennedy, the daughter of Robert and Patricia, became a professional golfer after attending Rollins College. She was on the Ladies Professional Golfers Association tour for several years, before becoming an instructor with the John Jacobs Golf Schools, then a teaching professional at the Phoenix Country Club.

Ruth Kennedy's niece, Nancy Bletzer, the only living descendant of the Zimmerman family, still operated her ranch in Tres Pinos, California. "Nancy is carrying forth the joviality she always shared with Ruth," Kennedy said fondly, referring to a black-tie dedication dinner she hosted inside a new horse barn completed in the spring of 1992.

Eddie Kennedy lived in Santa Fe, New Mexico, where he continued the outdoorsman interests dating to his childhood.

He and his wife, Zulika, had two young daughters, Alexandra and Debbie. Danny Kennedy worked with a law firm in Hollywood, Florida, and Patty attended school in New Jersey. Susanne Cook, who had graduated recently from Hamilton College, was working with a New York advertising agency to gain experience for a career choice.

As he had done during his entire career, Kennedy arranged travel schedules to include visits with family members whenever possible. Michael Kennedy always looked forward to seeing his uncle in Phoenix:

> When we got together, he was only interested in talking about my family and what I was doing in my law practice. He was such a humble man, I could only keep current on what he was doing in business or with university foundations by reading clippings from magazines and newspapers. We would talk some about the Navajos, or current events, but he quickly turned each conversation back to our family and the rest of the Kennedy clan. Uncle Edwin was the glue that kept the family united. Kay and I both went all the way back to Columbus for some of the Worthington Inn Thanksgiving gatherings.

Michael represented Charles Keating Jr.'s American Continental Corporation, not in one of the celebrated criminal trials, but in a civil suit at Washington, D.C., in which the infamous financier attempted unsuccessfully to regain his Lincoln Savings and Loan Company. During the course of lengthy proceedings, Michael met numerous East Coast investment bankers who knew his uncle. "It was a great ice-breaker for me," he said, "and it was interesting that under tense circumstances of that litigation, and in a business where there is not such profound respect for peers these days, those bankers always mentioned the great integrity of Ed."

In late December of 1992, Kennedy looked ahead with great anticipation toward progress of Stamet and NoRad, the two companies with which he had been closely associated since they were launched by Morton Winston and Donald Firth a few years earlier. Stamet's unique materials handling technology was receiving international recognition as the possible solution to an environmental concern. New coal-electricity technology promised major gains in combustion efficiencey, with nearly emission-free performance, if engineering could overcome the inhibiting difficulty of feeding coal reliably and accurately at the high pressures required with existing equipment. Because Stamet had successfully fed and metered coal continuously into such pressures without loss of accuracy, something never before accomplished, the U.S. Department of Energy awarded the company a $500,000 research grant to further develop its system. Utilities around the world were following this effort, as well as field demonstrations being planned for 1993 by the U.S. Electric Power Research Institute and by a group in the United Kingdom.

Meanwhile, NoRad had produced the world's only externally fitted device capable of substantially reducing low-end magnetic field emissions from computer monitors. Swedish researchers speaking at several international conferences recently had reported a direct link between such emissions and cancer, and the government of that nation, recognized for its exceptionally stringent emission standard known as MPR II, said NoRad's product was the only device—among hundreds that had been tested by its laboratories—to meet that standard of protecting computer users from radiation.

With these developments, progress of Ohio University's museum of American art, and the intrigue of a new federal administration, Ed Kennedy looked toward 1993 as "a year of great stimulation."

Documentation

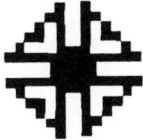

Taped interviews with more than seventy persons, most of whom have known Edwin L. Kennedy for many years, provided the principal reservoir of information that has been condensed into this book. Transcripts of these interviews alone make up a document three times as long as the book. Supporting material came from personal letters, corporate publications, records and correspondence, newspapers, magazines, and appropriate books. The names of publications and resource organizations not identified within the text are keyed to appropriate chapters in the following listing:

Chapter 1
The 1985 program of the Council for Advancement and Support of Education (CASE) was well chronicled in a nomination packet, letters, press coverage, and publications of supportive colleges and universities.

Chapter 2
Background information on Marion County and the Lust family is taken from *The History of Marion County and A History of Marion County and Representative Citizens*. One-room schools were researched in *The Old Country School* by Wayne E. Fuller (University of Chicago Press, 1982); *Rural One-Room Schools of Mid-America* by Leslie C. Swanson (Moline, IL, Swanson, 1976); and bulletins of the U.S. Department of Education. Data on the influenza epidemic of 1918 came from bulletins of the National Research Council, series 1. Material

concerning President Warren G. Harding and the recession of the early 1920s is from the *Encyclopedia of American History* (Harper and Row, New York, 1976), *World's Work* magazine (May 1921), and various newspapers. Biographic information on Professor Wilfred Binkley is from Ohio Northern University and the *New York Times* (December 10, 1965).

Chapter 3

The epigraph is a quote from Mark Hopkins, an influential nineteenth century teacher, long-term president of Williams College, and prolific writer of religious and educational works. Chautauqua information is from various newspapers; from the magazines *Outlook* (August 9, 1922), *Overland* (July 1924), *Scribners* (July 1922 and July 1923), and *World's Work* (May 1921 and August 1924); and from *The Chautauqua Movement* by Joseph E. Gould (State University of New York, 1961). Information on Albert R. Teachout and the Teachout Foundation was provided by the Historical Society of the Christian Church (Disciples of Christ).

Chapter 4

The epigraph by Ruth Nanda Anshen is from the preface of *The Family: Its Function* (New York: Harper and Brothers, 1959), which she planned and edited as volume five in a "Science of Culture" series. Nationwide celebrations marking the beginning of the twentieth century were reported in the January 1 and 2, 1901 issues of the *Cleveland Plain Dealer*. Some information on Massillon and the C. W. Zimmerman family was provided by the Massillon Museum.

Chapter 5

General information about the Great Depression is from the *Wall Street Journal* and the *New York Times; The Crash and Its Aftermath* by Barrie A. Wigmore (Westport, CT, Greenwood Press, 1985); *America's Great Depression* by Murray N. Rothbard (Richardson and Snyder, 1963); *The Great Depression* by Robert S. McElvaine (Times Books, 1984), and *What a Year* by Joe Alex Morris (New York: Harper, 1956).

Chapter 6

The epigraph is from Ohio State University Professor of Finance Henry Hoagland's book, *Corporation Finance* (McGraw-Hill, 1933). Du Pont family history was researched in *Du Pont Dynasty* by Gerard Colby (Secaucua, NJ: Lyle Stuart Inc., 1984); and *The Du Ponts of Delaware* by William H. Carr (New York: Dodd, Mead, 1964). Sources of material on the state of the economy, investment banking, Lehman Brothers, the oil business from 1936 to 1953 include the *Oil and Gas Journal, Scientific American, Business Week, Nation's Business, New Republic, Time, Fortune,* the *New York Times Magazine,* the *Wall Street Journal,* AP Wide World Magazine, Lehman Brothers publications, transcriptions by official stenographers for the U.S. District Court, Southern District of New York, and *The Merchant Bankers,* by Joseph Wechsberg (Boston: Little, Brown and Company, 1966). Information concerning Kerr-McGee comes from *Innovations in Energy* by John Samuel Ezell, (Norman: University of Oklahoma Press, 1979) and the records of Edwin Kennedy.

Chapter 7

Information on the P.E.O. and Ruth Kennedy's participation in its affairs was provided by that organization's executive office in Des Moines, Iowa.

Chapter 8

A preponderance of information concerning Ohio University during the administration of Dr. John C. Baker, as well as verification of material from interviews, was provided by the University Archives and Special Collections, the University News Services, and several issues of *The Ohio Alumnus* magazines.

Chapter 9

The epigraph by Frank J. Manheim appeared in *The Merchant Bankers* by Joseph Wechsberg (Boston: Little, Brown and Company, 1966). Lehman Brothers information supplementing that obtained from interviews and personal files of Edwin Kennedy is from records of the firm, as well as general publications. Details of TransCanada PipeLine's corporate structure, activities, and finances are from *Standard and Poors* reports; *Pipeline,* by William Kilbourn (Toronto, Vancouver: Clarke, Irwin & Company, 1970); and *The Murchisons,* by Jane Wolfe (New York: St. Martin's Press, 1989). Figures on oil exports, imports, and reserves in the late fifties and early sixties are from the nation's press and several issues of *The Oil and Gas Journal.*

Chapter 10

Background information in support of that received from interviews concerning Tosco, and general energy observations of the sixties are from several issues of *Duns Review, Fortune, The Oil and Gas Journal, Forbes,* and *Business Week.*

Chapter 11

The opening butcher shop narrative is related as told by Ruth Kennedy to Christa Cook. Details of Ohio University's teacher training program in Nigeria were published in *The Ohio Alumnus* magazine and a final report from the university's Office of International Studies to the USAID Mission to Nigeria, prepared by Edward Baum, professor of political science. Zane Grey's quoted observation of waters at the later site of the Tropic Star Lodge are from his book, *Tales of Fishing Virgin Seas* (New York: Grosset & Dunlap, 1925), with the location verified in research by film writer/director William L. Sprague.

Chapter 12

Material on Navajo history, culture, and art is from *Hosteen Klah: Navaho Medicine Man and Sand Painter,* by Franc Johnson Newcomb (Norman: University of Oklahoma Press, 1964); *The Song of the Loom,* by Frederick J. Dockstader (New York: Hudson Hills Press, in association with the Montclair Art Museum, 1987); *Evolving Designs,* and *Turquoise Jewelry,* both by Nancy N. Schiffer (West Chester, PA: Schiffer Publishing); *Walk in Beauty,* by Anthony Berland and Mary Hunt (Kahlenberg New York Graphic Society, 1977); and *Navajos: The Past and Present of a Great People,* by John Upton Terrell (New York: Weybright and Talley, 1970).

Chapter 13

The progression of developments within Lehman Brothers during the seventies, based primarily on interviews with persons involved, was supported by articles that appeared regularly in *Business Week, Duns Review, Newsweek, Time, Fortune,* and *Wall Street Journal.* Similar support on shale oil and Tosco activities is from articles in *Nation's Business, Forbes, U.S. News & World Report, Business Week,* and *Fortune.* Information on deregulation and its consequences is from issues of *Financial World;* a speech by Peter G. Peterson; *Phillips: The First 66 Years,* edited by William C. Wertz (Bartlesville, OK, Phillips Petroleum, 1983); and *Deregulation or Re-Regulation,* edited by Giandomenico Majone (London: Pinter Publishers 1990).

Chapter 14

Student unrest in the early seventies is documented in newspapers, magazines, college and university publications, and the *Encyclopedia of American History* (New York: Harper & Row, 1976). Information on

Panama politics in the seventies is from various newspapers, magazines, and *In the Time of the Tyrants,* by R. M. Koster and Guillerimo Sanchez (New York: W. W. Norton, 1990), which contained the specific quotation describing Manuel Noriega's infamous career.

Chapter 15

Periodicals provided a wealth of supportive information for examining investment trends and the evolution of Lehman Brothers in the eighties. Among those most frequently utilized were the *Wall Street Journal, New York, Fortune, Forbes, Business Week, Institutional Investor, National Review, U. S. News and World Report,* and the *New York Times.*

Chapter 16

Stamet and NoRad documents, publications, and news releases, and articles appearing in *Information Week, PC Magazine,* and the *New York Times* supplemented information received in interviews with executives of the two corporations.

Chapter 17

The epigraph is from a sermon by the famed nineteenth century clergyman, Phillips Brooks, whose spiritual, yet practical preaching made him one of America's best known personalities. Historical information is from *The Oberammergau Passion Play,* by Saul S. Friedman (Carbondale: Southern Illinois University Press, 1984).

Index

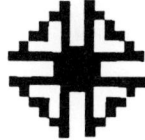

A & K Petroleum Company (Kerlyn Oil), 60
Abraham and Company, 153
Alden, Marion (Mrs. Vernon Alden), 87–88, 129
Alden, Vernon R., 87–88, 128–129, 138
Alden, Mrs. Vernon R. *See* Alden, Marion
American Express, 177, 183–84
American Potash, 188
Artic Star Lodge, 128, 172
Ashland Oil Company, 59, 113
Askland, A. E., 52
Atkins, Oren, 113
Athens, Ohio, 25–26, 30, 32, 37, 43, 77, 79, 81, 121, 124, 202. *See also* Ohio University
Athens Messenger, 203
Atlantic Richfield Corporation (Arco), 115, 157
Avon Refinery, 155–56
AZL Resources Corporation, 158

Baer, Raymond, 18–19
Baker, Anne, 207
Baker Day, 86
Baker, Elizabeth (Mrs. John C. Baker), 81–82, 85
Baker, John C., ix, 2, 6, 43, 77–87, 105–06, 115, 132–33, 189, 207; Baker Day, 86; Baker Fund,86, 124, 167; Baker Peace Conference, 213
Baker, Mrs. John C. *See* Baker, Elizabeth
Baker, William, G., Jr., 150
Ball, George W., 150, 152, 176
Banca Commerciale Italiana, 152
Banff Oil Company, 98, 109
Banking crisis, 37, 46–50; Banking Holiday, 49
Bankers Trust, 2
Barrow, James H., 133–35
Barton, Al, 63
Begay, Vera, 66, 203
Bell Exhibit Services, 199. *See also* Rick and Sue Bell
Bell, Rick and Sue, 199–200, 202
Bennett, William J., 7
Beta Gamma Sigma, 91
Big Inch pipeline, 56, 62
Binder, Frederick M., 170–71
Binkley, Wilfred E., 20
Black Thursday, 42. *See also* Wall Street crashes
Blanchard, Paul, 27
Blazer, Paul, 59

Bletzer, Helen (Mrs. Lloyd Bletzer). See Zimmerman, Helen
Bletzer, Lloyd, 36
Bletzer, Mrs. Lloyd. See Zimmerman, Helen
Bletzer, Nancy, vii, 36, 69, 127, 172, 215–16, 218
Bloomingdale's, 188.
Boesky, Ivan, xi, 185–86, 188
Bond, Mildred, vii
Booth, Alan R., 166
Brickman, Jeffrey, 164
Brody, J. J., 145
Brown, Robert A., Jr., 97
Bryan, Elmer B., 25, 28
Buffalo, Tom, 144
Bunting, Josiah, III, 173–74
Bush, G. Kenner, 203
Bush, George, 6–7
Bush, Gordon, 87

Calabogie Lake, ix, 73–75, 121, 160–61
Campeau Corporation, 188
Campus unrest, 138, 165–166. See also Vietnam War
Campbell, Robert, 97–98
Canada Oil Lands, 98
Canadian Delhi, 96–97
Carbondale Savings Bank, 47–48, 50
Carpenter, John. See Zimmerman, John
Carter, Jimmy, 155, 179
Chase Manhattan Bank, 64
Chautauqua Circuit, 22–25, 28, 29, 31–32, 37–38
Chenery, Christopher, 94–95
Christian Church (Disciples of Christ), viii, 14, 28
Clark, Howard L., Jr., 184
Clay, General Lucius D., 153
Cleveland Cliffs Iron Company, 113–15
Cohen, Peter A., 178, 183–84
Cold War, xi, 86, 210–11
Colony Development Corporation, 113, 155, 157
Columbus, Ohio, 13, 23, 30, 32, 37, 72, 121–22, 172

Cook, Mrs. Jeffrey. See Teichmann, Christa
Cook, Jeffrey, vii, 4, 125, 128, 130–31, 165, 209
Cook, Susanne, C., vii, ix–x, 4, 130–31, 165, 168, 171–73, 200, 218
Copeland, Lammot du Pont, 115
Cottey College, 6, 69, 174
Council for Advancement and Support of Education (CASE), 1, 6, 175
Crewson, Harry B., 165–66
Crissinger, Guthrey & Strelitz, 19

Daugherty, Jessie, 11–12
Davis, Walter R., 2–3, 87, 107–09, 127, 148–49, 213
DeBrul, Steven, 108
Delhi Oil Company, 96
Depression, Great, xi, 44, 47–51, 55, 78
Deregulation, 162–63, 186
Desert Storm, 210
Disciples of Christ. See Christian Church
Dice, Charles A., 37
Dime Bank-Lincoln Trust Company (Lincoln Trust), 46
DiSalle, Michael V., 83–84
Distinguished Professor Awards, 82–83, 86, 166. See also Ohio University
Dobbins, Earl, 20–21, 25–26
Drexel Burnham Lambert, 185
Duncan Refinery, 157
du Pont, E. I. de Nemours and Company, 52–53
du Pont family, 52–53

Eberhardt, Harry, 70–71, 73; Eberhardt Foundation, 71
Ehrman, Frederick L., 147–48, 151–53
"1804 Fund," 169. See also Ohio University
Eisenhower, Dwight D., 85, 89
Ellis, Jack G., viii, 175, 199–200
Emergency Banking Relief Act, 49
Exxon Corporation, 102, 157

Fairfield, Roy, 124
Fall, Paul, 89, 122

Farm Depression, 17–18
Federal Savings and Loan Insurance Corporation, 186, 189
Fell, John, 97
Findlay College, 6, 138, 174
First Boston Corporation, 116
Firth, Donald, 194, 196–97
Firth Solids Pump, 197
Flu Epidemic of 1918, 15–16
FMC Corporation, 197
Forster, William D., 161
Founders Citation, 167. *See also* Kennedy, Edwin L., honors and Ohio University
Frohring, Paul, 134–135

Gaddis, John, 210
Galion, Ohio, 71, 122
Gamma Sigma, 27
Gas exploration, 95–98
Geiger, Alan H., 201
Gerber, John H., 200–01, 205
Glanville, James W., 99–100, 153, 160–61
Glucksman, Lewis L., 149–51, 176–77
Gubitz, Albert C., 79
Gulf Oil Corporation, 116
Gutman, Monroe, 91, 94, 153

Halliburton Corporation, 153
Hampden-Sydney College, 6; Board of Trustees, 173–74
Hammer, Armand, 108–09, 148
Haning Hall, 199, 202–03. *See also* Ohio University
Hanson Trust Company, 196
Harding, Warren G., 14, 16, 18–19
Harvard University, 6, 43–44, 45–46, 87–88, 166
Hausa (African tribe), 7, 130
Hellman, F. Warren, 152
Heyman, George H., Jr., 147, 153–54, 189
Hiles, Michael L., 194, 196
Hiram College, vii, 5–6, 28–29 88–89, 121, 123, 133–138, 205–07, 215; Board of Trustees, 89, 174, 205; Field Station, 133–135, 171, 214; Foundation, 206; Kennedy Loan Fund, 88–89; Trustee Challenge, 206
Hiram Foundation, 206. *See also* Hiram College
Hoagland, Henry, 37, 51
Home Oil Corporation, 97
Hoover, Herbert, 42, 210
Hopi, 144
Huehner, Martin, 171
Hughes, Jeffrey, 190
Humble Oil Company, 65, 99–100
Husky Oil Company, 94
Hutton, E. F. and Company, 183–84. *See also* Shearson Lehman Hutton

Isaac, William, 186

Jagow, Elmer, 133, 136–37
Jergins, A. T., 63
Jergins Corporation, 62–65; "package," 63–65
Johnson, Fred H., 81, 86–87
Johnson, F. Ross, 184
Jordan, Harvey B., 83
Juniata College, 6, 105–106, 169–71, 174, 207–08; Board of Trustees, 133, 207
Junk bonds, 156

Katsina, Hassan Usman, 129
Keating, Charles, Jr., xi, 189, 219
Kele, C. G., 130
Kennedy, Alexandra, 218
Kennedy, Danny, 4, 121, 164–65, 218
Kennedy, Debbie, 218
Kennedy, Debra, 39, 218
Kennedy, Edwin Clarence, 8–9, 13–14, 18, 38–39, 71–72
Kennedy, Mrs. Edwin C. *See* Kennedy, Emma C.
Kennedy, Edwin DeWeese "Eddie," 4–5, 51, 70, 73–74, 88, 119, 121, 126, 128, 131, 164–65, 218

Kennedy, Mrs. Edwin D. *See* Kennedy, Zulika
Kennedy, Edwin Lust:
aging, views on, 182, 193; humor as buffer, 209; as role model, 217
as builder, 189
career, Standard Statistics Company, 4–44; Dime-Bank-Lincoln Trust Company, 46; Pennsylvania State Department for Banking, 46–50; Washburn & Company, 51; Young Management Company, 51–52; Mutual Associates, Inc., 52–53; Shields & Company, 53–54; Lehman Brothers, 54, 56, 65. *See also* main entries
childhood and youth, 8–9, 13–19, 38
collecting: Southwest Native American weavings and jewelry, 66, 144–46, 198–205, 216; Nigerian artifacts, 130. *See also* Southwest Native American Art Collection, Navajo weaving, Navajo jewelry, and Hausa tribe.
college: Ohio Northern University, 19–20; Ohio University, 21, 25–30; Ohio State University, 37, 41; Harvard University, 43–44. *See also* separate entries
college jobs, 20, 24, 29, 31
corporate directorships, 93, 109; view on, 109–11
decision-making process, 210
diversification, views on, 101–03
education, philosophy of, 3, 40, 86, 93–94, 173–74, 216
education endowments, 4, 6; Cottey College, University of New Mexico, Utah Southern University, 174. *See also* main entries for Hiram College, Hampden-Sydney College, Juniata College, and Ohio University
education, primary and secondary, 10–12, 15–19
education, support of, 76, 138–39, 167, 175, 215–16; praise for, 211

energy, views on, 112–13, 167–68, 179–80; technology, views on, 112
ethics, xi-xii, 2, 37, 57, 100, 181–82, 188–89, 219
family: children (*see* main entries on Edwin DeWeese Kennedy and Christa Teichman); grandchildren, 121, 130–31, 164–65, 217–19; grandparents, 8–9; parents, 8–9, 12–13, 39, 71–72; siblings, 10,12, 39–40, 71–72, 217–18; wife (*see* Ruth Zimmerman)
family life, 68–76, 118–21, 164–65, 172–73, 209; views on, 5–6, 40
and forecasting, market, 59, 101, 191
friendship, views on, 212
greed, views on, 190
and Hampden-Sydney College: Board of Trustees, 173. *See also* main entry
health, 58, 71
and Hiram College: Board of Trustees, member, 89, honorary member, 205; Edwin and Ruth Kennedy Center, 136–37; Field Station, 133–34, 214; fundraising, 205–07; Kennedy Loan Fund, 88; Nature Observation Building, 134; Northwoods Field Station, 135; Ruth E. Kennedy Memorial Nature Trail, 171. *See* separate entries
honors: Volunteer of the Year (1985), Council for Advancement and Support of Education, 1, 175; Ohio University Alumni Certificate of Merit, 81; Ohio University Beta Gamma honorary business society, 91; Ohio University honorary doctorate, 129; Juniata College honorary doctor of human letters, 132; Findley College honorary doctor of business administration, 138; Ohio University Alumnus of the Year

(1971), 164; Ohio University Founders Citation, 167

influences, major: Wilfred E. Binkley, 20–21; Chautauqua, 32; Jessie Daugherty, 12; Roy C. Martin, 4, 45; Oberammergau Passion Play, 209–10; Pansy Rauhauser, 16; Albert R. Teachout, 28–29; Arnold Toynbee lecture, 124; Ruth Zimmerman Kennedy, 3. *See* separate entries

investment banker, description of, 91–92; praise as, 152, 189

and Juniata College: Board of Trustees, 133, 207; Century II Commencement speaker, 169; honorary doctorate of humane letters, 132; "Margin of Difference" honorary chairman, 169; Ruth E. and Edwin L. Kennedy Sportsrecreation Center. *See also* Hiram College

and Lehman Brothers: specialist, research and investing division, 54, 56–65; partner, 65–66; head of Oil Department, 91; managing director, 150; retirement, 181; semi-retirement, 181. *See also* main entry

liquidator of banks, 47–50, 191

marriage as partnership, 3, 68, 82, 101, 127–28. *See also* Ruth Zimmerman

as mentor, 99–100, 182

and NoRad Corporation, 193–96. *See also* main entry

and Ohio University; Sesquicentennial Scholarship Fund, 77, 80–81; Alumni Association, president, 82; establishment of Distinguished Professor Awards, 82; appointment to Ohio University Fund, 83, 166; Board of Trustees, member, 84, 129, 165–66, chairman, 129, 165, views on, 84; endowment of John C. Baker Fund, 86, 167; Edwin and Ruth Kennedy Lectures, 86–87, 166; Alumni Certificate of Merit, 81, 128; honorary doctorate, 129; Alumnus of Year, 164; Founders Citation, 167; "1804 Fund" honorary chairman, 169. *See also* main entry

and oil industry, 48, 56–66, 93–103, 107–09, 111–16, 152–59, 178–80; expertise, 54, 55–56, 91–103, 111–16

personal traits: curiosity, 66; even temperament, 100, 154, 158; modesty, 5–6, 152–53; patience, 147, 190; persuasiveness, 21, 93; optimism, 190; retentiveness, 57, 217; shyness, 3, 19, 27, 105; thoroughness, 57, 61, 105, 133, 190–92

philanthropy, philosophy of, 1, 4–5, 21, 81, 215–16

retirement, 192, 213

risk-taking, views on, 58–59, 154, 182, 191

and Solids Transport and Metering Corporation (Stamet), 196–98. *See also* main entry

as sportsman, ix, 70–71, 73, 75, 128, 131–32, 168

teaching jobs, 30–31, 49, 50

and Christa Teichmann (Mrs. Jeffrey Cook) as member of family. *See* main entry

underwriting, views on, 59

volunteerism, views on, 2

and Ruth Zimmerman (Mrs. Edwin L. Kennedy): initial meeting, 31–32; courtship, 37, 42–43; marriage, 46–47. *See also* main entry

Kennedy, Mrs. Edwin L. *See* Zimmerman, Ruth

Kennedy, Emma C. Lust (Mrs. Edwin C. Kennedy), 9–10, 12, 14, 39, 71, 122

Kennedy, Frank, 9–10

Kennedy Mrs. Frank. *See* Kennedy, Olive

Kennedy, Gladys (Mrs. Fred Linville [elder]), vii, 8, 13–14, 18, 38–39, 72–73, 121, 173, 192, 217
Kennedy, Helen (Mrs. Edgar Likens), 10, 12, 16, 18, 38, 218
Kennedy, John F., 106
Kennedy June (Mrs. Richard Kennedy), 218
Kennedy, Kay, 40, 218
Kennedy Lecture Series, 86, 124, 166, 211. *See also* Ohio University
Kennedy Loan Fund, 88–89. *See also* Hiram College
Kennedy, Margaret Johnson (former Mrs. Edwin D. Kennedy), 119, 131, 164–65
Kennedy, Michael, 40, 218–19
Kennedy, Olive McCurly (Mrs. Frank Kennedy), 9–10
Kennedy, Patricia (Mrs. Robert Kennedy), 218
Kennedy, Patty, 4, 131, 165, 168, 173, 218
Kennedy, Peggy Jean, 39, 218
Kennedy, Richard, vii, 18, 38–39, 71, 218
Kennedy, Mrs. Richard. *See* Kennedy, June
Kennedy, Robert, vii, 18, 39–40, 71, 218
Kennedy, Mrs. Robert. *See* Kennedy, Patricia
Kennedy, Troy and Edith, 66–67, 144–145, 205
Kennedy, William, 9
Kennedy, Zulika (Mrs. Edwin D. Kennedy), 218
Kent State University, 121
Kerr-McGee Oil Company Industries, viii, 60–61, 66, 72, 103, 115, 144, 157, 159–60, 178–79, 181, 188
Kerr, Robert S., 60, 72–73
Keystone Custodian Funds, 62
Kidder Peabody, 181–82
King's College, 125, 131
Kirkpatrick, Ohio, 10–12, 14, 17, 19–20, 37–38, 172

Kohlberg Kravis Roberts & Company, 184
Koolsbergen, Hein I., 114, 156
Klah, Hosteen, 144, 204
Krantz, LaVern L., 85–86
Krueger, Harvey M., 159
Kuhn, Loeb, 159, 162

Lackawanna County, Pennsylvania, 45, 47
Lake Erkshine, New Jersey, 73
LaVan, Pete, 95
Lazard Freres & Company, 160, 176
League for Industrial Democracy, 26–27
Lehman Brothers, 1, 3, 54–65, 68, 70, 75, 90–104, 107–16, 147–63, 176–192; Lehman Brothers Kuhn Loeb Incorporated, 159, 176; Lehman Brothers Limited, 150; Lehman Commercial Paper, 150; Lehman Corporation, 64, 91–92, 150, 184; Lehman Government Securities, 150; Lehman Special Services, 150; Oil Department, 91–92, 99, 101, 107–08, 113, 153, 161; One William Street Fund, 92, 150, 162; Shearson/American Express, 177–78; Shearson/Lehman Brothers, 178, 180–81; 183, 193; Shearson Lehman Hutton, 183–84
Lehman, Emanuel, 54–55
Lehman, Henry, 54–55
Lehman, Mayer, 54–55
Lehman, Robert "Bobbie," 55, 90, 108, 116, 147–48, 159
Lentz, Jack, 161
Levine, Dennis, 185
Leverage buy-outs, 156, 184–88, 190
Likens, Edgar, 19
Likens, Mrs. Edgar. *See* Kennedy, Helen
Likens, Helen (Mrs. Edgar Likens). *See* Kennedy, Helen
Lin, Henry, 204
Lin, Maya, 204
Lincoln Trust, 46. *See also* Dime Bank-Lincoln Trust

Linville, Fred (elder), 39, 72, 75, 121–22
Linville, Fred E. (junior), 39, 72–73, 121, 172, 217, 218
Linville, Mrs. Fred (elder). *See* Kennedy, Gladys
Linville, Mrs. Fred (junior). *See* Linville, Pat.
Linville, Gladys (Mrs. Fred. [elder]). *See* Kennedy, Gladys.
Linville, Pat (Mrs. Fred E. Linville [junior]), 218
Linville, Saundra (Mrs. Lawrence Theis), 39, 72–73, 121, 217
Lion Oil Company, 155
Lubanko, Walter, 161, 189, 213
Lust, Jacob, 9, 39
Lust, Rosa (Mrs. Jacob Lust), 9, 39
Lust, Lucy, 16

McCabe, Robert, 148
McCutcheon, Bill, 212
McGee, Dean, 60–61, 160, 178, 181. *See also* Kerr-McGee Oil Company
McNeal, Lyle, 146
McPherson, Frank A., 178–79
Madison, New Jersey, 51–52, 68
Manheim, Frank J., 90
Marathon Oil, 100
"Margin of Difference," 169. *See also* Juniata College
Marion, Ohio, 12–19, 26, 38–39
Marion County, Ohio, 8–9, 12, 26
Martin, Roy C., viii, 4, 44–45, 48, 52–53, 87
Materials handling technology, 196–98, 210
Mathews, Elbert G., 129
Maxwell, Charles, 111, 195–96
Maxwell, Gilbert, 145, 199
Maxwell Museum, 145, 174, 198–99, 203. *See also* University of New Mexico
"May Day," 162
Mazur, Paul, 153
Mellon, Andrew W., 116
Memorial Auditorium, 25, 78, 80. *See also* Ohio University

Messenger, James, 17
Middle East, 115, 152–53, 156, 210
Milken, Michael, xi, 185–86
Milliken, Russell A., 129
Millimet, Erwin, 105
Mobil Oil Corporation, 64, 100, 111
Monnett, Ohio, 12, 18, 38
Monsanto Corporation, 155
Monterey Oil Company, 64–65, 88, 100
Morgan, J. P., 42, 116
Morgan Stanley & Company, 116
Morris, Griffith R., 181–82
Morris, William C., 153–54, 156, 159, 161, 193
Murchison, Clint, 95–97
Murphy, Charles, Jr., 93–94
Murphy Oil Corporation, 93, 102–03
Museum Advisory Committee, 202, 204. *See also* Edwin L. Kennedy collecting, Ohio University, and Southwest Native American Art Collection
Mutual Associates Incorporated, 52–53

National Alumni Association, 81–82
Navajo culture, 67, 140–43, 198–200, 202, 205. *See also* Navajo jewelry and Navajo weaving
Navajo jewelry, 140, 142, 144, 146, 198, 202–03
Navajo sand paintings, 143
Navajo Sheep Preservation and Development Project, 146. *See also* Utah Southern University
Navajo weaving, 4, 66, 140–46, 198, 202–05; chant weaves, 143–44, 203
Neff, Robert, 207
New Deal, 51, 55–56; agencies, 51, 56; regulation of oil and gas industry, 56. *See also* Depression, Great
Newmont Mining, 196
New Vernon, New Jersey, 75, 106, 118, 124–25, 165, 172, 181
Nez, Despah, 201, 205
Nielson, Glenn E., 94
Nigeria, 7, 85, 129–30, 212. *See also* Hausa tribe

Niles, Ohio, 30–31
Nippon Life Insurance Company, 183–84
Nixon, Richard M., 149, 165
NoRad Corporation, 194–97
Noreiga, Manuel, xii, 168–69
Northwest Territory, 25, 199
Northwoods Field Station, 135. *See also* Hiram College

Oberammergau Passion Play, 173, 209–10
Oberlin, Edna Zimmerman (Mrs. Howard Oberlin). *See* Zimmerman, Edna
Oberlin, Howard, 36–37
Oberlin, Mrs. Howard. *See* Zimmerman, Edna
Occidental Oil Company, 108, 147–48
Ogunsola, Albert, 130, 212
Ogunsola, Femi, 212
Ohio General Assembly, 200, 203
Ohio Northern University, viii, 6, 19–21, 174
Ohio, Southeastern, 25, 79
Ohio State University, 30–33, 37, 39, 41, 105, 121–22
Ohio University, vii–viii, x, 2, 6, 21, 24–32, 35, 37, 42, 67, 76–88, 91, 121–22, 124, 128–30, 138, 164–67, 168–69, 175, 198–205, 210–13, 216; Board of Trustees, 83–84, 165, 198–99, 202; 1804 Fund, 169; Haning Hall, 199, 202–03; Sesquicentennial Scholarship Fund, 76–77, 79–81; Siegfred Hall, 200–01; Third Century Campaign, 200–01, 212
Ohio University Inn, 203
Ohio Wesleyan College, 20
Oil industry, 48, 54, 56–66, 93–99, 107–08, 111–16, 152–62
Oil shale, *See* shale oil
Oil Shale Corporation, The (Tosco). *See* Tosco.
Oliver, G. Benjamin, 205–06
O'Neill, William, 83–84
One William Street Fund, 92, 150, 162

Organization of Petroleum Exporting Countries (OPEC), 100, 180, 152–53, 156, 180
Ott, Emil, 117–18

Panama, ix, xii, 7, 131–32, 168–69
Paul, James, 47–48
Peabody Coal Company, 196
Pennsylvania Department of Banking, 46–58. *See also* Edwin L. Kennedy as liquidator of banks.
P. E. O. Sisterhood, 69, 126
Permian Corporation, 107–08
Peterson, Peter G., 151–52, 159–60, 162, 176–77
Phillips Petroleum, 48, 60, 155, 188
Ping, Charles, Jr., x, 6, 164, 166–67, 175, 199–201, 204–05
Plymouth Oil Company, 100
Prairie Oil Royalties, 98
Public Utility Holding Company Act, 53
Pueblos, 140–41

Rankhauser, Pansy, 16, 216
Reagan, Ronald, 1, 6–7, 180
Redpath Circuit, 23, 28–29, 31–32. *See also* Chautauqua Circuit
Rhodes, James A., 129
Ridges, The, 203, 205. *See also* Southwest Native American Art Collection
RJR Nabisco, 184
Roberts, Donald, 204
Roehl, Ora C., 2, 62, 68, 87, 213
Roosevelt, Franklin D., 48, 49, 55
Roosevelt, Theodore, 23
Rowe, Mr. and Mrs. Charles, 17
Rumley, Fred 107

St. Thomas College (University of Scranton), 45, 49, 50
San Ardo oil field, 63–64
Salomon Brothers, 184
Savings and loan crisis, 186
Schaefer, Laurel Lee, 164, 212
Schultz, Frank, 96–97
Schwarzman, Stephen, 177
Scranton, Pennsylvania, 44–47, 49–51

Seligman and Company, J. & W., 54, 193
Sesquicentennial Scholarship Fund, 76–77, 79–80. *See also* Ohio University
Shale oil, 94, 112–15, 155–57, 179–80, 196
Sharp, Hugh R., 53, 115
Sharp, Paul, 122–23
Shearson/American Express, 177–78. *See also* Shearson/Lehman Brothers and Lehman Brothers
Shearson/Lehman Brothers, 178, 180–81, 183, 193. *See also* Lehman Brothers
Shearson Lehman Hutton, 183–84
Shephard, Bessie, 25, 26
Shields & Company, 53–54
Short Hills, New Jersey, 68–69, 72, 192
Shotten, Mr. and Mrs. Donald, 47
Siegfred Hall, 200–01. *See also* Ohio University
Signal Oil & Gas Corporation, 154–55
Silent Unity, 70
Sinclair Oil, 95
Sohio, 113–16. *See also* Standard Oil of Ohio
Solids Transport and Metering Corporation (Stamet), 196–97, 216
Song of the Loom, 140, 204
Southeastern Ohio Cultural Arts Association, 202
Southern Production, 94–95
Southwest Native American Art Collection, 198–205
Sowle, Claude R., 138, 165
Spaulding, Henry, 174
Sputnik, 86. *See also* Cold War
Standard Oil of Ohio, 102, 113–16. *See also* Sohio
Standard Statistics Company (Standard and Poors), 41–44, 48, 52, 80
Sunderland, Klare, S., 207
Sunlite Oil Company, 98, 109
Sun Oil Company, 157

Tanner, Anna Mae, 201
Teachout, Albert R., 28. *See also* Teachout Foundation

Teachout Foundation, viii, 28–29, 76, 88
Teichmann, Christa (Mrs. Jeffrey Cook), 4–6, 117–21, 124–28, 130–31, 165, 168, 171–73, 192, 200–01, 209, 216
Teichmann, William and Klara, 118, 125
Theis, Lawrence, 217
Theis, Mrs. Lawrence. *See* Linville, Saundra
Theta Chi, 27–29
Third Century Campaign, 200–01, 212. *See also* Ohio University
Thomas, Alberta, 201
Thomas Joseph A., 147
Tidewater Oil Company (Tidewater Associated), 48, 50
Torrijos, Omar, 168–69
Tosco (The Oil Shale Corporation), 105, 112–15, 154–59, 194
TransCanada Pipeline Limited, 95–98
Tropic Star Lodge, 131–32, 168–69
Trustee Challenge, 206. *See also* Hiram College
Tuppers Plains, Ohio, 30
Turnage, Martha A., 201
Turpen Tobe, 144–45, 201, 205

Union Oil, 58, 188
Utah Southern University, 6, 146, 174
University of New Mexico, 6, 146, 174, 199. *See also* Maxwell Museum

Vedder, Richard K., 211
Vietnam War, 138, 165. *See also* campus unrest
Virginia Military Institute, 5

Wall Street crashes: October 24, 1929, 42; October 19, 1987, 183
Warburton, Philip L., 206
Washburn and Company, 51
Western Kentucky University, viii, 45, 87
Western Oil Transportation, 107
Western Pipelines, 96–97
Wheat, Joe Ben, 204
Wilmington, Delaware, 52–53
Williams, Clark E., 77, 79, 81

Wilson, Mark, 135
Wilson, Robert, 62
Winston, M. Winston, 114–15, 156–59, 193–98, 216
World War I, 15–16, 18, 25, 55
World War II, 37, 39, 62, 56–58, 101, 117, 209
Worthington Inn, 172, 219

Yankey, Sylvia, viii, 206
Young, Gene, 138
Young Management Company, 51–52

Zambia, 132
Zimbabwe, 132
Zimmerman, Cyrus, 33–34, 37, 72.
Zimmerman, Mrs. Cyrus. *See* Zimmerman, Sadie
Zimmerman, Edna (Mrs. Howard Oberlin), 34, 36–37, 44
Zimmerman, Helen (Mrs. Lloyd Bletzer), 34, 36
Zimmerman, John (John Carpenter), 34–35, 37, 68
Zimmerman, Ruth (Mrs. Edwin L. Kennedy):
childhood and youth, 34–35
death, 171
education, 35
education, philosophy of philanthropy, 126
health, 163–64, 170–71
honors: Ohio University Alumnus Certificate of Merit, 128; naming of Ruth E. Kennedy Memorial Lectureship, University of New Mexico, 146, 174; naming of Ruth E. Kennedy Memorial Nature Trail at Hiram College, 171
as hostess, 132
musicianship, 32, 69, 76
personal traits, 36; sense of humor, 2–3, 7, 128, 170; thriftiness, 50, 126; lack of pretense, 69, 126–27, 135; determination, 106
and Christa Teichmann (Mrs. Jeffrey Cook), relationship, 118–21, 124–27
Zimmerman, Sadie (Mrs. Cyrus Zimmerman), 33–34, 36

A Note About the Author

David Neal Keller received both his B.S. and M.S. degrees from Ohio University. He was a newspaperman, industrial writer, and public relations director at Ohio University, before becoming a full-time freelance writer and filmmaker in 1967. He has written and produced more than a hundred sponsored films and videotapes, and his byline has appeared on a variety of magazine articles. This is his fourth book. He and his wife, Marian, also an Ohio University graduate, live at Keowee Key in South Carolina. They have three married children and eight grandchildren.